The Films of Werner Herzog

The Films of
Werner Herzog
Between Mirage and History

Edited by

Timothy Corrigan

METHUEN
New York and London

First published in 1986 by
Methuen, Inc.
29 West 35th Street, New York NY 10001

Published in Great Britain by
Methuen & Co. Ltd
11 New Fetter Lane, London EC4P 4EE

Library of Congress Cataloging in Publication Data
The Films of Werner Herzog.
    Filmography: p.
    Bibliography: p.
    Includes index.
    1. Herzog, Werner, 1942 – Criticism and
interpretation.   I. Corrigan, Timothy.
PN1998.A3H443   1986   791.43′0233′0924   86–12430

ISBN 0 416 41060 X
    0 416 41070 7 (pbk.)

British Library Cataloguing in Publication Data
The Films of Werner Herzog: between mirage
    and history.
    1. Herzog, Werner – Criticism and
    interpretation
    I. Corrigan, Timothy
    791.43′0233′0924   PN1998.A3H4/

ISBN 0 416 41060 X
    0 416 41070 7 Pbk

For the Corrigan family

Contents

Notes on the contributors

Dana Benelli is presently completing his doctoral degree at the University of Iowa where he is researching the relationship of the Hollywood cinema of the forties to documentary film practice.

Timothy Corrigan is Associate Professor of English and Film Studies at Temple University. His most recent book is *New German Film: The Displaced Image*. He has also written on British and American literature, film theory, and contemporary American cinema.

Thomas Elsaesser has published a wide range of essays on classical and contemporary international cinema, film theory, genre, and film history. He is the former editor of *Monogram*, and his work has appeared in *Screen*, *Wide Angle*, *Sight & Sound*, *New German Critique*, and many other journals.

Jan-Christopher Horak has, among other publications, just completed a lengthy study of German filmmakers in exile during the Third Reich. He is presently Associate Curator of Film at the George Eastman House.

Gertrud Koch is the co-editor of *Frauen und Film*. Based in Frankfurt, she has published monograph studies on Louis Malle and Carlos Saura, articles on pornography and film, Jacques Tati, Yasurjiro Ozu, and feminist film theory.

Judith Mayne is an Associate Professor of French and Women's Studies at Ohio State University. Her previous publications include work on feminism and film, New German Cinema, film and literature.

Brigitte Peucker is an Associate Professor of German at Yale University and is currently chair of film studies. She has published on issues connected with German Romanticism, as well as numerous articles on the German cinema.

Eric Rentschler is Director of Film Studies at the University of California, Irvine. He is author of *West German Film in the Course of Time* and editor of *German Film and Literature: Adaptations and Transformations*.

Alan Singer is the author of *A Metaphorics of Fiction* and a forthcoming novel titled *The Charnel Imp*. His work on contemporary fiction and aesthetics has appeared in *Enclitic, Sub-Stance*, and *Contemporary Fiction*.

William Van Wert is a Professor of English at Temple University. His work includes *The Film Career of Alain Robbe-Grillet* and essays in *Film Quarterly, Wide Angle*, and *Sight & Sound*.

Amos Vogel teaches at the Annenberg School of Communications, University of Pennsylvania. Author of *Film As a Subversive Art*, he is a founder and former director of Cinema 16 and the New York Film Festival.

Acknowledgments

Several organizations provided very important assistance as this book was being researched and assembled: New Yorker Films for screenings, Temple University for a grant-in-aid, and the Museum of Modern Art Film Stills Archive (Mary Corliss in particular) for the stills used. Two essays in the volume are reprints and one a revised version of a previous article. I am grateful to the following individuals for permission to use that material: Sigrid Bauschinger (*Film und Literatur: Literarische Texte und der neue deutsche Film*), Amos Vogel (*Film Comment*), Richard T. Jameson (*Movietone News*). Antje Masten and Mercedes Pokorny helped considerably with the necessary translations; Rick Rentschler has, as usual, been a rich and much appreciated source for ideas, debate, and facts about Herzog and his films; and Robin Nilon was my extremely valuable research assistant. To Marcia Ferguson: thanks for everything else.

I
INTRODUCTION

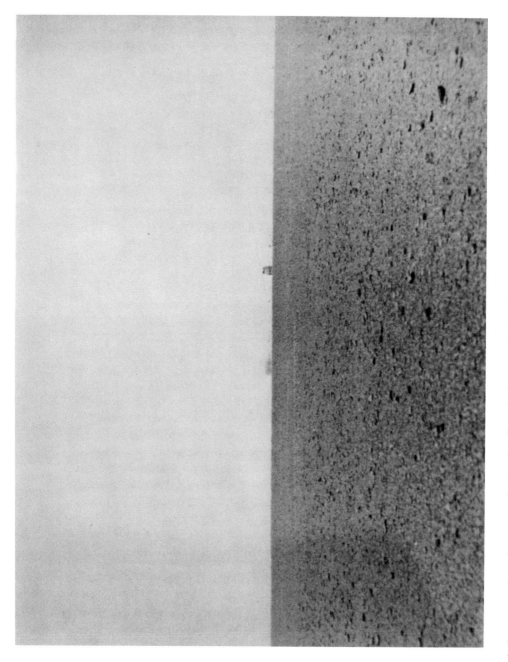

1 A perspective always producing itself and always refusing the position it produces (*Fata Morgana*)

1

Producing Herzog: from a body of images

Timothy Corrigan

> We have to articulate ourselves, otherwise we would be cows in the field.
>
> Werner Herzog

Enigmas, flying doctors, ecstasies, fanatics, dwarfs, sermons, wood-chucks, and phantoms: the perverse menagerie of images and abstractions that form the body of Werner Herzog's mesmerizing and exasperating films. Eating one's shoe: the raw emblem of a critical response to filmmaking, offered by a filmmaker who hopes to rescue the world with images, while claiming that "film is not the art of scholars, but of illiterates" (Greenberg *et al.*, 1976, 174). Indeed, the last surprise should be that Herzog and his films, perhaps more than the films of any other contemporary director, suffer from the very excessiveness which distinguishes them and their histrionic director, distorted equally by extreme adulation and extreme condemnation.

In many ways, the most demanding challenge of these films is therefore not their purported density or idiosyncrasies but the difficulty of negotiating and mediating the extremities that they represent and provoke. Fascinated by images of outsiders, iconoclasts, and strange other worlds, various audiences on university campuses and beyond have, since the early 1970s, turned to Herzog as the latest freedom from the dull round of commercial cinema. Yet, as part of that difference and distinction, these audiences have also discovered the guilty trace of a shared regression to adolescence and childhood. Along with the startling rebellion Herzog's images represent for many, these same films carry the aura of romantic naiveté and self-absorption which tends to mark them as little more than Hollywood fantasies disguised as high seriousness and to prompt an equally reactionary dismissal of them. As Eric Rentschler has recently remarked, critics "have, by and large, not found a way out of this hermeneutical impasse – nor have they begun to perceive it as a problem worth their attention" (Rentschler, 1984, 87).

That this critical impasse exists in such opposed terms is, it seems to me, neither an accident nor an unusual position in the reception of a filmmaker or film today – Hollywood or otherwise. Rather, Herzog's monolithic performance of himself and his films is entirely consistent with commercial filmmaking of the last two decades, whether one points to the career of Michael Cimino or the person of Francis Coppola. At least since 1970, commercial movies have primarily been an occasion to make the real the ingenuous, to let history begin at the box-office, to discover singular genius in the most innocent ability to see things, and to play and play again the pleasures of regression and youth. For all their differences, *The Cotton Club, Das Boot,* and *Rambo* have shared a sense that history is fundamentally a star's spectacle which reveals itself through the immediacy of images; contemporary movies, from *Star Wars* to *The Never Ending Story*, have increasingly become narratives which map a course back to the future and toward the massive teenage audience outside the theater. With typically little awareness, the movies today have transformed that traditional tension between physical reality and formative image into the resolved equation of physical reality as celluloid image. More importantly perhaps, distinctions between so-called art cinema and the commercial movies start to become, at best, academic and, at worst, politically useless: Godard plans a version of *King Lear* with Hollywood producers Golan and Globus, and in Germany the Bavaria Studios can easily accommodate both *Moscow on the Hudson* and *Berlin Alexanderplatz*.

Presented with these terms, a critical spectator's ability to distinguish or debate what must present itself as self-evident has become a treachery or pomposity equivalent to asking a child "why?" when the only answer can be "because." A self-dramatizing athlete, Herzog is a romantic artist, in short, only that he is, by chance or design, a totally contemporary moviemaker: all is image, and the density and flamboyancy of those images have established themselves as the only vehicle for significance. The resistance that Herzog thrives on thus may be not so much the physical world that he so often celebrates but the physical body of images that define the world for him. In these terms, measured leery of Herzog's appearance (Herzog, 1980, 43). Herzog's antipathy toward the broad mass of the human race, his hatred of authority figures of all kinds, especially bureaucrats and teachers, is amply demonstrated in the pages of his diary, and, of course, in his films which abound with caricatures of such figures. In *Burden of Dreams*, for example, the intensity of Herzog's revulsion for/fascination with the jungle is matched in intensity only by his hatred for modern man, whom he imagines as coming out of "a cheap, suburban novel."

As in his films, some of his negative feelings toward human beings in *Of Walking in Ice* are transferred to animals, which, as surrogates, are given human attributes. Herzog now discovers his ambivalent feelings toward sheep, mixing both the Christian and Marxist denotations, allowing the sheep to believe that he is the Messiah:

> During the worst snowstorm on the Swabian Alb, I encountered a provisional enclosure for sheep, the sheep freezing and confused, looking at me and cuddling against me as if I could offer a solution, The Solution. I have never seen such expressions of trust as I found on the faces of these sheep in the snow. (Herzog, 1980, 63)

At another point a flock of sheep stares at Herzog, "standing in rank and file," fearfully moving "closer in formation," causing Herzog to flee, because "such closing-in became so embarrassing" (Herzog, 1980, 75). These human/animal equivocations, although appearing absurd at times, are meant to be taken seriously; they are symbolic representations.[2] They signify Herzog's revulsion with modern civilization's evolution toward institutionalization and mass culture, and more specifically, all those persons (sheep) who have not resisted their integration into that structure.

Herzog, like the German romantics, remains apart from both man and nature, because he cannot help but imbue both with symbolic meaning, perceiving nature as a hostile and sometimes violent force. In *Burden of Dreams* Herzog notes: "Nature is vile and base, I wouldn't see anything erotic here. I see fornication, and asphyxiation and choking and fighting for survival, growing and just rotting away." In *Of Walking in Ice* the narrative's central conflict involves a struggle between Herzog's physical and mental capacity for pain and the punishing indifference of nature's snowstorms, early winter rains and coldness, just as *Burden of Dreams* documents Herzog's attempt to overcome "the curse of the jungle," to survive in "a land god created in anger." Only four days into his journey, nature revolts against Herzog's

Samaritan undertaking, as if aware of the fact that Herzog intends to cheat death itself by walking to Paris for Lotte Eisner:

> The storm grew so fierce that I can't recall having experienced anything like it. A black morning, gloomy and cold, a morning that spreads itself over the fields like a pestilence, as only after a Great Calamity. The side of the shed facing the wind is piled high with snow, the fields are a deep black with white lines of snow ... I have never cast my eyes upon such a gloom-laden land. (Herzog, 1980, 28)

Yet the magic can only work if he struggles on, sleeping less and less as he approaches Paris, until he gives up sleep all together, walking continuously the last twenty-five hours. Herzog's narrative takes on a trance-like quality in these final pages, a story of his grandfather from his childhood, other seemingly unconnected observations and hallucinations strung together in a stream of consciousness form. The fever of his quest, its intensity increasing as he nears his final goal, is like a fever in the movies that subsides in the early hours of the morning, forecasting a return to health.

Clearly, Herzog's diary is far from a documentary description of an observed reality. Just as his non-fiction films seldom adhere to the "objectifying" convention of documentary film practice, so too is his diary a subjective depiction of both factual and fictional events in which Herzog as narrator and hero is allowed to play the central character. Obscuring the boundaries between fact and fiction, dream and reality, Herzog's narrative is obviously unreliable. He continually relates events and information regarding local history to which he could not possibly have been privy as a stranger passing through: the unexplained disappearance of a factory owner, the collapse and death of a young girl on the steps of a church, an accidental manslaughter when a girl falls out of a moving bus. Whether fact or fiction, they are presented – like many of Herzog's film scenes – as aestheticized moments of death and loss.

Without any previous notification of a shift in space or time the reader may also find him/herself transported from the snow-covered fields of Swabia to the palace of Lon Nol at the height of the Cambodian War. At other times the transition to a Herzogian dream state will not be immediately discernible until seemingly plausible events become more and more unreal:

> A train races through the land and penetrates the mountain range. Its wheels are glowing. One car erupts in flames. The train stops, men

try to extinguish it, but the car can no longer be extinguished. They decide to move on, to hasten, to race. The train moves, it moves into fathomless space, unwavering. In the pitch blackness of the universe the wheels are glowing, the lone car is glowing. (Herzog, 1980, 44)

Herzog's perception of dreams and reality indivisibly intertwined again remind us of both romantic fiction and expressionist cinema. The objective and subjective exist on equal terms, each mitigating the other, the meanings of their messages equally important. For Herzog, scientific empiricism, like modernity itself, is a sham. In his films it is the soothsayers, the mystics, the dreamers and clairvoyants who have recognized the essential truths of existence.

In *Of Walking in Ice* Herzog himself becomes a visionary prophet. He reinforces the images with a continual series of cryptic statements, worthy of the prophet's supposed profundity: "Only if this were a film would I consider it real" (Herzog, 1980, 9); "It is a field called death" (Herzog, 1980, 12); "The morning emerges from utter blackness, this is not a dream" (Herzog, 1980, 35); "Friendship is possible with mice" (Herzog, 1980, 49); "Rain can leave a person blind" (Herzog, 1980, 66). While such phrases have always been a part of Herzog's cinematic stock in trade, their essential banality has usually been undercut by the truly arresting visual images accompanying them. In a prose text such as this they stand mercilessly alone. Yet Herzog, whose self-perception as a visionary prophet seems to have increased with each new success, hardly seems to notice.

In his interviews, in fact, Herzog often seems unaware of his own posturing, claiming for example that he "created" his son "through an act of spiritual concentration," and noting that he remained celibate during the first years of his marriage (Rummler, 1975, 195). Herzog, the prophet and guru, claims to have left behind him the needs and desires of the flesh, allowing him to connect more directly to the godhead:

> I don't know ... sometimes it happens to me by chance that I capture something like this. It's like a grace, like a gift of God that has fallen into my lap. (O'Toole, 1979, 41)

According to another interview, Herzog in fact met God at the age of 3; it was Christmas and God wore a brown suit and worked for the Electric Company. Herzog not only has an acute, God-given gift of prophecy, according to his own statements; as a filmmaker he can communicate with others, blessing them with his wisdom: "I know that I have the ability to articulate images that sit deeply inside us, that I can make them visible" (Hoberman, 1985, 61). In *Burden of Dreams* he tells us: "All these dreams are yours as well, and the only distinction between me and you is that I can articulate them."

Yet, as Herzog tells us elsewhere, he never dreams. Instead, his visions come to him while walking. In fact, the act of walking takes on religious significance in the world of Werner Herzog. Thus, walking to Paris becomes an act of healing for Lotte Eisner, because Herzog attaches to the act a ritualistic significance; walking as a spiritually and physically therapeutic activity. In interviews Herzog notes again and again that while filmmaking is self-destructive, leading to emotional, if not physical, burn-out, walking rejuvenates the soul:

> Walking on foot brings you down to the very stark, naked core of existence. We travel too much in airplanes and cars. It's an existential quality that we are losing. It's almost like a credo of religion that we should walk. (O'Toole, 1979, 48)

Like the German romantics who revered walking as a symbolic union with nature, Herzog's cult of walking carries with it a strain of anti-intellectualism. Herzog's tirades against intellectuals, academics and critics are a well-known element of the Herzogian persona, steeped in a mystical anti-rationalism. Directly commenting on Herzog's mystical hodge-podge, Herbert Achternbusch entitled his book on German filmmakers, *It's Easy When Walking to Touch the Ground* (*Es ist ein leichtes, beim Gehen den Boden zu berühren*). (Herzog once forced an interviewer to look at the various physical scars he had acquired in his pursuit of images. His scars are symbols of his suffering and success.)

Again we are confronted with the paradox of Herzog venerating the symbolic significance of his actions. Yet is not that also the central drama of many of Herzog's protagonists, their quest in the name of principles, dreams, and symbols? Herzog, like his characters, will sacrifice all, even submit to mortal danger, for the sake of his (their) obsessions. Interestingly, death remains strangely abstract. In his films, Herzog often aestheticizes death: the extreme long shots in *Signs of Life* and *Woyzeck*, the swirling camera in *Aguirre* and *Heart of Glass*, the off-camera deaths in *Kaspar Hauser* and *Stroszek*. In *Burden of Dreams*, Herzog hardly considers his culpability in the deaths of his Indian workers: "It (the jungle) becomes questionable, because people have lost their lives, people have been in a plane crash, and five of them in critical condition. One of them paralyzed. And those are all the costs you have to pay." In *Of Walking in Ice* Herzog represses the thought of Eisner's possible death, preferring the immortality of her symbolic representation. Herzog's insistence on the primacy of the

symbolic over actual human life, coupled with an aestheticization of death, mark him as dangerously close to fascistic tendencies. The German fascists in fact promulgated the cult of heroic sacrifice for the sake of state symbols, aestheticizing death as a glorious fate (Horak, 1981, 205–18). Nazi filmmakers, too, created a whole genre of "historical biographies," in which the protagonist suffers, often dies, for his ideals, succeeding against all odds, transcending death. The structural differences between such epics and *Fitzcarraldo* are unfortunately not great.

Where does this leave us in our evaluation of Werner Herzog, the narrator of *Of Walking in Ice*, the filmmaker of the New German Cinema? As a prose work, *Of Walking in Ice* is of little literary merit, indeed Herzog's prose has never been stylistically eloquent or philosophically deep. That the English translation is exceedingly inelegant and at times inept certainly does not help matters. Those passages which attempt flights of fancy are turgid at best, utterly banal at their worst, never achieving the beauty and mystery of Herzog's film images. Part of the problem lies in Herzog's inability to convey the intense physicality of his experience. His film images, even when they are fraught with symbolic meaning, convey a strong sense of the physical, of natural elements, simply because Herzog allows for a certain "physical redemption of reality," to use Kracauer's phrase. Herzog's prose lacks the depth of his cinematic space, leaving the reader with a one-dimensional and symbolic view of reality. In fact, Herzog's prose is but a pale imitation of the writing of his Bavarian colleague, Herbert Achternbusch. As Eric Rentschler has pointed out, Herzog may be nothing more than second-rate Achternbusch (Rentschler, 1985, 1).

While such a view may be a bit too harsh, given his undeniable film achievements, a comparison between Herzog and Achternbusch is instructive in pointing out some of Herzog's more glaring deficiencies.[3] All of Achternbusch's films and prose center on a fictional persona played or narrated by Achternbusch, just as Herzog places his persona at the center of his diary, *Of Walking in Ice*. Both Achternbusch and Herzog share – at least superficially – a strain of anti-authoritarianism which seems indigenous to the Bavarian Free State, possibly having its roots in a popular, anti-Prussian spirit. Each in his own way has created a persona which displays anarchic tendencies, living outside the restricting confines of bourgeois society, a quasi-outlaw, contemptuous of uniformed police, teachers and bureaucrats. Yet, while Achternbusch's characters are truly abrasive, never avoiding either cultural or political taboos, disregarding with abandon all the rules of social discourse in bourgeois society, Herzog presents in *Of Walking in Ice* a prefabricated, romantic outlaw, who dares to break and enter, to walk 600 miles living off the land. Where Herzog's film heroes attempt feats worthy of the gods, Achternbusch's Herbert merely attempts to survive the murderous ineptitude and small-mindedness of those persons socializing him.

Both Herzog and Achternbusch perceive film as a dream experience, expecting as spectators to see images which in their startling newness soothe the psyche. The cinema becomes essentially a liberating and regenerating force. Achternbusch writes in *The Hour of Death* (*Die Stunde des Todes*): "The cinema was always necessary to keep me alive. Too much has disappeared into my dreams." (Achternbusch, 1978, 119). Herzog concurs: "We are surrounded by images that are worn out, and I believe that unless we discover new images, we will die" (Cott, 1976, 56). The difference between Achternbusch and Herzog lies in their respective styles and themes, in the proportions of the individual dreams. Achternbusch's images, grounded in the *Heimatfilm* of his mind's eye, concentrate on the microcosm, on the nightmares and dreams of an immediately experienced reality. Herzog's films, especially his later works, strive for the gargantuan, the exotic, the supernatural and the mystical, attempting to evoke metaphysical responses. While Achternbusch's cultural pessimism is funneled into absurdist recreations of our cultural reality, which in the Bakhtinian sense are truly grotesque and thereby liberating in their satire, Herzog's notion of the absurd originates in a dire romanticism and cosmic existentialism. By his own admission, Herzog has no sense of the ironic (Ebert, 1984, 120), while Achternbusch is irony incarnate.

Herzog's lack of ironic distance, his strained seriousness, ultimately has political repercussions for the reception of his work. The very construction of a mystical biographical persona on Herzog's part cannot but color the reception of images whose ambiguity further reinforces our belief in the artist's magical aura. Herzog, the filmmaker willing to go to any lengths to produce films – be it to hell and back – shows us persons in *Fitzcarraldo*, or *Of Walking in Ice*, whose aspirations and achievements are not only meant to dwarf our own, but also to emphasize the smallness of our lives. There is something antihumanistic in his view of ordinary mortals as sheep, or ant-like figures hauling a ship up a mountainside, according to the master's plan. Herzog's mystical cult of the overachiever fosters an extreme individualism, which can be aligned to reactionary politics. Likewise, his extreme stance against the modern, against institutionalization and industrialized society, must be viewed as counterproductive, given world society's essential need to cooperate at the global level to insure survival. Herzog's perceived images of endless Bavarian woods and streams may blot out the reality of Turkish workers in grungy Swabian towns, his fast-motion cloud banks billowing over mountaintops in *Heart of Glass* may reinforce the mystical power of nature over human beings, but they can hardly liberate the viewer from the realization that mankind has within its power the means to utterly annihilate our natural environment. In such a world, symbols must be compromised and the physicality of death confronted. Sadly, the modesty of *Kaspar Hauser*, of sowing with cress a name in the soil, has given way in the Herzogian universe to the megalomania of bulldozers ripping mile-wide gashes in the virgin rain forest, so that ships can traverse mountains, as if in a dream.

Notes

1   One of the few exceptions was Alexander Kluge, who worked as an assistant director for Fritz Lang on *Der Tiger von Eschnapur* (1959).
2   Other critics have argued for Herzog's sense of the absurd, interpreting him as a Bakhtinian satirist; a point of view I cannot share. See Cleere (1980).
3   Many thanks to Rick Rentschler for pointing out Achternbusch's *Land in Sight*, as well as making a copy of Achternbusch's published works available to me.

Works cited

Achternbusch, Herbert (1978) *Die Atlantikschwimmer*, Frankfurt/Main, Suhrkamp Verlag.
—— (1980) *Es ist ein leichtes, beim Gehen den Boden zu berühren*, Frankfurt/Main, Suhrkamp Verlag.
Cleere, Elizabeth (1980) "Three Films by Werner Herzog: Seen in the Light of the Grotesque," *Wide Angle*, 3 (4), 16.
Cott, Jonathan (1976) "Signs of Life," *Rolling Stone* (November 18), 48–56.
Ebert, Roger (1984) *A Kiss Is Still a Kiss*, Kansas City, Andrews, McNeel & Parker.
Eisner, Lotte (1955) *Die dämonische Leinwand. Die Blütezeit des deutschen Films*, Wiesbaden-Biebrich, Der neue Film.

—— (1969) *The Haunted Screen*, Berkeley CA, University of California Press.

—— (1973) *F. W. Murnau*, London, Secker & Warburg.

—— (1978) *Fritz Lang*, London, Secker & Warburg.

—— (1979) *Die dämonische Leinwand*, Frankfurt/Main, Kommunales Kino.

—— (1984) *Ich hatte ernst ein schönes Vaterland. Memoiren*, ed. by Martje Grohmann, Heidelberg, Verlag Wunderhorn.

Herzog, Werner (1978) *Vom Gehen im Eis. München – Paris 23.11. bis 14.12.1974*, Munich, Carl Hanser Verlag.

—— (1980) *Of Walking in Ice*, trans. by Martje Grohmann and Alan Greenberg, New York, Tanam.

—— (1982) "Die Eisnerin, wer ist das?" *FILM-Korrespondenz*, (7), 1.

—— (1983) "Schwanger gehen mit ganzen Provinzen," *Süddeutsche Zeitung*, (126), 101.

Hobermann, J. (1985) "Obscure Objects of Desire," *Village Voice* (February 19), 61.

Horak, Jan-Christopher (1979) "Werner Herzog's *Ecran absurde*," *Literature/Film Quarterly*, 7 (3), 223–34.

—— (1981) "Liebe, Pflicht und die Erotik des Todes," in Axel Marquardt (ed.) *Preussen im Film*, Reinbek bei Hamburg, Rowohlt Verlag.

Limmer, Wolfgang (1979) "Leben eines Untoten," *Der Spiegel*, (3), 128.

O'Toole, Lawrence (1979) "The Great Ecstasy of the Filmmaker Herzog," *Film Comment* (November–December), 34–9.

Rentschler, Eric (1984) *West German Film in the Course of Time*, Bedford Hills NY, Redgrave.

—— (1985) "Herbert Achternbusch. Celebrating the Power of Creation," in Klaus Phillips (ed.) *New German Filmmakers. From Oberhausen through the 1970s*, New York, Ungar.

Rummler, Fritz (1975) "Zum Filmen notfalls in die Hölle," *Der Spiegel* (November 17), 194.

Strasser, Sylvia (1979) "Indianer wollen keine Filmstatisten sein," *Frankfurter Allgemeine Zeitung* (December 19).

Wetzel, Kraft (1976) "Interview mit Werner Herzog," *Herzog/Kluge/ Straub*, Munich, Hanser.

III
READINGS

3 An archetypal landscape of the mind (*Fata Morgana*)

3

On seeing a mirage

Amos Vogel

1970

Basic philosophical issues in cinema were brought home with a vengeance on a recent revisit to Werner Herzog's *Fata Morgana*. Herzog is one of the masters of the modern cinema, and *Fata Morgana* is one of his key films. In its shimmering opacity it occupies a unique place in the director's oeuvre, quite separate from his deceptively "realistic," plotted films (*Aguirre, Signs of Life, Woyzeck, Kaspar Hauser, Stroszek, et al.*). *Fata Morgana* is the paradigm of Herzog's more overtly experimental films (such as *Even Dwarfs Started Small, Precautions Against Fanatics, Last Words, The Unparalleled Defense of Fortress Deutschkreutz*). It provides a key to the director's universe, and could only have emerged from a country ravaged by two world wars, total fascism, the traumas of scientific genocide and saturation bombings.

Fata Morgana is a sardonic, melancholic comment on mankind's shaky position in the universe. Its elusive, hallucinatory images (accompanied by sacred sixteenth-century Guatemalan creation myths and Herzog's avant-garde texts) coalesce into devastating dream tableaux that cunningly exploit trappings of conventional reality.

The land, though Africa, is an archetypical landscape of the mind. The inhuman grandeur of primeval dunescapes and horizons reveals man's triumphant and empty rape of nature. Factories (their initial purpose unfathomable) abandoned in the desert; decomposing vehicles, military supplies, rotting symbiotically with animal cadavers in intimate, frozen embraces that melt into the soil before our eyes; emaciated black children; flies and insufferable sun.

"In Paradise," says the narrator, "man is born dead" – a typical Herzog line. Herzog, privately, refers to Hieronymus Bosch's *Garden of Earthly Delights*; his paradise, too, "contained God's fatal errors from the start ... visible only in corners, so that the painter would not be branded a heretic." The result is an obsessive, hypnotic, iconoclastic interior travelogue that attempts to project chaos and irrationality in a direct, unmediated form. ("Chaos is in all of my works ... it has positive aspects.")

Among the filmmaker's ideological weapons are absurd, bizarre, goal-directed tableaux that address themselves to the unconscious. A determined young German teacher stands knee-deep in water with her black flock, senselessly forcing them to repeat the phrase "Blitzkrieg is madness" in German. A ridiculous, yet threatening frogman, equipped with grotesque fins and snorkels, desperately holds on to a huge turtle and breathlessly informs us that it has flippers to move, a mouth to take nourishment, and "a behind where it all comes out again." A sweating, fascist German lizard-lover, in a hopeless desert, (obviously affected by years in the African sun) – his square-jawed German visage distorted by madness and black glasses – sadistically manipulates a lizard, comments on its habits, and continuously attempts to avoid getting bitten by it, while flies hover over festering wounds on his hands.

The strongest sequence may be a catastrophic metaphor of hell on earth: a catatonic drummer and a tacky female pianist on a tiny stage in a brothel perform a piece they have played a thousand times without any emotion, endlessly, off-key. "In the Golden Age, man and wife live in harmony," the commentator says, as they are photographed head-on, with all the merciful cruelty of a humanist filmmaker who must show everything. At the end of the piece, they remain immobile. There is no applause.

Fata Morgana emerges as a sardonic comment on technology, sentimentality, despoliation of land and people, projected by a suffering visionary tremblingly aware of our limited possibilities, outrageous perseverance, and almost bearable ridiculousness.

It was with this film that Herzog progressed from the promise of genius implicit in his earlier films to a level of artistry at once more subversive and more inaccessible; for here, working solely with the materials of reality, Herzog, in a cosmic pun on cinéma vérité, recovered the metaphysical beneath the visible. It is only in such works that we achieve intimations of the radical humanism of the future.

1980

Not having seen the film for ten years, I was more than eager to expose myself again to the acidity and black humor of this monument of icy subversion. The outcome was disaster.

Not that the indispensable, courageous repertory theater was empty. It was packed, for by 1980 (with the customary decade or two of delay) Herzog had finally become a cult figure. Viewers just born when he had started in films waited expectantly for further revelations in the Herzog canon.

Here is what they and I experienced. Having originally been exposed to the crystal clarity and sharp-edged photography of a first-generation 35mm print projected on a large screen, I found myself peering uncertainly into the dim, contrastless recesses of a cheap 16mm print, decorated with striations and scratches. The tones – the gross and subtle details so central to the film – were gone, reconfirming that its magical power derived from a profusion of dream images that are subliminally responsible for those profound psychic shocks inevitably associated with all great moments of visual cinema. There were protagonists of central tableaux suddenly "missing" because of lack of contrast; there were black areas that had turned gray, and white areas that had turned gray as well. There had been those unforgettable, shimmering reflections of heat waves connected with an important object in the far background, shuttling back and forth impotently, obsessively, in several separate sequences – a symbol considered basic to the film by Herzog; this was missing. There were the identical shots, obsessively repeated, of a huge jetliner (technology itself) touching down at least seven times in "primitive" Africa amidst hallucinatory blazes of polluted grandeur; a threat; a monster; its impact was now entirely obliterated by lack of detail. There was the abandoned factory, its blood-red steel girders squatting threateningly against a black, incongruous, pre-industrial background, a bloodstain upon nature; its colors were now washed out of existence.

Simultaneously, within the theater, one stared, unbelievingly, into brightly lit, red exit signs, situated in front of the viewer, an incessant anti-illusionist onslaught on the entire film. The projectionist – perhaps underpaid and undertrained, "doing a job," not particularly concerned with Herzog's philosophical musings nor helped by the murkiness of most of the images – tantalizingly projected the entire work just sufficiently out of focus to make the viewer unable to feel the magic and power of the sharply defined graphic compositions. The audience, non-comprehending for all the obvious reasons, had grown restless, moving about in their squeaking seats, embarking on equally squeaky trips across ancient wood floors to bathroom or exit or lobby conversations, dimly overheard inside the theater, as were the projectionist's muttered imprecations and the rattling of an under-serviced 16mm projector. The tired screen was overlaid with the grayness of generations of films; it was also pathetically small in respect to the size and shape of the theater, creating the infamous postage-stamp effect which reduced this subtle visual work to a series of dim messages from afar – imperfectly grasped, spectral projections of Kafkaesque situations with just enough visibility of possibly portentous but inexplicable events to create disorientation.

In an act of supreme irony, Herzog's lament for the unfulfilled promise of a Genesis and a Paradise that somehow failed had been turned against him. *Fata Morgana* refers to a magnificent, false mirage for desperate travelers; the condition of print and exhibition subverted the film itself into what it successfully deplored: the failure of a planned piece of perfection.

It is, of course, entirely questionable whether customary modes of commercial exhibition are suitable for meditative, non-narrative works closer to Robert Wilson or Richard Foreman than to John Ford. Perhaps *Fata Morgana* needs to be seen, in 35mm only, from third row center, on a large screen, one to ten spectators at a time, none in adjoining seats. Perhaps such works demand detailed program notes, to explicate background and context. Or must the magnificent powers of human imagination forever be yoked to the requirements of commerce?

What kind of art is this that depends so heavily on the nature of its presentation, and to which access in a form close to its "original" becomes ever more impossible? What shall we do with the evanescence of film stock (technologically and economically based), with cheap laboratories (inevitable in a profit-oriented society), with businessmen "understandably" skimping on making appropriately timed prints of meritorious works that have proven unprofitable? What shall we do with equally praiseworthy exhibitors only able to operate in ancient theaters, with tired projection systems, again, and inevitably, responding to profit-loss considerations? What shall we do with visual cinema if we cannot see the visuals? What kind of art is this, in which an exhibitor, laboratory worker, distributor, and projectionist have the power to determine the nature of one's experience of a work, acting as unwelcome mediators between viewer and artist?

It is as if *King Lear* were available only one day per decade in one city per continent, in fiftieth-generation, pirated, Hong Kong copies of which entire pages were missing, individual paragraphs not quite readable, portions of characters obliterated with frustrating intimations of potential greatness; the stuff of Borges, of Kafka, of Marquez.

What, then, is this film *Fata Morgana*? Where is "the text" to be deconstructed? Is it the original stored in a vault for no one to see? Or am I to report my "knowledge" of the closest approximation to it – a 35mm print – to readers and students, as if I were Marco Polo, bringing back (ten years after) my "impressions" of certain stupefying riches of the east fleetingly glimpsed but once?

To be resigned to what is being broached here (and therefore to the fate of *Fata Morgana*) is in consonance with Herzog's somber world view; he is explicit about this. Great works will arise in every generation (less often since the conglomerates have taken over); they live for a moment of historical time, then slowly fall back into the undifferentiated flux – itself a symbol of recurring birth, maturity, and death. They are flashes of brilliance that temporarily "light our ways" along the corridors of darkness until extinguished by the great Indifferent Projectionist in his crochety booth, muttering obscenities to himself as he brings the uncertain discourse to an end amidst squeaks, misunderstandings, and obtrusive exit signs.

And yet, in every audience, there is one young person, as if struck down by what he sees, who ultimately will once again perform the eternal dance of divine madness: the creation of masterpieces. Briefly carried in triumph on the shoulders of believers, he, too, is ultimately slain by mortality and indifference.

CONSONANCE

4 *The Great Ecstasy of the Sculptor Steiner*

4

Last words: observations on a new language

William Van Wert

At first glance eclectic, obsessive and renegade, the documentaries of
Werner Herzog do, finally and inevitably, fit into the elaborate intertextual fabric of his fiction films. Even as Herzog was gaining notoriety
outside of Germany for feature films like *Signs of Life, Even Dwarfs
Started Small* and *Aguirre, the Wrath of God*, he was simultaneously
submitting short films to major film festivals like Oberhausen. These
documentaries are not considered "lesser" works by Herzog himself,
and, in fact, they are crucial to understanding the creative trajectory of
this most important of the filmmakers to have emerged from the so-
called New German Cinema.

Many other internationally known filmmakers, Herzog's contemporaries, began their careers in the documentary form, then moved into
feature-length fiction films, only to abandon documentaries, by and
large, after commercial success: Jean-Luc Godard, Nagisa Oshima,
Sembene Ousmane, for example. For these filmmakers, the documentary film seems to have been an apprenticeship, dictated more by
financial constraint than by personal preference. Why, then, has Herzog
persisted in making documentary films, especially when they are time-
consuming and questionable in terms of reputation, distribution, and
financial rewards? The reasons are many and provocative.

One of the reasons for Herzog's persistence in the documentary form
has to do with distribution. Whereas his documentaries, by subject
matter and running time, are excluded from traditional film-booking
circuits, they are appropriately suitable for film festivals, where German
shorts got their first breakthrough in the international market, and for
television, an industry much stronger in Germany than the film industry
because it is government-subsidized. While Herzog may promote the

myth that he has been obscured in his own country, he quietly continues to make documentaries whose running times fit the requirements of German national television programming.

Another reason has to do with influence. It is perhaps fashionable, as a question of national cinema, to see Werner Herzog as a neo-expressionist, especially since the making of *Nosferatu* and *Woyzeck*, to find links between his themes and those of Wiene, early Murnau and Lang, and even to trace a film like *Fata Morgana* back to Todd Browning's *Freaks*. But the documentary Herzog, both in composition and in irony, derives from the French surrealist tradition, from the biting *Land Without Bread* of Luis Buñuel to the documentaries of Chris Marker.[1] The romantic sensationalism to which Herzog is sometimes prone in his approach to his fictional subjects is curbed in the documentaries by the same cerebral wit and sudden irony that informs the French surrealist shorts. As for them, so too for Herzog, the documentary is not strictly referential or simply derivative of reality, but a simultaneous exploration of subjects' lives and cinematic forms.

Other reasons for Herzog's documentaries, however, can be found in the particular temperament of Herzog himself. First, the experimenter in Herzog can best be satisfied in the documentaries. The very same inclinations that have gotten him into trouble in the fiction films (hypnotizing actors in *Heart of Glass*; the repeated use of former asylum inmate Bruno S. in *Kaspar Hauser* and *Stroszek*; the strained manipulation of native Indians in *Aguirre* and *Fitzcarraldo*) are much less problematic in the documentary form, where the question of manipulation is more subtle, more obscured, because Herzog himself often "acts" in these films as interviewer, filmmaker or *engagé* spectator. He "manipulates" himself, then, in terms of compositional positioning, inserts and point of view, while his found subjects are ostensibly encouraged to play themselves, not some preordained role.

Thus, there is no need to confront the labor practices of the feature films in his documentaries. There is, instead, a valorization of the documentaries in the fact that Herzog "controls" them better than the fiction films, from concept to post-production and distribution. Shy, estranged, reclusive and idiosyncratic behind the camera, Herzog emerges as something of an exhibitionist, even a narcissist, in front of the documentary lens. At the same time, with the smaller crews required for the documentaries, he can maintain, and often enhance, the intimate bond he has with Jörg Schmidt-Reitwein, Thomas Mauch and Ed Lachman, his cinematographers; with Beate Mainka-Jellinghaus, his editor; and with musical coordinators like Florian Fricke and Popol Vuh;

an intimacy which is often strained during the long ordeals of the more problematic fiction films.

Finally, Herzog seems to require the documentaries as a way to exercise (exorcize?) his *idées fixes* while maintaining his sanity for the fiction films. It is no coincidence that he is fast-working, frenetic and prolific with the documentaries, while he is slow, brooding and meticulous with the features. He conceived *Last Words* while working on *Signs of Life*. Almost as a parody of his critics of *Signs of Life*, he made *Precautions Against Fanatics* in the same year as *Last Words*. He stumbled onto Fini Straubinger and the relatively easy making of *Land of Silence and Darkness* while grappling with the immense logistical problems in making *Aguirre*. In 1974 he produced both the documentary *The Great Ecstasy of the Sculptor Steiner* and the supposedly fictional *The Mystery of Kaspar Hauser* (*Every Man For Himself and God Against All*), the result of which was a further blurring of the lines between documentary and fiction, since Herzog creatively ennobled Steiner on the one hand, while asking Bruno S. to "act out" a largely autobiographical plot in *Kaspar Hauser* (beatings, deprivation, abandonment, treatment as a social curiosity or freak), itself based on an historical figure and document. Then again in 1976, Herzog surrounded the making of a fiction film, *Heart of Glass*, with a flurry of documentaries: *How Much Wood Would a Woodchuck Chuck, No One Will Play With Me* and *La Soufrière*. Finally, in 1980 he again made two documentaries, both in America (*Huie's Sermon* and *God's Angry Man*), while trying to work out the immense problems involved in making *Fitzcarraldo* (Mick Jagger and Jason Robards Jr pulling out of the project, the clash of temperaments between Herzog and Klaus Kinski, the logistical problems and prohibitive expenses necessary to building boats and pulleys in unfriendly terrain). Most recently in 1985, Herzog documentaries (*The Dark Glow of the Mountains* and *Ballad of the Little Soldier*) were still accompanying the release of fiction films (*Where the Green Ants Dream*).

If I can exaggerate the dynamic at work in this dizzy listing of projects, I see two Herzogs at work here: the one who hurries through a hands-on documentary project with fervor, enthusiasm and humor, and the one who broods over the fictional project, more obsessive for that brooding, more tyrannical with collaborators, more desperate for financing, almost lost in the labyrinth of problems. Almost always the question of Herzog's sanity arises around the fiction films, against which the documentaries can be seen as frenetic therapy, safe exorcisms of his personal demons.

The final motivation in Herzog's predisposition toward the documentary form has to do with a vision of himself, with which most audiences are unfamiliar. Just as Herzog facilitated the playing out of Bruno S.'s autobiography in films like *Kaspar Hauser* and *Stroszek*, so, too, has Herzog been able to access his own autobiography in the documentaries. His passion for ski-jumping as a teenager was responsible for *The Great Ecstasy of the Sculptor Steiner*. He acknowledges an affinity of projection with Fini Straubinger as well, in terms of the deprivation and misunderstanding she has suffered and which he chronicles in *Land of Silence and Darkness*. His claim that he once had a vision from God as a child helps to explain his fascination with the fringe preachers in *Huie's Sermon* and *God's Angry Man*. And his vision of himself as an archeological journalist is the source of a documentary like *La Soufrière* as much as the fictional expeditions in *Aguirre, Fitzcarraldo* and *Where the Green Ants Dream*.

Given the attraction of a realist's autobiographical exploration in the documentary shorts, one would reasonably expect to know a great deal about Herzog's inner self from them. But this is not the case. These films are neither personally direct nor politically consistent. Herzog substitutes artifice for vulnerability, irony for frankness, and a joking metaphysics for coherent politics. As with the Magritte adage that "an image is more like another image than like the thing it represents," the showman Herzog shows his sleight-of-hand more than he shows himself or his subjects.

Even when we appreciate the importance of the documentaries for understanding Herzog's creative impulse and total body of work, we must still distinguish between the various kinds of documentaries he makes. They seem to be of three kinds: (1) the self-conscious shorts like *Last Words* and *Precautions Against Fanatics*, those which are more telling of Herzog's formation and style than of their actual subject matter; (2) the road-show sketches like *Woodchuck, Huie's Sermon* and *God's Angry Man*; and (3) the full-length documentaries like *Land of Silence and Darkness, The Great Ecstasy of the Sculptor Steiner* and *La Soufrière*, those documentaries whose brilliant interplay of language, image and musical soundtrack make them the most compelling of Herzog's films, and without which this study would be suspect, even superfluous, to the present volume of texts.

I propose now to examine that interplay of language, image and musical soundtrack, elaborating upon the last three films to justify the importance I have given them in the overall body of Herzog's work.

The spoken text

It is my contention that language, itself, is the main character in most of Herzog's films, and especially in the documentaries. Whether characters talk too fast (*Woodchuck*) or not at all (*Land of Silence and Darkness*), Herzog is fascinated with their speech, their dialect, their lack of speech, their reasons for silence, their compensatory gestures. He called the machine-gun rhythms of the auctioneers' rapping in *Woodchuck*, albeit naively, the "poetry of latent capitalism,"[2] and he subtitled the film: "Observations on a New Language." This particular example can be extended to all of these diverse cinematic texts, in which Herzog is searching, almost in the manner of a folklorist, for the last poetry possible, and for a language, or refusal of language, that merges with music. It is at this level of language-as-main-character that one can trace, zigzag-fashion, complex intertextual references between the films, documentary and fiction alike. Often, though, the individual film contains characters who run the gamut from silence to idiosyncratic speech to multiplicity of speech or babel. For the purposes of this study, however, I shall isolate and exaggerate the three categories.

(1) Silence. It is important to note that Herzog seems to have a devotee's loyalty to characters whose speech has been lost, interrupted, arrested, or willfully discarded. He resists calling them extreme characters or marginal beings. Instead, he refers to them as *pure* beings, and he includes himself in their company:

> Yes, all the rest are eccentric. And I think that individuals like Kaspar Hauser are not so much "marginal" figures. They are just very *pure* figures that have somehow been able to survive in a more or less pure form. Sometimes, of course, they are under very heavy pressure, like, let's say, Steiner, or like Fini Straubinger, or even like myself when I was making *La Soufrière*. But, under this sort of pressure, people reveal their various natures to us. It's exactly the same that is done in chemistry when you have a particular substance that is unknown to you. When this happens, you must put this substance under extreme conditions – like extreme heat, extreme pressure, extreme radiation – and it is only *then* that you will be able to find out the essential structure of this substance which you are trying to explain and to discover and to describe. (Walsh/Ebert, 1979, 7–8)

So, the purest of the pure figures, then, must be the entirely silent ones.

In *Last Words*, Herzog's earliest available documentary, a man is found on the evacuated islands near Crete and brought back to Greece. Even before the credits sequence is finished, the man is saying his supposed last words: "I'm supposed to say 'No,' but I'm not even saying that. This is my last word." On the surface, the joke is self-reflexive, a postmodernist joke, like the John Barth short story in which the writer announces that his last word will be his last word, and so forth. But Herzog goes beyond the nihilist simple sentence of a supposedly silent man. He is interested in the causes, the compensations, and at least one leap into poetic association. The causes are explained by a man at the pier: "I don't know what was wrong with him. When the police found him, they found a pile of severed heads. . . . He must have eaten lizards. . . . When they removed the lepers, he stayed behind." Another man repeats that he must have eaten lizards, which sets up the pattern of artificial repetitions in the film. Herzog has two policemen, facing the camera, repeat a dozen times: "Hello. How are you keeping? We got him over here. We rescued him." In so doing, Herzog stacks the argument in his favor. The redundancy of other people makes a devalued mockery of language, whereas the found man has already learned to compensate for his refusal of language: he is known as the best lyre player in all of Crete.

It is typical of Herzog in all his films that the next step beyond the stoppage of speech is not always silence, but sometimes music. When he is not playing the lyre, the man throws up his hands in repeated emblematic gestures, not unlike those of the deaf-blind in *Land of Silence and Darkness*, the choreography of auctioneers' hands in *Woodchuck* or the power-broker hands of preachers in *Huie's Sermon* and *God's Angry Man*.

After Herzog has shown the causes and compensations for the refusal of language in *Last Words*, he "fictionalizes" the document by revealing, in poetic fashion, that the man may very well be delusional. One of the policemen states that when they seized the man and put him on the boat, the man said: "You can't do anything to me. I've got a whole fleet behind me." And then the policeman adds: "But his boats were all scratched in rock." This last touch, suggesting the man's delusion, seems to ennoble the character for Herzog, turning him into one of those pure figures, like Kaspar Hauser and Fini Straubinger.

The malady of Fini and the other deaf-blind in *Land of Silence and Darkness* is both real and imagined at the same time, and Herzog approaches his subject with more than his usual respect and invention. Fini Straubinger narrates her first memories, the lost visions of her

childhood: a ski-flier, animals at a zoo, the feel of inanimate objects like chairs. She continues to narrate as Herzog shifts to a thematic section entitled "Memories," comprised of photographs of Fini and her parents when she was a child. We see what she can no longer see, but can only narrate through memory. Gradually, all of Fini's impairments are explained, and once again Herzog makes sure that the causes are followed with the unexpected complications or compensations. Silence, then, is anything but silent: "People think deafness means silence, but that's wrong. . . . It's a constant noise, going from a gentle humming . . . to a constant droning, which is the worst."[3] The cinematic structure of various voice-removals helps the spectator to appreciate both the deprivation and the compensation of Fini and her friends. With Fini's interpreter's voice controlling the spoken text and Herzog inventing the visuals to accompany that text, we as spectators are gradually made to realize that, just as Fini and her friends are deprived of our sensory world, so too are we deprived of theirs. And, when Fini is thus "recuperated" as a healthy being, she becomes our guide in visiting more extreme cases, two of which are noteworthy here. The first is Else Fehrer, whose mother, the only person with whom Else could communicate, has died. By way of commentary Herzog adds: "Since no charity or old people's home would accept Else Fehrer, she was sent, out of necessity, to an insane asylum, where she doesn't belong at all. Else Fehrer withdrew completely into herself. She never spoke again." The second is Heinrich Fleischman, a man "so neglected by his parents that he forgot to speak and write," and "rejected by society, he looked for the company of animals and lived in a stable for a long time." This is the man who hugs the tree at the end of the film. Deprived and then compensated, both Else Fehrer and Heinrich Fleischman are partial mirror-images of Bruno S., the former asylum inmate who had already gained some acclaim as a street-musician in Berlin when Herzog found him.

Causes, compensations and poetry again. Both Fini and Miss Julie present poems, which are marked by strong visuals and a lack of logical transitions. The incomprehensibility of their poems does not, in this case, signify bad poetry so much as private poetry, whose effect we able-bodied spectators can never fully grasp.

Herzog began filming *Aguirre* upon completion of *Land of Silence and Darkness*, and the dynamic of the latter is fully evident in the former. The screenplay is littered with indications of "prolonged silence" and "Aguirre is silent." Attacks by Indians are almost always announced by profound silences: "The jungle lies in horrible silence, maliciously still, the woodland waiting" (Herzog, 1980, 59). There is even a character with an unpronounceable name, Quauhtlehuanitzin, which means "the one who speaks," who does not speak. Even the Bible, the "Word of God," causes death by silence.

> Carvajal, waiting impatiently all this time for his turn, asks the Indian if he had heard of our Savior Jesus Christ and of the True Word of God. The Indian is very confused and gives no answer. This, here, is a Bible with the Word of God, and they had come to carry God's Light into the darkness. While saying this he shows him a Bible. The Indian is dumbstruck and does not comprehend a thing. Yes, within this book is the Word of God, Carvajal insists. Deeply disturbed, the Indian picks up the Bible and puts his ear to it, listening. "It does not speak," he says and casts the Bible to the floor. Highly incensed, some Spaniards seize him at once and kill him on the spot. (Herzog, 1980, 75)

Three of the four people on display in the "Riddles of the Spheres" sequence in *Kaspar Hauser* are similarly language-stunted. Mozart suffers from Mallarmé-like blank spaces.

> The director shouts out that Mozart didn't start to talk until the age of three, but once he did, he asked for nothing but the music of Mozart. Night and day he longed obsessively for Mozart. By the time he was five he knew all the scores by heart. Now he doesn't talk anymore, as he is only interested in dark holes in the ground, in cave entrances and drainage ditches that capture his attention and enable him to meditate upon the blackness within. He stopped speaking altogether at the age of five when they tried to teach him how to read and write at school. He couldn't do it, he said, because the bright whiteness of the paper blinded him. Since then he has refused to speak. (Herzog, 1980, 135)

And Hombrecito, the Indian on display, "doesn't speak a word of any language other than his Indian dialect," but he is the only living member of the original Native and Indian Show that once toured Europe. So, he, too, is silent.

Finally, Kaspar Hauser, who was beaten, abandoned and raised with animals in caves, speaks, when he speaks at all, in his own logic and syntax. The three of them – Mozart, Hombrecito and Kaspar – embody the various deprivations, both physical and psychological, that result in language-loss, silence and music-acquisition that we have already seen in earlier films.

In *God's Angry Man* Dr Eugene Scott refuses to speak on the air when his television fundraiser stalls. "Not one more word tonight until that thousand comes in," Scott roars. There is a difference, though, in Herzog's treatment of this silence. The cause is rendered, but no compensatory language, like music, takes the place of speech, nor does Herzog interject any poetic commentary to layer the narrative. Scott may be fascinating, but he is no pure figure, no foundling of the jungle or cave. There is nothing deprived about him, his person or his evangelical empire in southern California. Instead, he seems to represent the abuse of silence.

ABUSE of silence

Herzog populates both fictions and documentaries with these silent characters. When they appear in the fiction films, as in *Aguirre, Kaspar Hauser* and *Where the Green Ants Dream,* their effect is both surreal (because they are not assimilated into the rest of the narrative) and documentary-real, because they demand attention more than immediate analysis, like found objects.

(2) Dialect. Herzog shares with Godard a fascination with the way languages are spoken by non-native speakers and the permutations on pronunciation in any given language system: the clipped rhythms of the antagonists in *Precautions Against Fanatics*; the slurred half-syllables and wailing of some of the impaired in *Land of Silence and Darkness*; the Swiss-German of the ski-flier Steiner; the slang of Kaspar Hauser; the drawl of auctioneers in *Woodchuck*; the pidgin French of the three survivors in *La Soufrière*; and the frenetic sing-song pitch of preachers in *Huie's Sermon* and *God's Angry Man.*

DiAlect permutations on pronunciation NON NAtive SpeAkers

Put another way, Herzog is interested in these *pure* forms of speech and does not consider them bastardizations. The screenplay for *Kaspar Hauser* does not include the soft-focus shots of wavy wheat fields to the accompaniment of the Pachelbel Kanon. Instead, there is a long monologue by Kaspar in the cave, a monologue full of slang and made-up words, and the awkward English translation renders them this way:

> I want to say myself how hard it be for me. There, where I was always lokked in, in this prison, it seemed there wel to me, becos I knew naught of this world, and so long as I was lokked in and never seen no human being. I had two wood orses and a dog, and with these I always played. (Herzog, 1980, 100–1)

Of his own diaries, Herzog states that their major interest derives from the lapses into Bavarian dialect, with "wrong" (read: poetic) German:

It's probably the *best* single work that I've ever done in all my life. Perhaps that sounds easy to say without my having the proof here to show to you. I hope that it will be translated into English soon, but it will be *very* difficult to translate because the text lapses quite often into the Bavarian dialect. There are many expressions in it that are "wrong" – wrong German in a grammatical sense – and to discover how to translate this "wrong" German into wrong English that will still make sense is going to be very difficult. For example, there's one sentence towards the end of the book that says in German: "Together we shall cook fire, and we shall stop the fish." Well, you can *cook* a meal, but you cannot *cook* fire; and you can *stop* the traffic, but you cannot *stop* the fish. You can *catch* the fish but not *stop* the fish. This kind of expression sounds "wrong" and very, very strange even when you read it in German, but, even so, in German still there is a definite feeling behind these words that somehow they express the absolute truth. Translated into English, however, as literally "together we shall cook fire, and we shall stop the fish," these words lose everything. They *only* sound wrong and nothing more beyond that. This means that there will be a very, very deep problem in translating this book ... and so I must ask you all to learn German. (Walsh/Ebert, 1979, 33)

Herzog has already circumvented this translation problem, following the example of other New German Cinema directors, most notably Wim Wenders,[4] by making films directly in English. Three of his documentaries – *Woodchuck, Huie's Sermon* and *God's Angry Man* – were made in English. *Stroszek* is a mix of German and English. And there is an English-language version of *Nosferatu*, with slightly different footage, coexisting with the German-language version.

(3) Babel. If Herzog has chosen to make three documentaries directly in English, it is not out of any love of the exotic or as a way of catering to English-speaking audiences. The spoken text in *Woodchuck, Huie's Sermon* and *God's Angry Man* often begs for subtitles in English. The auctioneers' rap is more fascinating for the sound and the rhythm of the speech than for any phrases or clauses to be caught and comprehended. Herzog's format is that of the episodic sequence, broken into three cumulative times: the various auctioneers, one by one, give a brief presentation of how they got started, how they practice at home or on the road, why they continue to be auctioneers; then, again one by one, they compete at the Thirteenth World Championships near

Lancaster, Pennsylvania, in Amish country; then they give speeches, again one by one, at the awards banquet. And, if Herzog chooses to think of their rap as the last poetry of latent capitalism, that bias does not come through to the spectator, who witnesses the straightforward chronology without added commentary from the filmmaker.

Auctioneers World Championships

Huie's Sermon is like *Woodchuck*, in that the language used in the sermon is fast, repetitive, cumulative and enchanting, more like an incantation for emotional expression than a vehicle for straight communication. Periodically, the text slows down enough so that the viewer knows the object of Huie's attacks: government, homosexuality, abortion, artificial insemination. But, more often, Huie's words come out as song, the constant litany-like humming, not unlike the jungle droning that plagues and enchants Aguirre and his men. What sets *Huie's Sermon* apart from *Woodchuck* is the contrast-statement of Herzog's camera at the end of the film, which will be covered in the next section of this study.

God's Angry Man is the most interesting of the English-language documentaries, not because Dr Eugene Scott is any more interesting than Huie or the auctioneers, but because Herzog, himself, takes a more active role as interviewer, which necessitates a more interesting structure of sequences and transitions in the film.

This active role of Herzog as interviewer is not to be understated in the overall importance of the documentaries to his film output. In *God's Angry Man* Herzog seems to play the goad to Scott, asking potentially insipid questions that seem more like beginning therapy sessions than like cinéma vérité. "Do you want to have children?" Herzog asks. "Do you cry?" Herzog prods. "You seem to be very lonesome," Herzog leads. The questions are geared to beg either an emotional response from Scott or a demonstration of his lack of emotionality away from the camera.

I find it interesting, and even a support of my contention of Herzog's narcissism, that references made to Herzog's presence or to the fact of a German film being made, are not edited out of the final film. Steve Lipshay, the winning auctioneer in *Woodchuck*, tells people at the awards banquet that a German film is being made and suggests that he wants to go to Germany to see it. Huie, in his diatribe against money as a kind of anti-Christ, says the following: "Every time you go overseas and put out a dollar and they say that ain't no good ... Gimme a German Mark or something." In the work of other filmmakers, such comments would be edited out. In Herzog they are left in.

But it is Herzog's role as interviewer that makes *Land of Silence and*

Darkness, The Great Ecstasy of the Sculptor Steiner and *La Soufrière* the best of his documentaries. He leads Fini Straubinger in *Land of Silence and Darkness* from topic to topic, from patient to patient, filling in the gaps where the characters, themselves, are often prone to falling silent. In *Steiner* it is Herzog, himself, both visible and audible, who encourages Steiner's paranoia, who runs around Planica, Yugoslavia, infusing neutral ramps and jumps with menace. One is quite aware of the former aspiring ski-flier in Herzog, dogging Steiner, even when Steiner turns his back, becomes moody, wants to avoid interviews. And, when Steiner falls and hurts himself, a visually shaken Herzog asks his observers on the crew if this injury will jeopardize their film. Once again, the narcissism of Herzog is not edited out. He allows this frantic self-serving concern to show.

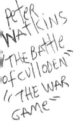

Herzog is a frenetic interviewer in the way Peter Watkins is anxious and agitated in documentaries like *The Battle of Culloden* and *The War Game*, but, whereas Watkins intrudes upon the actors, insists himself in battle zones and gets quite politically righteous and strident to the accompaniment of hand-held camera and jerky visuals, Herzog is both less political and less composed. Rather, Herzog seems to project himself into the project, so that he ceases to be simple interviewer and becomes alternate conscience or alternate ski-flier in *Steiner* or yet another endangered inhabitant in *La Soufrière*. The second half of *La Soufrière*, the interviews with the three men, would be consummately boring, without Herzog's interjections, not just as interviewer, but also as someone equally endangered by the eruption that never comes. And it is Herzog's admission of embarrassment, that he has chronicled a catastrophe that never happened, that ironizes the ending of *La Soufrière*, with those majestic aerial views of mountains, sea and clouds, to the musical accompaniment of Wagner. Herzog playing meek and mild next to grandiose visuals and the surge of classical music, that is what is finally memorable about the film, not the fact of the volcano or its hypothetical eruption.

The image

Herzog speaks eloquently on the subject of the image, perhaps too eloquently at times. If he can be believed, he is even more messianic about the need for new images than he is on the subject of pure figures and extreme languages:

At the present time, I think that we do not know very much about the process of vision itself. We know *so* very little about it, and, with this kind of experimental work that I have been describing, we might soon be able to learn a little bit more. This kind of knowledge is precisely what we *need*. We need it very urgently because we live in a society that has *no* adequate images anymore, and, if we do not find adequate images and an adequate language for our civilization with which to express them, we will die out like the dinosaurs. (Walsh/Ebert, 1979, 21)

Still, it is precisely what Herzog does with the image that makes his documentaries so worth studying. The reputation that Herzog enjoys as a "visionary" filmmaker derives from the beautiful *idée-fixe* images in his films: the close-ups of dwarfs in *Fata Morgana*; the deaf-blind fondling the animals with such unrestrained joy in *Land of Silence and Darkness*; the endless turns in the Amazon and low-angle up shots of lianas in *Aguirre*; the overcranked (slow-motion) photography of Steiner flying like a weightless bird through the air in *The Great Ecstasy of the Sculptor Steiner*; the wavy wheat fields and the visions of the Caucasus and the Sahara in *Kaspar Hauser*; the haunting opening of *Heart of Glass*; the final aerial views of shrouded volcano and mountains in *La Soufrière*; the RVs and carnival at the end of *Stroszek*; the eerie humanness of his *Nosferatu*; those weighted husks of rusty boats in *Fitzcarraldo*; the Aborigines in the supermarket in *Where the Green Ants Dream*, casting spells. These are the emblematic images from Herzog's films, each one as memorable as the entire film which houses it.

And yet there is a perceivable methodology to Herzog's vision, and perhaps more transparent in the documentaries than in the fiction films. If *Last Words* is a documentary in which all people face the camera frontally, and rigidly so, then the last image of the leper/lyre player, seen in silhouette and in profile through the window of the cantina, is a wonderful ironic touch for repeating his earlier pronouncement that he will no longer speak.

Precaution Against Fanatics employs a similar structure. Throughout the film the major visual metaphor has been that of circling, the fanatic walking horses around a tree and supposedly protecting the horses from other fanatics, only to be interrupted by a short fat man who chases him away from the racetrack. The same circling of the figure before a static camera takes place in the park, where our fanatic is now protecting the flamingos from other fanatics. But what separates the two circlings is a straight-on lesson in phenomenology, in which the fanatic says:

[handwritten margin notes: Beautiful idée-fixe images in his films; endless turns in the Amazon and low-angle up shots of lianas in Aguirre; emblematic images each as memorable as the entire film which houses it; Circling; Precaution Against Fanatics]

Here I stand. I cannot do otherwise. And this here is my hand.... You gotta see me.... When you see this fist, you gotta see me.... This fist is joined to this body.... Have you ever wept blood?

Have you ever wept blood(?)

Those static pronouncements set up the ending, in which our fanatic is still begging the spectator to be seen, while the camera circles the fat man from an aerial point of view.

These structures are rather straightforward, even a bit simplistic, but they foreshadow a visual leap in consciousness for *Land of Silence and Darkness*. The opening sequences of that latter film are poetic and associative, in much the same way that Alain Resnais conveys memory achronologically and associatively in films like *Night and Fog* and *Hiroshima mon amour*. The opening image, the haunting image of the ski-flier, is given a context in the narrative by the commentary from Fini Straubinger: "When I was a child, before I was like this, I watched a ski-jumping contest." Like Godard before him, who used images emblematically in one film, only to make them major themes in later films (Vietnam, prostitution, sexism, the city as wasteland, Marxist-Leninist criticism), Herzog foreshadows *Steiner* in this opening image of *Land of Silence and Darkness*.

Alain Resnais conveys memory achronologically and associatively in films like Night + Fog and Hiroshima mon amour

But the key to this image and succeeding images is associative. Herzog moves from the *jumping* of the ski-flier to Fini Straubinger jumping, with the note: "I always jump when I'm touched." And from the mention of touching, we move to Fini, Miss Julie and friends touching the animals at the zoo, with an interesting especial emphasis given to birds like woodpeckers and pheasants. The next sequence begins with Fini and Miss Julie touching airplane wings, with the title "The First Flight," which title brings us back to the ski-flier and the arena of memories of the beginning. Their airplane ride is like an animated silent movie, full of gestures, signing, hand-holding for speaking into the palms and fingers, smiles, approval and clapping of hands. And the next title, which ends the cluster of sequences, is entitled "Memories," with commentary as an overlay to the photographs of Fini and her parents from her childhood. Ski-flier/memories to jumping/touching to touching animals (including birds) to the airplane/flying/touching to memories again. The images, themselves, and the editing between images are so much more sophisticated than those in *Last Words* and *Precaution Against Fanatics* that it is difficult to believe they were made by the same person and three years apart from each other.

But the cinematographic structure to *Land of Silence and Darkness* is like that of Resnais' *Hiroshima mon amour* in another way. The first half of *Hiroshima* is a Proustian first-person narrative, with associative intercutting and overloading of images, until the point in the film where the Japanese lover says that they have some thirteen hours to kill until her plane leaves. "Real time" seems to set in, and the second half of the film is a much less interesting, sometimes tedious account of their approach-avoidance, with impromptu arrivals, sudden departures, and many slow chase scenes in between. Likewise, in *Land of Silence and Darkness*, Herzog overloads the images with stark shots like photographs or emotional shots of fondling animals and signing in palms. Thus, the first half of the film is the interior exploration of Fini Straubinger: how did she become deaf-blind, what are her hopes and fears, how has she compensated for her impairment, what is she now, after thirty years of lying in bed. But, once Fini and Miss Julie have rendered their poems, "real time" enters the film structure: we stay outside the consciousness of Fini until the very end of the film, when she tells us that, if another world war were to break out, she would not even know it. Fini "emerges" halfway through the film as an integrated being, more healthy than her peers, and she becomes our guide through the visits to the less fortunate, like Else Fehrer, the wild child Harald and Vladimir Kokol, the most impaired of them all. As in *Hiroshima,* these sequences of visits in *Land of Silence and Darkness* are usually straightforward, benign, observant, sometimes even tedious. But the dazzling intercutting and intertitling of the first half now serve as "memories," our memories of Fini, who in the second half is quite shut off from the spectator and totally focused upon her contemporaries and on how best she can bring them joy. This sharp demarcation between beautiful point-of-view shots and static silent-observer shots is a calculated risk on Herzog's part, but one which I think works well enough to make *Land of Silence and Darkness* a masterpiece.

The Great Ecstasy of the Sculptor Steiner is also a masterpiece for quite the opposite reasons. The action sequences of actual ski-flying are breath-taking by themselves, and *Steiner* is one of the best sports films ever made, for them alone. But the complexity of the film derives instead from the tension between Steiner and Herzog, who, having failed at ski-flying himself, insists himself so obtrusively into Steiner's life and moods, with an equal balance between reverence for Steiner's accomplishments and a total lack of respect for privacy when Steiner clearly wishes to withdraw.

I am aware, watching the opening sequences of *Steiner,* even before the short scene of wood-carving and metal-sculpture, not so much of space but of time. Soft-focus shots in slow motion make the ski-flying, an apparent contradiction in logic, seem real. The slow-motion images stretch spectator credibility, without ever breaking tension. I am made to think of Norman McLaren's *Pas de deux* and Chris Marker's *La Jetée* in watching those opening shots, precisely because time, itself, is as much the main character as Steiner. The question is not so much "Who is this stick-man soaring through the air on skis?" but "When will he ever come down?"

These opening sequences to *Steiner* are associative in much the same way as those in *Land of Silence and Darkness*. The image of ski-flying is fixed first, without commentary or context, followed by the brief scene of Steiner sculpting, and Steiner reports: "For instance, I have this knowledge ... and the way the shape recedes.... It's as though an explosion happened." The next sequence proves his explosion as it returns to the slopes and ramps, and in succession three jumpers fall, to be helped up or carried off on stretchers.

These repeated falls serve to announce the organizing principle of the film as episodic sequences, even as they foreshadow Steiner's own fall at Planica on his second jump. And still they seem a team, Steiner supplying the drama, Herzog adding the ironies. First irony: Steiner's jumps cannot be measured accurately and they are often disqualified, because they exceed the anticipated marked-off areas. Second irony: Steiner sets a world record at Planica, but it does not count, because he fell in doing it. Third irony: Steiner suffers a momentary loss of memory in the fall, so that even he does not know what he has accomplished. Fourth irony: others laugh at him and say he broods too much, while Steiner adds: "I have to break my skull before they believe me ... they probably won't listen until I give up ski-flying." One can almost hear Herzog speaking here, with the substitution of filmmaking for ski-flying. And yet Herzog's evocative imagery more than makes up for his lack of objectivity in the film, and from that imagery the most memorable image has to be the repeated pose of Steiner in the air, completely parallel to the ground, his mouth open and reminiscent of "The Shriek" by Edvard Munch.

Causes, costs and compensations all detailed, there remains only the ending. Herzog is not content merely to chronicle Steiner's eventual victory at Planica. Instead he crowds together the various images of flying to form a more personal, more poetic ending. Daylight ski-flier, followed by night helicopter, followed by the trophy (in the form of a soaring bird, wings at glide), followed by Steiner's memory of the young raven when he was a child:

I once had a young raven.... I raised it on bread and milk, and, when it could fly, it would meet me.... I whistled and it flew on my shoulder. Unfortunately, he kept losing more and more feathers.... The other ravens plagued it. So, I'm afraid, I had to shoot it.... It was a torture to see him being horrified by his own kind because he couldn't fly anymore.

Inference with the raven drawn, Herzog lets Steiner babble on about wanting to be all alone in the world, to the coda of Popol Vuh music. Steiner, too, is clearly horrified by his own kind, but because he flies too far, too well for the rest, and the cost is both in terms of physical danger and mental derangement. For his part, Herzog seems to intend a haunting more than a screening.

The same is true for *La Soufrière*, in which Herzog exerts all his skill to infuse absence with drama. The town of Basse-Terre completely deserted, Herzog and crew focus on the eerie ongoing signs of inanimate life: traffic lights still functioning in deserted streets; air-conditioners still running; television sets still turned on; price tags in windows; doors banging in the wind; dogs that have taken to the streets and have stopped barking, already starving from the lack of garbage; the long blank vista of pier, devoid of ships.

I think of Buñuel's *Land Without Bread* as I watch *La Soufrière*, with the substitution of Herzog's joking metaphysics for Buñuel's acerbic politics. The dictum in both films seems to be: if no drama presents itself, invent one. Herzog informs us that the sea was full of dead snakes: they had crawled down from the burning mountain only to drown in the sea. In the same vein, Herzog refuses to give us the usual eye-level shots. His mobile camera moves through the streets, running red lights, tilting at corners, conveying the houses at diagonal slants.

And, just as Buñuel had interrupted the narrative of *Land Without Bread* with shots from a textbook, and a treatise on which mosquitoes carried malaria and which did not, so too Herzog interrupts his narrative to meditate upon the catastrophe at Martinique in 1902, in which the only survivor was a thief in prison, who later was exhibited as a side-show attraction in American circuses. This insert gives Herzog the opportunity to show more shock shots of spaghetti transformed into metal sculpture, a loaf of bread turned into a black coal, a half-sunken Canadian refugee ship. "Fear became anonymous," Herzog says, after which he finds three survivors to interview, none of whom is as interesting as Sabatti, the thief from the Martinique catastrophe. These three are too apathetic, too full of so-what fatalism, too interested in being on camera to be dramatic figures. One sleeps with his cat, another strikes a pose of waiting for disaster, and the third says he is tending the cattle, but would gladly go with the film crew.

And, in a provocative (but unsubstantiated) parting shot, Herzog comments: "In my memory it is not the volcano which remains, but the neglected oblivion in which those black people live."

A similar shift in point of view occurs at the end of *Huie's Sermon*. Most of the film is shot indoors, full of close-ups of Huie, the congregation, his preaching, their clapping and singing. But, when we leave the brownstone church in Brooklyn, it is with a lateral camera, devoid of commentary, panning block after block of wasted tenements, empty churches, gutted homes and alleys filled with debris.

The musical soundtrack

Music is perhaps the strongest organizing principle in Herzog's films. On a conscious level, the spectator may very well marvel at "haunting" visuals in Herzog's films, but, I contend, the music that accompanies those visuals is what charges them, providing the "haunting," as much as the camera or editing. Often, the musical soundtrack is made memorable only by its incongruity with the visuals: the accomplished lyre-playing of an inarticulate leper in *Last Words*; the electronically modified folk-song of a 12-year-old girl singing in a cave in *Fata Morgana*; the sudden reprise from Hans Eisler's score for *Night and Fog* in *Land of Silence and Darkness*; the plaintive violins on the ski ramps for Steiner's fall in *The Great Ecstasy of the Sculptor Steiner*; the piano concertos in *Kaspar Hauser*; Rachmaninoff against empty streets and Wagner against the aerial shots of the volcano that never erupted in *La Soufrière*; country music in *Stroszek*, classical music in *Nosferatu*, the urge toward aleatoric music in *Woyzeck*, opera in *Fitzcarraldo* and *Where the Green Ants Dream*. The Pachelbel Kanon does not simply blend with wavy wheat fields in *Kaspar Hauser*; it calls attention to itself. And one does not expect opera in the jungles of *Fitzcarraldo* or in the barren Australian outback in *Where the Green Ants Dream*.

These instances are not isolated examples nor are they accidents. Herzog labors over the music for his films. The music is usually the "last words" to his films:

> Most of the time I work very, very long on the music. Sometimes it even takes me more time to work on the music than to work on the

editing. Almost all of my films are shot in direct sound, but, even so, normally it takes me more time, more energy, more precision in preparing the sound than for working on the camera to establish the shots and the movement of the camera. Just to set up all the reflectors always takes you hours, but to prepare the sound I take even more time. On most occasions it is the sound that decides the outcome of the battle. (Walsh/Ebert, 1979, 29)

Herzog seems always to be suggesting a musical structure: in the spoken text, from the silences, which can be understood as musical silences or "rests," to the babel of *Woodchuck* and the sermons in *Huie's Sermon* and *God's Angry Man*; in the images (the fugue structure of the first half of *Land of Silence and Darkness* or the contrapuntal editing in *Steiner*); and in the soundtrack as well, whether it be the direct and expected lyre-playing in *Last Words* or the Buñuelian dialectic in *La Soufrière*.

Music can in fact serve as a measure of why I think *Land of Silence and Darkness*, *The Great Ecstasy of the Sculptor Steiner* and *La Soufrière* are Herzog's best documentaries.

Just as Alain Resnais employed musical themes in *Hiroshima mon amour* to embody visual themes (Nevers, Ota, etc.), so, too, Herzog gives Fini Straubinger her own theme in the first half of *Land of Silence and Darkness*. The same musical theme links the opening image of the ski-flier with the later intertitle "The First Flight," when Fini and Miss Julie take the airplane ride. Similarly, the Eisler reprise from *Night and Fog* serves to sandwich the sequences in the second half of the film, coming as it does after the zoo visit and at the intertitle "The Deaf-Blind by Birth" and foreshadowing Fini's last words: "If a world-wide war would break out now, I wouldn't even notice."

There would seem to be little place for music in the vast expanse of snow and silent ski-jumps in *The Great Ecstasy of the Sculptor Steiner*. If music were used at all, one would expect it to convey the "ecstasy" of the title. Far from it. Herzog uses music to interrupt the silent episodic sequences of jumper after jumper, soaring after soaring, fall after fall. In fact, the closest emotion one can find to name the music used is fear. Steiner spends a great deal of time in the beginning of the film, explaining his fear, his ways of coping with fear (including a substitution of "respect for conditions" for "fear," so that fear, itself, is never named). Herzog's use of music names it for Steiner. After the first episodic sequence of terrible falls, Herzog pulls the spectator away from a direct identification with the jumpers in two ways: the plaintive violins, a

[handwritten margin notes:] fugue structure · contrapuntal editing in Steiner · fear · respect for conditions · plaintive violins

symbolic insertion not unlike Eisenstein's fourth remove in the ensemble of montage, the sounds substituting for the visuals, but more like the shriek of wounded birds than the screams of aching men; and the equally sudden insertion of an extra lens, the camera now filming, not the direct fall of the men, but the removed fall on a TV screen, replete with distortion lines. The violins by themselves would constitute a romantic effect. The TV screen by itself would result in a strictly ironic effect. But the convergence of the two, I contend, constitutes a double irony, referring us both to Steiner's perilous jumps and falls and to Herzog's film.

The Popol Vuh score for *Steiner* does not simply imitate the jumps; rather, it seems to shadow-box with the visuals: it drops off when the jumpers soar, it rises in crescendo when they fall. In its own musical terms, the Popol Vuh score runs the same kind of perilous risks that Steiner does, with the same kind of tenuous rewards.

With *La Soufrière* Herzog uses classical music as an empty swell, an outrageous insult, a sardonic commentary, in the same way that Buñuel used a Brahms score in *Land Without Bread*, to emphasize the discrepancy between culture and the destitution, by government neglect, of the inhabitants of Las Hurdes. The difference is this: in the Buñuel film, the contrast is polarized from the outset, directed, in keeping with the arrogance of the narrator, who calls the Hurdanos cretins and idiots, whereas in the Herzog film, the musical score accompanies inanimate objects, feels more like an afterthought, a post-production overlay, and so is doubly ironic, since the satire is frankly a beautiful much ado about nothing.

Herzog announces: "This is the pier, devoid of ships." What follows is an aerial panorama of Basse-Terre, naming places devoid of things in a visual way. Finally, the romantic Rachmaninoff piano score invades the film, where before there was silence, and announces in musical form the reference to the sea full of dead snakes.

The Wagner at the end of the film is equally interruptive. It seems to fit the majestic sweep of aerial views of volcano, clouds and sea, but it makes an ironic mockery of Herzog's admission of embarrassment about having filmed "a report on an inevitable catastrophe that did not take place." I laughed and felt exhilarated at the end of *La Soufrière*, at the convergence of Wagner, vacant volcano and Herzog confession, at such a sumptuous montage, straining to be cliché.

Documentary films are often meant to be archive instruments: the simple recording of an event. They do not often pretend to aspire to the density of narrative or complex ambiguity of meaning in fiction films. *Land of Silence and Darkness, The Great Ecstasy of the Sculptor Steiner* and *La Soufrière* have this density and ambiguity. By their layered language, cinematography and musical scores, these three documentaries do more than record events: they *invent* them. The tenderness in *Land of Silence and Darkness*, the passionate tension between ski-jumper and filmmaker in *Steiner*, the sheer inventiveness of the spoof that is *La Soufrière*, all are remarkable. I am reminded here that even the worst circus barker can often emcee the most extraordinary spectacle. So, too, with Werner Herzog. The hype of Herzog the visionary, he of the hallucinatory images, the madman at his manicure, carving out and colonizing unknown territories, is finally just that: hype. But the Herzog who can make these three films is a documentarist of enduring value.

Notes

1 Chris Marker has restricted himself, almost exclusively, to the documentary form. Among his most interesting documentaries are the following: *Letter from Siberia* (1957), *Sunday in Peking* (1957), *Le joli mai* (1962), *The Koumiko Mystery* (1965), *Far from Vietnam* (1967), *Cuba: The Battle of the Ten Million* (1970), *The Train Rolls On* (1972) and *The Loneliness of the Long-Distance Singer* (1974). Like Herzog's documentaries, Marker's documentaries are simultaneously explorations of their subjects and essays on cinematic form.
2 For an interesting critique of Herzog's claims for "the last poetry of latent capitalism," see J. Hoberman (1978) "Over the Volcano," *Village Voice* (May 22).
3 Werner Herzog (1980) *Screenplays,* translated from the German by Alan Greenberg and Martje Herzog, New York, Tanam. This edition includes the screenplays for *Aguirre, the Wrath of God; Every Man for Himself and God Against All: The Mystery of Kaspar Hauser;* and *Land of Silence and Darkness*.
4 I refer here to Wenders' English-language films, most notably *Hammett* and *Paris, Texas*.

Works cited

Herzog, Werner (1980) *Screenplays,* translated by Alan Greenberg and Martje Herzog, New York, Tanam.
Walsh, Gene (ed.) (1979) "'Images at the Horizon': a workshop with Werner Herzog," conducted by Roger Ebert, Chicago. Facets Multimedia Center (pamphlet).

5 A paralyzed pathos that contradicts its own longings for extreme experiences (*Land of Silence and Darkness*)

5

Blindness as insight: visions of the unseen in *Land of Silence and Darkness*

Gertrud Koch

In 1964, under the title "Rebellen in Amerika," Werner Herzog wrote about the New American Cinema: "What makes the work of this group so significant has long ceased to be an experiment. It is the move towards the self-reflection of film on its inherent means.... And here mere seeing no longer suffices: the films usually have a deeper, visionary referential radius" (Herzog, 1964, 57). Indeed, Noël Carroll has convincingly traced these lines of thought to Stan Brakhage's *Metaphors of Vision*, and, according to Carroll, Herzog's characteristic quest for a visionary expression for that which lies outside the experience of everyday consciousness and denotative language leads to a central paradox:

> On the one hand, Herzog, and other celebrants of experience, seek to acknowledge the unexpressed or ineffable aspects of experience that have been filtered out and suppressed by routine forms of schematization, such as language. For them, there are more things in heaven and earth than are canvassed by our dictionaries. Most of us, I think, would assent to this. However, what the celebrants overlook is that by pointing to unacknowledged properties and feelings, they not only make them salient for others to experience, but they also make them available to language. (Carroll, 1985, 39)

To be sure, the paradox Carroll describes exists only as long as author and work are considered identical and not when the self-imagined role of the artist is examined alongside that paradox: a role which in this case is clearly not a communicative-mediating one, but that of a prophet, an enlightened one. Here, the artist is not concerned with the undiscovered in an empirical sense, but, rather, he must track down those very phenomena that purportedly hold "higher truth." In a narrow sense, this is very much a theological concept, and not one based on aesthetic experience as a central category. In this context it also becomes possible to reconstruct why Herzog – rather uncere-moniously, it seems – detached himself from the narrower bounds of the aesthetic avant-garde and the sensual notion of experience found in Brakhage and others, and concentrated on the telling of tales, almost all of which deal with the will to absolute faith and the visualization of inner enlightenment.

Asked about the religious motifs in *Fata Morgana*, Herzog himself said: "There is also a religious rage inside of this film. This also has a decidedly biographical dimension for me, that is, precisely this intensely religious phase that I had, with conversion to Catholicism followed by a radical antitheism. Such things occupied me much more than others of my age. This rage over the absurdity of the universe, over these blunders, these shortcomings implanted from the cradle, this rage is in there too, of course" (Wetzel, 1976, 125). This "antitheism" which is grounded on the question of the theodicy and the "short-comings implanted from the cradle" is developed through the most diverse motifs by Herzog – though never in a materialistic-heretical sense as in Buñuel who lets the beggars and lepers gather around the table of the Lord to consume his bread in a literal sense or who, in *Viridiana*, secularizes the Lord in the material master of the house whose main loss is his property. Herzog remains, rather, under the spell of the theodicy. Thus, he describes how he transposed the music from *Fata Morgana* to *Even Dwarfs Started Small*:

> On the Ivory Coast, there's a man who says he is the Messiah. He performs miracles and preaches by a lagoon, where fishermen live, and there he has a little theocracy. There on the sand the fishermen built a giant cathedral; 4000–5000 people fit in it. On Sundays they come together and sing chorals in there. These were recorded, because I immediately thought that this will be my music for the dwarf-film. (Wetzel, 1976, 125)

Religious motifs can also be found on several levels in *Land of Silence and Darkness*: in the use of music, of language and in a few scenic accents. This is not to say, of course, that Herzog is a religious filmmaker, or that his films characteristically stand in a religion-based context. Rather, my argument aims to show what separates Herzog from the aesthetic avant-garde with whom he is often mistakenly associated and to indicate which aspects of his work let him flicker in the spectrum of neo-romantic regression.[1]

In this context it seems unavoidable to refer to Benjamin's much-cited essay on "The Work of Art in the Age of Mechanical Reproduction," where he develops his concept of the aura, and to determine more closely its transformation through the history of the concept and the phenomenon it designates.

Benjamin developed his concept of the aura from the sacred origin of art. The aura arises from the unique existence of a cult object in time and space: *this* altar-piece exists only in *this* church, at *this* location, and is quite possibly shown only on a single day of the year. The conditions of uniqueness are then preserved in secularized modernity, without being bound to ritual functions. In more recent discussions, the conceptual framework of the Benjaminian aura has been expanded considerably, and can now be understood in terms of actual experience.[2] Here, the sense of uniqueness, of here and now, no longer depends on the location of the original object, but takes place at the moment of reception, the experience of an object, even when this is a mechanically reproduced and reproducible one. This development is especially important for film theory, because it offers the possibility of understanding the auratic moments of the cinema differently from the negatively cast notion of the "pseudo-aura," which seems culturally and critically reduced through recourse to empirical developments in art itself. Applying this distinction to the New German Cinema, I find Alexander Kluge's bricolage-aesthetic[3] to be, in a certain sense, the real exponent of democratic, emancipated romanticism, while Werner Herzog has become the exponent of neo-romantic regression. By neo-romantic regression, I mean the second tendency developing out of Benjamin's historical aura-concept, namely the re-sacralization of the aesthetic sphere, the transformation of artist as prophet, a tendency whose newest developments Jörg Drews has also uncovered in recent German literature from Peter Handke to Botho Strauß.[4]

Those who have nothing to gain by the recasting of the aura in terms of experience must then turn to a notion of the aura that does not arise from a specific situation (the iron as *objet d'art* in the museum), but is part of the art object itself. Herzog's endless and manic quest for stories, people and situations that already in and of themselves carry the mark of auratically unique existence thus becomes, as it were, his return to a para-sacred aura. Appropriately, he regularly returns to the visible signs of the bodily stigmatized: dwarfs, the deaf-blind, and the retarded. Or, he creates situations that are formed by exceptional conditions: hypnotized actors in *Heart of Glass*, and the island of *La Soufrière* the day its volcano was predicted to erupt. Herzog's accounts of extreme situations faced during shooting also fit into this pattern. He talks about his films as "unmediated life, filmed on the spot, without mediation": "One can no longer speak of my life, and the things that fascinate me, collected and worked up into a film, but this process itself coincides with the process of fascination and experience" (Wetzel, 1976, 127). That such an aesthetic program necessitates an unmediated continuity of action in front of and behind the camera, by those chosen ones selected for this action, is also made clear in Herzog's characterization of Fini Straubinger, the central figure in *Land of Silence and Darkness*:

> Those are people in which a fire is burning that glows, and one can see this from far away. This can also be seen in Bruno, this strong light from within. In both of them there's this radical dignity that they radiate, and this radical quality is due to the suffering they have gone through. They give off a radiance, like one once painted saints with haloes in the late Middle Ages. That is how I see it with such people.
> (Wetzel, 1976, 127)

Herzog's quest for the unmediated proves itself consequently to be a quest for the sacred and vice versa; and such terms clearly place Herzog much more in the tradition of Heideggerian philosophy than in the radical aestheticism of modernity. In the words of Jürgen Habermas, "this reveals itself in the undialectical nature of being: the sacred, through which the being within the poet's word comes into its own, is looked upon, as in metaphysics, as the absolutely unmediated" (Habermas, 1985, 181). In his lecture on Heidegger, moreover, Habermas again provides a focus for the question of Herzog and the avant-garde by pointing to the difference between an autonomization of the aesthetic that aims at subjectivity and the conception of art as unveiling of the sacred:

> A comparison with Walter Benjamin could show how little contact Heidegger ever had with the genuine experience of avant-garde art. That is why he could never understand why only a subjectivistically determined and radically discriminating art that persistently develops the stubbornness of the aesthetic recommends itself as inaugurator of a new mythology. So much easier is the leveling out of the aesthetic phenomenon and the assimilation of art into metaphysics.

Being is illuminated by the beautiful: "Beauty and truth both relate to being, namely in the sense of unveiling the being of the one who is." (Habermas, 1985, 122)

Perhaps no Herzog film exposes this dilemma better than *Land of Silence and Darkness*: a documentary film that so engages the viewer precisely because it purports not to treat the deaf-blind people standing at its center from the outside, as social cases, but shows them in the context of their day-to-day existence. The most important figure in the film is Fini Straubinger, a deaf-blind woman injured as a child by falling down a flight of stairs who, at age 18, lost her sight completely and became deaf. In this film Herzog makes her the "blind seer." The title comes from a remark made by Fini Straubinger that is part of the film. On the occasion of her birthday party she declares: "But even this group must be looked after, so that it is not cast overnight into the land of silence and darkness." The designation "land of silence and darkness" is obviously a poetic metaphor referring to an image of expulsion: one is driven from one land to another, a foreign one. The metaphor Herzog uses as the title for his film thus carries within it the image of two different realms, of belonging and of strangeness, much more than it characterizes the empirical-sensory condition of the deaf-blind, which Fini Straubinger also describes. Indeed, her commentary reveals that the deaf-blind by no means live in a poetic land of silence and darkness, but rather in an irritating chaos of noise and color perception:

It is like this: people think deafness is complete silence, but they are mistaken. A constant noise fills one's head, from the faintest ringing, something that sounds like trickling sand, to cracking sounds. But the worst thing is, that when one's head is ringing, one never knows where one must turn. This is a great torment for us, and that is also why we are sometimes so touchy, and can no longer manage. The same is true for blindness. It is not complete darkness, there are often very odd colors in front of one's eyes. Black, gray and white, blue, green, yellow. It all depends.

Of course Herzog does not make the attempt to translate these descriptions into filmic images and sounds. The only time he films linguistically expressed conceptions of images is at the beginning of the film, which starts with black frame and the voice of Fini Straubinger, who says: "In front of me I see a field path that leads across a ploughed-up field, over which clouds are moving." After this description of an "inner image," Herzog cuts to the gloomy, flickering, out-of-focus view of a field path above which clouds are drifting. These first shots and the film titles that follow are underscored with soft music. This is followed by more black frames, and Fini Straubinger's voice: "Once as a child, when I could still see and hear, I watched a ski-jumping event. I cannot get the image out of my mind. How those men were soaring in the air. I concentrated on their faces. I wish you could also see this some day." Already during Fini Straubinger's last words, the music sets in again, before the ski-jumper appears in the middle of the frame and opens the dark into light. The camera follows him until he gently touches down on the slope. Both of the images evoked by Fini Straubinger are filmed without sound, even though both of them strongly suggest synaesthetic sense perceptions of wind. Instead, Herzog uses music, and this illustrates that it is not Herzog's primary concern to give sensual expression to the inner world but to realize the elevation to the "spiritual," with the music indicating this change of spheres. As we know, Herzog later made a film about a ski-jumper, *The Great Ecstasy of the Sculptor Steiner*, that makes evident the transfiguration of spirituality and death. Herzog himself discusses this film in the unmistakably Heideggerian categories of "Being onto Death": "Ski-jumping is not only something athletic, but rather a mind set, i.e. how has one already overcome death. It is a question of solitude, of surrendering oneself to the utmost imaginable still remaining for a human being" (Wetzel, 1976, 130). If the "utmost imaginable still remaining for a human being" is death, and death itself must be stylized into a spiritual reality, then this also indicates that for Herzog, death does not lie with Eros, as in radical romanticism, but with ascetic transfiguration. Still to be examined is how, particularly in *Land of Silence and Darkness*, all manifestations of sensual perception end in the sphere of transfiguration into the spiritual. This becomes especially clear in another sequence dealing with flying, with breaking away from the earthly dimension of life.

This central sequence of *Land of Silence and Darkness* is once again filmed without sound and accompanied only by music. The first shot shows Fini Straubinger, Julie, and another woman at an airport, touching the wings of a small plane. The music begins at the moment when their arms stretch out onto the rising keel. The next shot is already taken from inside the plane, and above the clouds, showing a panoramic view of snow-capped alpine peaks. In this sequence Herzog does not mediate what the seeing companion communicates to the others by tactile alphabet but only his own gaze over the majestic beauty of the sublime, the peaks above the clouds. Once again, Herzog is not concerned with the strong physical effect of flying, of the take-off, but uses the image as a metaphor: a metaphor of a rapture carried by music and pictoral motif, not by the sensual experiences of the deaf-blind, whose blissful smiles now appear as inner radiance.

When the camera sets free the gaze that the blind are debarred from, when the soundtrack switches over to music, then the viewer is carried off to an unreal realm, in which he hears and sees what the individuals on the screen cannot hear and see. Their feeling of happiness, as their smiling faces make clear, unfolds as the riches of an audible and visible world, which is not the world of the deaf-blind. The auratic sequences of the film are thus unmistakably the subjective construc-tions and world views of Werner Herzog, who, precisely in these sequences, transposes the otherness of a sensual realm of experience hardly accessible to us into cultural models of the aesthetically sublime. Ironically, Herzog scarcely acts differently from those people that Fini Straubinger characterizes in her remembrances as too impatient really to communicate on the terms of the deaf-blind: the childhood visitors at her sick-bed, who did not adjust themselves to her reduced facility of comprehension, but talked over her head with her mother. This is certainly not Herzog's intention; yet precisely in the "beautiful" passages of the film, the impression is that the plight of the deaf-blind is used mostly as a screen onto which the need for "inner riches," enlightenment, and redemption is projected. Even in the sequence where the camera accompanies Fini Straubinger's deaf-blind birthday guests through the botanical garden, there is a subjective camera movement through the dense crowns of the palm-lined passage. In the rustling foliage of the trees, preceded by the detached image of the deaf-blind fingering the cacti, sensual and visual tangi-bility describes the longing for plenitude, for immersion in a fleshly luxurious world which in the framework of the film acts as a severed dimension of life suddenly pushing its way in: a dimension that the film, in all of its metaphysical transfigurations, otherwise does not allow itself to enter. A similar split is already apparent in Fini Straubinger's descriptive characterization of the empirical-sensory sensations registered by the audio-perceptual apparatuses of the deaf-blind, a characterization which, within the overall structure of the film, is shifted to the poetic transfiguration of metaphor.

At another point, Fini Straubinger portrays the fate of the deaf-blind with a poetic reductionism typical of the votive panels found in

Bavarian chapels and characteristic of her and Herzog's fundamentally pre-modern perspective:

> If I were an inspired painter, I would depict the fate of being deaf-blind in the following way:
>
> Blindness is a dark stream flowing slowly and melodically but surely towards the falls. On its banks are beautiful trees, flowers, and sweetly singing birds.
>
> The other stream, coming from the other side, should be clear and transparent. It should flow slowly, but without any sound. Far below there would be a very deep and dark lake. Then, on both sides, where the streams, the dark and the clear, empty into the lake, there are rocks against which the water dashes, foams, and eddies. This happens ever so slowly, and very, very gently. This water would also be very still, but from time to time it would have to spray into the air. That would represent the mental agony endured by the deaf-blind. I don't known if you have understood this correctly, the tumbling and breaking of the water against the rocks is, as it were, the mental depressions experienced by the deaf and the blind; how it feels to be deaf-blind. I cannot portray it differently; it is within me, but it cannot be just put into words.

Fini Straubinger's naive piety, the faith in which she seeks solace and refuge from her fate, becomes more obvious in such poetic condensations than when she comments directly on her relation to religion. And later Herzog makes even more explicit this double-edged relationship to religiousness in a curious interplay of observation and staging. In his visit with Else Fehrer, a deaf-blind woman who had been sent off to a mental hospital where she lost her ability to communicate, Herzog stages the opposition between the deaf-blind woman and the seeing and hearing inmates as one of exhibitionism versus inwardness. Already upon entering the day room the inmates gather around the deaf-blind woman like curious spectators, relating to the camera and surroundings through a dramatically visual orientation. Herzog cuts from this room to a medium close-up of the dormitory: a woman dressed in black, sitting on the white sheets of her bed, faces the camera; behind her another woman is sitting on a parallel bed; from the left, the sun is falling through an open window casement, bathing the whole scene in a luminous light. The woman in the foreground begins to pose in front of the camera. She looks up obliquely, folds her hands over her breast with a mawkishly malicious smile, and then strikes this tableau vivant in order to set up another. Tenderly she leans her chin upon her right hand, raising the left one with the forefinger extended in the gesture made by apostles or Jesus-figures in religious images. Finally, she assumes another pose, laying her right hand over her breast, and lowering her gaze, as if about to make a vow, or absorbed in sorrow, like a *pietà*. In between, though, she always shifts her position with a veiled-sardonic smile, as if she is making fun of the onlookers.

Herzog contrasts this performance with a close-up of Else Fehrer, now sitting in the foreground and pensively looking into the camera. Unlike the other deaf-blind, her eyes do not have the visible, outward signs of blindness, and when she looks out at us from the screen, we forget that she sees nothing, that her gaze is sightless. In this montage of the imitative, religious theatrics that the madwoman performs for the camera, Herzog once more denounces the superficiality of a purely mimetic relationship to the world vis-à-vis the intensity of an inner sight. From this isolated close-up, the camera draws back steadily to a long shot of the dormitory: on each bed a woman is sitting in such a way that all of them are visible to the camera, while the window beams against the far wall form black crosses. Not only does Herzog's perspective of private spiritualism behind the documentary material become clear in such staged sequences, but it also becomes clear that the documentary material serves, at best, as a point of departure for developing personal world views. In Wilhelm Roth's words:

> Directors like Herzog, Schroeter, Praunheim, or Wenders are taking it upon themselves to revalue the concept of documentary film: for them it is not a bastion of objectivity, but the possibility for radically personal self-representation. Some appear in their own films, yet they do not altogether dispense with the mask of fictionality: in the camera work and elements of the mise-en-scène, these films come close to their fiction films. The reverse also holds true. *Fitzcarraldo* is, for long stretches at a time, a documentary film. (Roth, 1982, 205)

Thus Herzog engages the mentally ill as the industrious image-copiers of the world, and depicts the blind as the seers, whose gaze should touch us. To be sure, this self-representation not only hides behind the mask of fiction, but disguises itself through the position of he who presents the sights, who mediates the initiation into higher truths like a priest, who exorcises the false gods of the graven images. The alternation between fictional and documentary footage is part of the Herzogian aesthetic in which the artist is not at all a radical subjectivist, but a privileged interpreter whose fiction reflects the rays emitted by its haloes back onto reality.

The emphatic quest for extreme situations, the transfiguration of mortal fear into existential experience of human existence, takes however a morbid turn in a sequence from *Land of Silence and Darkness.* In the part of the film dealing with children who are deaf-blind by birth, Herzog accompanies Fini Straubinger into a home where teachers and therapists work with differing methods. One sequence begins in a gloomy indoor swimming pool – brown tiled walls, pale light, icy blue water, barren branches appearing in shadowy outline through the steamed-over window panes. The sequence begins with a shot of the teenaged Harald under the shower. Emitting sounds of obvious well-being, he stretches his thin body under the shower-water. His teacher, wearing Spartan black bathing trunks, gives him to understand by the tactile alphabet, that he should now detach himself from the warm shower, and go into the swimming pool. Harald begins to climb down the ladder into the water. A pan past a tiled column reveals Fini Straubinger and her companion sitting on the far edge of the swimming pool. The camera pans back to its original position, and the voice-over commentary takes over: "Harald had a mortal fear of water. It had taken over a year until he let himself be moved to follow his teacher into the swimming pool." Herzog gives this commentary without further comment. We do not learn what macabre ideals stand behind this program of overcoming mortal fear. At any rate, the swimming pool scenes disagreeably call to mind those unfortunate German traditions of physical training, Prussian toughness, tests of courage and initiation unto death. Why an individual should prove his humanity through overcoming mortal fear, by quivering in cold water – in short, the inhumaneness of such an idea that is in keeping with Herzog's conceptual world – is not even called into question by this morbid scene. With the coldly observing voice of a commentator, the teacher outlines his pupil's conduct: "He is hesitating a little, the water is a bit cold today. Now I am going to try and get him to walk through the pool on his own." While the boy hesitatingly walks through the pool, soft, solemn string-music sets in. A musical countervoice at this point could no doubt achieve a doubly critical function. It could, for instance, appear self-critically, letting the beautiful appearances of affirmative culture burst against the sorry natural substratum of mankind, referring to itself in a negative sense. As an expression of this terrible fear and coldness it could also voice a critical protest against what we see, picking up the Herzogian commentary on mortal fear, and taking it seriously. All of this does not happen. Rather the music affirmatively underscores Herzog's commentary to celebrate the overcoming of mortal fear, becoming the resonance of the spheres that sound in extreme situations, a medium of transfiguration and spiritualization just as in the earlier sequence, "the First Flight."

This move toward transfiguration, the affirmative celebration of alleged proximity to death, sheds light on Herzog's relationship to inner and outer nature. For him nature is a frontier: the mountain, the jungle, the desert, the river, the island, the volcano, the bare rocks, the by-nature-limited body of the disabled. Peter W. Jansen has formulated the relationship between individual and nature as represented by the landscape imagery in Werner Herzog's films this way:

> In Werner Herzog's films, landscapes exist as a feverish dream (*The Mystery of Kaspar Hauser*), an obsession (*Signs of Life*), and in the minds of people (*Land of Silence and Darkness*). Above all, it passes by them, above them, without taking notice of their presence or leaving its mark on them, devoid of people, appealing directly to the viewer's emotions, consciousness, memory, and frame of mind....
>
> The cinema of subjectivity offers itself as poetic-mystical refuge for the self, that sees itself as torn from the *unio mystica* with nature and irreparably wounded since its rude awakening at birth. The image of the landscape becomes a vague and unsettled distant memory of a lost primal state, in which idyll and might, the individual and the world, the self and the other are still facets of one and the same sensation, and neither moral nor political categories. (Jansen, 1976, 69 and 84)

Herzog proceeds no differently with the body-pictures of the deaf-blind: when he confronts the playful, theatrical expressiveness of the schizophrenic woman's body with the dull massiveness of Else Fehrer's, whose gaze, although sightless, seems to come from within nature itself; when he exponentially heightens the image of the boy's thin, trembling body moving through the water by giving it musical expression. The last sequence of the film is fittingly the most effective representation of such an iconographic metaphor of longing for the *unio mystica*. Here a deaf-blind farmer's son walks away from the conversation between the three women and into the garden where he tenderly embraces and touches a tree, as if it were human.

The dimension of showing human bodies in front of and for the camera, bodies that in and of themselves are a piece of blind and deaf nature, and never letting this corporeality tend toward sensuality in the mise-en-scène, but only toward spiritualization, indicates that in Herzog's aesthetic cosmos nature itself has become the foil of the *deus absconditus* – its substance is coldness and absence. The unbridled pathetic realm of the senses that Herzog masterfully banishes is also overcome by this coldness. This is the redeemable moment in Herzog's films: the pathos that strikes out into the void, like Else Fehrer's gaze. But where this coldness as theological transfiguration should be purified by the frost-flowers of modernity, it lapses into neo-romantic regression.

The coldness in Herzog's films, this paralyzed pathos that contradicts its own longings for extreme experiences, keeps its nature (human) pictures from slipping into the idyllic lowlands of a *locus amoenus,* of a neo-romantic Biedermeier. In view of the tendency toward re-sacralization and affirmative transfiguration already apparent in *Land of Silence and Darkness*, and more so in his recent films, I, at any rate, find a reading of the film as an example of the humane representation of our fellow (human) beings unsatisfying and negligent of its aporias. The stylistic intent that subjugates human beings and situations to the role of material and not the aesthetic construction remains, at its core, pre-modern. In response to the question, "Why don't your films show history as an event that has an effect on people as in Ivens and Nestler?," Jean-Marie Straub replies with what might serve as the fundamental criticism of Herzog's films:

> For me the answer is very clear: I believe the deception is due to giving people the impression that something is happening in the moment the film is running, something they call "action." This is not true. When a film not based on deception runs, then nothing at all happens. Whatever happens can only happen inside the viewer, and this only through the combination of images and sounds ... of forms that then enter into the viewer through his eyes and ears, his brain and his reflection. (Witte, 1976, 209)

[translated by Antje Masten]

Notes

1   Eric Rentschler (1981/2) "American Friends and the New German Cinema: Patterns of Reception," *New German Critique*, nos 24–5 (Fall/Winter), 34: Rentschler explicitly points out that the experimental parts of the dream sequences in *The Mystery of Kaspar Hauser* were not filmed by Herzog: "Wyborny prepared the dream

sequences, ones numerous critics freely attribute to Herzog, lauding him for his visionary powers."

2   Martin Seel (1985) *Die Kunst der Entzweiung. Zum Begriff der ästhetischen Rationalität,* Frankfurt/Main, Suhrkamp, 219:

> Even the most modern art-experience is often, if not always, auratic: the more or less unique the experience of an experience appearing from an object, whose situation is removed from our perception, the nearer the realized experience is. Below I will try to show, why this modified definition of the aura even describes the aesthetic frame of reference for Hollywood film comedies or pictures by Barnett Newmann. What changes radically in the history of aesthetic perception is the constructive and receptive application of aesthetic-auratic materials and phenomena. On this point, aside from esoterical sensitiveness, Adorno, not Benjamin, was right. (Seel, 1985, 219)

3   Compare also Miriam Hansen's work on Alexander Kluge. She describes Kluge's montage-aesthetic as follows:

> In terms of the textual make-up of Kluge's films, the tension between narrative and history is not merely an effect of the overall structure of the film, but is generated on the level of its shot-by-shot articulation. Again and again, an incipient action is invaded by montage sequences, associational clusters of images that exceed narrative and diegetic anchoring. These clusters assemble a variety of materials – illustrations from nineteenth-century children's books or popular magazines, panopticum prospects, still photographs, film footage shot from the editing table – which often share a thematic undercurrent and, more importantly, convey their own historicity as "used," "second-hand" images. (Hansen, 1985, 23)

From Hansen, M. (1985) "The Stubborn Discourse: History and Story-Telling in the Films of Alexander Kluge," *Persistence of Vision,* 2 (Fall), 23.

4   Jörg Drews (1984) "Über einen neuerdings in der deutschen Literatur erhobenen vornehmen Ton," *Merkur,* 8, 950 ff.:

> Those things that Handke's project, a renewed "hallowing" of the world, would not like to have described, named, or simply *to be.* Instead, they should once again actively "mean." ... Of course Handke must construct a language for his project, a language that

since the *Left-Handed Woman* or thereabouts is, not putting it critically, "not of today," but builds on Goethe, Stifter, Heidegger, and Rudolf Steiner. The result is an unmediated construction: self-celebration in seclusion as expression, the attitude of self-ordained priesthood. (Drews, 1984, 950 ff.)

Works cited

Carroll, Noël (1985) "Herzog, Presence, and Paradox," *Persistence of Vision*, 2 (Fall), 30–40.

Drews, Jörg (1984) "Über einen neuerdings in der deutschen Literatur erhobenen vornehmen Ton," *Merkur*, 8, 950ff.

Habermas, Jürgen (1985) *Der philosophische Diskurs der Moderne. Zwölf Vorlesungen*. Frankfurt/Main, Suhrkamp.

Hansen, Miriam (1985) "The Stubborn Discourse: History and Story-Telling in the Films of Alexander Kluge," *Persistence of Vision*, 2 (Fall), 19–29.

Jansen, Peter W. (1976) in P. Jansen and W. Schütte (eds) (1976) *Herzog/Kluge/Straub*, Munich, Hanser.

Roth, Wilhelm (1982) *Der Dokumentarfilm seit 1960*, Munich, Bucher.

Wetzel, Kraft (1976) in Jansen and Schütte (eds), *Herzog/Kluge/Straub*.

Witte, Karsten (1976) in Jansen and Schütte (eds), *Herzog/Kluge/Straub*.

6 History and narrative preserving the traces of heroic vision (*Aguirre, the Wrath of God*)

6

The cosmos and its discontents

Dana Benelli

Stating that his films are always about the same subject, Werner Herzog once described himself as a "limited" filmmaker.[1] A variety of textual characteristics readily provide persuasive confirmation for this claim of continuity of interest on Herzog's part: his films' consistent creation of central characters out of synch with, if not in open rebellion against, the societies within which they live; the repeated casting (and acting styles) of Bruno S. and, especially, Klaus Kinski as these characters; the mysteriously evocative landscape-and-music punctuation of the narratives; and, even, literal references to earlier films in later works, for example, the recurrence of the name "Stroszek" (in *Signs of Life* and *Stroszek*), the circling vehicles of *Even Dwarfs Started Small* and *Stroszek*, or the side-show of *Kaspar Hauser* (*Every Man for Himself and God Against All*) whose attractions are drawn from all of Herzog's earlier features, including an unrealized project on the young Mozart.

The mere fact of repetition, however, does not necessarily index the presence of "limitations" such as obsessive conceptual monomania or slavish adherence to an obscure, solipsistic film language.[2] Herzog's comment, in fact, would misleadingly distract his audience from recognizing the creative potential provided by repetition. For increasingly precise expression of ideas may derive from formal repetition across a series of texts. Auteur and genre criticism derive their analytic method precisely from an appreciation of the dynamics of repetition and difference operating within and between texts. From the perspective of these two forms of criticism the fact of repetition is not a limitation at all. Rather, it provides a basis for textual analysis which then proceeds to take the measure of accompanying variations in order to account for two kinds of film meaning: first, the significance of the text itself and, second, the text's contribution to an increased understanding of the auteur or genre intertext in relation to which the individual text stands.

Auteurism, in particular, attends to this latter aspect of textual significance. For the play of similarity and difference in a particular film provides insight not just into a continuity of interest on the part of the auteur, but also into the evolution of the auteur's thinking about that ongoing preoccupation. The discussion to follow considers the relationship between Herzog's *Signs of Life*[3] and *Aguirre, the Wrath of God* from such an auteurist perspective. *Signs of Life*, shot in Greece, is Herzog's first feature film, a low-budget black-and-white production seemingly (and literally) contemporary in its imagery of Greek life and locations despite a narrative set in the early 1940s. *Aguirre, the Wrath of God*, on the other hand, is a color period piece set in 1560 and more ambitiously designed for international art houses and commercial success. Yet, three shared formal characteristics of the films provide a basis for comparative analysis: first, the films' use of and reliance upon landscape to articulate a description of "the human condition"; second, their narratives of rebellious response to such an existential condition; and, third, the functions of the leitmotifs of motion, stasis, circles, and lines in structuring a narrational attitude toward the films' narrative and thematic concerns with history, nature, civilization, individuality, heroism and madness.

The choice, or privileging, of *Signs of Life* and *Aguirre, the Wrath of God* is based upon their notable narrative correspondences as well as the thematic concerns and stylistic visual traits which they share with other Herzog films. Both film narratives center on a soldier who finds himself becalmed in a location distant from his homeland. The circumstances of the military mission lead both into rebellion, first against military and social authority and, subsequently, against the universe itself (Stroszek, for example, commands the sun not to rise). In both cases a quality of nobility is ascribed to the hero and his doomed revolt. Thus, both films thematically center on forms of romantic rebellion in which the line between heroic vision and madness is blurred. Furthermore, the representation of these characters' conditions is graphically informed by the association of motion and stasis with themes of life and death, and a related linkage of circularity with entrapment and madness. In these respects, then, *Aguirre, the Wrath of God* invites consideration as a "remake" of *Signs of Life*.

Simultaneously, the complement of textual differences between the two films, specifically in their narrational points of view, can be interpreted as indicating a substantial change of thinking on Herzog's part.

From a purely formal standpoint the two films share their narrative starting points (in winding character movement within a vast landscape) and then diverge in their assessment of the rebellion which follows. *Signs of Life* concludes with Stroszek's visual diminishment as a linear trajectory carries him into the distant landscape, while *Aguirre, the Wrath of God*'s endpoint is structured with the camera circling the still-defiant Aguirre. Most immediately, these endings signal a radical shift away from "god's-eye" objectivity and toward a more partisan narrational (i.e. authorial) alignment with the subjectivity of the main character. Hence, it becomes possible to describe a change of attitude in Herzog, by the time of his making *Aguirre, the Wrath of God*, regarding the fate of the visionaries who populate his films. He accords transcendent value to lives lived in keeping with alternative (that is, non-traditional or "uncivilized") forms of consciousness, regardless of the literal outcome of those lives. In *Kaspar Hauser* Herzog picks up on and more explicitly confirms such a belief.

Despite the immediately compelling uniqueness of the central figures of Herzog's films, these characters remain significantly inaccessible when considered in terms of the poetic riddles of their scripted dialogue and their often "illogical" narrative actions. They are, by design, enigmatic characters, part madmen and part visionaries, with the meaning and differentiation of either aspect of their identities difficult to fix in mind. Neither is the fleshing out of the script, in performance, a solution to this interpretive dilemma. Performance style reinforces the cryptic quality of Herzog's characterizations. The lack of affect in Bruno S.'s speech and movement, the hypnotizing of performers in *Heart of Glass,* and Klaus Kinski's (natural?) tendency to suggest distraction by something out of frame, all function to noticeably repress conventionally psychologized behavioral expressiveness. Such a strategy, of course, appropriately suits Herzog's interest in representing individuals whose consciousness is unconventional and, hence, cannot be expressed "normally."[4]

The interaction between scripted and performed characterizations and their contextual physical and aesthetic environments, however, does provide the means for opening up Herzog's characters for critical analysis. His characters are very much "figures in a landscape." A viewer's understanding of character identity, character motivation, and dramatic action proves to be dependent, first, on an understanding of the world the character moves in and, then, on a sense of the character's relation to and awareness of this world as he acts. Thus, both *Signs of Life* and *Aguirre, the Wrath of God* open with landscapes, then recognize the presence of humans in the landscape, and, finally, differentiate one specific individual as the main character to be observed within or followed across the landscape/world of the film.

Herzog's mastery of landscapes lies in the degree of conceptual significance he can wrest from visualized physical space. There is evident care in his choice of landscape settings, in his positioning (or withholding) of characters in these spaces, and in the aesthetics of his filming of these locations. As a result, Herzog's landscapes dynamically perform several distinct textual functions: they sketch simple thematic descriptions of "reality"; they reveal information about character; and they are expressive of a narrational perspective which is related to, but also extends beyond, the specific character encounter with reality which is at the center of the film narratives.[5]

Both *Signs of Life* and *Aguirre, the Wrath of God* literally begin in voids – one with an image of an expanse of rather nondescript terrain, the other with clouds. Then the camera responds to a movement in the environment, a "sign of life" generated by the presence of people in the framed space. In a sense, this is a moment of "birth" for the character whose experience the viewer will watch and follow to a concluding situation in which that individual's fate is undeniably materialized, recognized and ordained. Even though Stroszek's and Aguirre's physical lives extend before and after the duration of the film narratives these narratives span the entirety of their vital "lives" as beings consciously discovering and reacting to the structures of their worldly existence. Previously Stroszek and Aguirre were naive (civilized); subsequently they are madly alone.

But in both films, before there is character there is landscape. The viewer's first observations of the diegetic locations of the narratives coincide with the thematic articulation of several metaphysical "first principles" about the nature of "reality" and the human condition. The world is displayed as vast, natural (ahistorical) and indifferent to humanity. The individual is presented as a minuscule element of this whole, ever in danger of being engulfed and lost in the world's vastness. The use of extreme long shot renders individuals and human activity as insignificant in terms of their visual dynamism, even as that movement succeeds in attracting viewer attention. Such visual tenuousness becomes an immediate metaphor for the characters' mortality, a fated fact and ever-present possibility which lurks just beyond all succeeding frames and events. It is always a possibility that a cut could return the viewer to extreme long shot, a "cosmic" vantage point, which would undercut the importance, the compelling specificity, of character, time, place, and narrative event attentively observed a moment earlier. In fact, the futility of Stroszek's rebellion in *Signs of Life* is signaled in precisely this form; the film shifts to extreme long shots and the images cease to be scaled to Stroszek's humanity (instead, he is likened to the trapped fly).

Thus, camera distance comes to be one indicator of an elemental experiential alienation between an individual and the world he must live within. This unbridgeable estrangement haunts Herzog's cinema and is additionally addressed by several of his films in terms of a "fall." Kaspar Hauser, for example, states explicitly: "It seems to me that my coming into this world was a terrible fall." In the opening of *Aguirre, the Wrath of God* the expedition moves downward out of the fog/clouds. Later Pizarro and Aguirre confer by the river and both refer to the journey ahead as "downhill" (a direction linked to death/mortality by Aguirre's preceding observation that "no one can get down that river alive"). The extreme long shots of *Signs of Life* are from a high-angle perspective. The latter two films acknowledge the Oedipal implications of the above metaphor through the topic of the hero's relationship to the sun. Stroszek claims equality with the sun by demanding that it not rise. Aguirre and his men are identified by the Indian/jaguar as the long-awaited "sons of the sun." They have entered this land at Christmas. And in proclaiming himself "the wrath of God" Aguirre confirms his belief in this kinship. His last line, "Who else is with me?", is followed (answered or mocked) by a shot of the sun overhead.[6]

If the world view of inescapable mortality posited by Herzog in his first feature film is reaffirmed in *Aguirre, the Wrath of God*, it is also amplified and intensified as an immutable fact of life in the latter film. The ever-present possibility of being devoured or lost in the landscape, which is expressed almost entirely in aesthetic and metaphoric terms in *Signs of Life*, becomes a literal aspect of the landscape and drama in *Aguirre, the Wrath of God*. In this film the shift from extreme long shot to a closer perspective does not allow viewers to humanize their perspective by effecting a reduction of mortality to a haunting, but only potential, accompanying alternative fact of life. "Reality" is no longer a cut away; it is one with the jungle which is a material presence in every frame. The viewer confronts characters who are in a state of constant and intense struggle with their world. The way down the mountainside is treacherous. Foliage entangles the march and mud threatens to halt its progress. And the jungle is saturated with lethal menace; lives may be suddenly, and inexplicably, lost, as when the soldier is yanked up out of the frame by a snare, or when cuts and pans reveal new and unsuspected corpses in hitherto off-screen areas. Even the Indian slaves, so frequently able to melt into the jungle, are killed by it. Such events happen ineluctably, regardless of vigilance. Though Aguirre's men are mindful of omnipresent danger, their attempts to understand anything beyond the fact of the hostility of their world are confounded. "We lose men but never see the enemy," comments Gaspar. Indians are diegetically the enemy responsible for the deaths of the Spaniards, but they are visually absent or indistinguishable from the jungle when most deaths occur (and usually benign when they are in view). Narrationally, silence and jungle landscape eclipse the Indians as significations of mortality. Gradually, the characters themselves concur in this reading: death takes the form of an arrow issuing from the foliage or of disappearance into the landscape (the chilling mid-frame erasure by trees of the war horse abandoned to the shore, and Ursua's wife's suicidal walk into the jungle); a catastrophic narrative crisis occurs simply when the raft drifts into branches at the shoreline; and, at film's end, Aguirre and his dying, or dead, daughter gaze, transfixed, toward the killing shore. The jungle ultimately cannibalizes life; Aguirre and his men learn that they have been reduced to mere "meat" in this world.

If landscapes function to articulate a world view for Herzog's films, then it logically follows that character experience within these landscapes metaphorically and literally indexes the possibilities for human behavior and identity in the world. The early extreme long shots of *Signs of Life* and *Aguirre, the Wrath of God* which define the world also establish a correlation between life and motion. In the vast spaces of these shots it is only in movement that individuals distinguish themselves from indifferent nature and signal their existence. Motion is an elemental life sign; to stop moving is to disappear (to fail to attract and hold attention in the frame). In both films the central figures are travelers. Stroszek is a salesman who had wanted to emigrate. He is first glimpsed in the course of being moved to a new post. Later, he is textually linked to the gypsy. And, still later, during his rebellion, he can be viewed running and dancing about the fort. Aguirre, too, is first seen during a journey, as an explorer. Eventually, his will alone keeps the quest for El Dorado from being stopped or turned back.

As movement becomes visually associated with being and staying alive, stasis correspondingly suggests entrapment and death. Stroszek is depressed by the frozen photographic images of individuals and families. And he feels increasingly anxious about his own confinement in the Greek fort. The Spanish expedition finds movement through the jungle tortuous and finally impossible. With the exception of Aguirre, those sent on ahead by way of the river become so enervated by despair and illness that it is impossible to say with certainty whether anyone other than Aguirre remains alive in that film's final shot. In both films silence serves as an aural equivalent for such deadening passivity. In *Signs of Life* silence is environmentally indicative of lack of eventfulness and, as a character trait (of the little boy at the pier and the little girl with no one to talk to), it is associated with existential isolation. In *Aguirre, the Wrath of God* the absence of sound or voice (in moments prefacing death, from the Bible which the Indian holds to his ear, or when the river smothers the cries of the men trapped on the raft in the whirlpool) has similar significance, a fact (at least in the first example) recognized but deferred to by the men and challenged by Aguirre and his order that the guns and cannon be fired, even without a target.

The dramatic core of both *Signs of Life* and *Aguirre, the Wrath of God* concerns their heroes' confrontation, however brief and however ill-fated, with the universe's vast antipathy, nature's indifferent silence, and the fact of their "meatness." But if these characters' resistance to stasis, and impulses to move and to make noise when others are still and subdued, constitute signs of life, are these also signs of hope for deliverance from the fact of mortality asserted by the films' landscapes? To assess Herzog's narrational attitude toward his heroes' rebellions it is useful to pay close attention to the motifs of circles and lines in the representation of human activity.

In *Signs of Life* Herzog's use of the motif of the circle leads the viewer, with Stroszek, toward the discovery that all aspects of normal human existence are inherently stifling of human potential. Circular forms, whether literal or figurative, and the textual "circles" created by narrative repetition, become associated with themes of meaningless passivity (the boredom of routine life in the fort), vitiating containment (the exhausted fly in the toy owl), entrapment (the buried rooster), a world utterly permeated by these sorts of experiences (the strikingly long pan of the valley of windmills), and, ultimately, madness (the windmills, again). The circular motif pervades images of nature (the fish eating and spinning the pieces of bread, the caterpillars following each other in circles, the little girl's reference to circling vultures) and civilization (man-made objects like the owl, the roach trap and windmills, and the repetitive day-to-day routines which structure people's lives). Even the innocent play of the children recapitulates the world's metaphysical structure as they surround the rooster and imprison it in earth. In this film Herzog's vision is almost unrelentingly pessimistic; passivity has become a timeless way of life, imposed naturally, and embraced culturally by the people of the island in their traditional lifestyle. History has given way to routine; the hieroglyphs in stone report that the same civic idyll was lived in ancient times. The film admits of only a few breaks in this systematic subordination of humanity to mortality: the earthquakes which occasionally collapse civilization into nature, the crown on the mountainside which mysteriously testifies to the existence of an ongoing resistance, and Stroszek's mad rebellion. The film minimizes the challenge to this universe undertaken by Stroszek by representing him in a narrative circle; at the end of the film he is in the same state (gravely ill and being transported through the landscape by a truck) that marked his arrival.

In *Aguirre, the Wrath of God* the circle remains, with the same lethal connotations. A whirlpool strands a raft of men and it is claimed that they are sickened by going in circles. The next morning they are dead. At film's end Gaspar's last journal entry states: "I can write no more. We are going around in circles" in another whirlpool. Strikingly, the last shot of the film circles around Aguirre and his floundering quest. Yet, in this film the overwhelmingly oppressive encirclement of *Signs of Life* can be seen to be further challenged and modified. In *Signs of Life* the possibilities of change, history and human initiative are eclipsed by structures of natural and social repetition. Change and resistance are admitted only as illogical, and therefore necessarily mysterious and absurd, alternatives. In *Aguirre, the Wrath of God* the bleakness of *Signs of Life* is substantially qualified. In the latter film history has not been negated; the example of Cortés is invoked as an indisputable precedent for heroic vision which leads to successful disobedience of the constraints of existing social practice. And Aguirre anticipates the future existence of others who will act if he fails, or fulfill what he may succeed in beginning (even if it is only the conquest of water and jungle). Nature and society are, thus, no longer presented as necessarily coincident in their repressive effect on the individual. It becomes more plausible for individuals to have occasion to rebel, and a chance of succeeding in that endeavor.

In accounting for this change there is a differentiation made in *Aguirre, the Wrath of God* between Old and New Worlds. The Old World, of Spain, is linked to existing institutionalized civilization, while the New exists in the jungles which "God never finished" and into which the expedition descends from the "last pass" between known and unseen lands as the film opens. In this opening sequence the Spaniards bring with them into the new land guns, animals, slaves, women, royalty, and religion. It is a catalogue of their civilization and of the tools it places faith in and can muster for the existential task of meeting new possibilities. Ominously included is a wheel (a circle) shot from above in a way that emphasizes the awkward, imperiling burden which it (and, by extension, the civilization it is part of) places upon these people in treacherous circumstances. The expedition, Spanish civilization's organized attempt to deal with the (extensive) margins of their world and subordinate its value (El Dorado) to their needs, subsequently fails, grinds to a halt and, at least figuratively, dies. Gaspar's journal records that it is the last day of the year and "we are exhausted." Narrative recapitulates history; the viewer witnesses the end of Spanish imperialism, its world view, and those who allowed themselves to be bound by its forms of dealing with reality. Only the advance party continues. And when its leader, Ursua, orders Christian burial for the dead men on the raft his decision jeopardizes any further progress of that initiative by privileging the rights of the dead over the living and by losing more lives to the jungle. The priorities of his choice indicate a (civilized) blindness and inadequacy in the face of both the unfamiliar perils and new potential (El Dorado) of the world he has entered. The collapse of traditional power which the viewer witnesses in such moments is at once particular and historical as well as general: Spain's failure to cope with the Amazon jungle, and an existing culture's inability to generate new responses to "the human condition." In adverse circumstances cultural vision yields to established values and practices. Pizarro commissions the advance party to gather information about El Dorado, the Indians, food and cities. His main concern, however, is the survival of his expedition and its safe passage, or return, to Christian civilization. The advance party is to serve this primary goal by limiting the extent of its venture and then returning, regardless of what it may learn of El Dorado. In *Aguirre, the Wrath of God*, though, cultural constraints on individuals are not as inexorable as in *Signs of Life*; institutional lack of vitality is countered by Aguirre's mutiny, specifically his refusal to return, to circle back, to what is already known and failed ("I don't turn back"). New experiential possibilities are potentially indicated by this breaking of the circle; Aguirre's behavior, now with an honored and indisputable precedent (Cortés), cannot be immediately dismissed as madness. And, further, the river seemingly affords a path through the landscape which has defeated the original expedition. It is a means of apparent escape from the jungle, continuation of the quest, and possible access to El Dorado. Correspondingly, the Old World's encounter with the New coincides not only with the end of the old year but also with Christmas, the day of a messiah's entry into the world.

For Aguirre, the river provides release from the fate of failed civilization, at a standstill in the jungle. In a sense, nature now offers resources for willed action on the part of individuals who can see beyond their culture. The river, then, becomes like the earthquakes and the crown on the mountainside in *Signs of Life*, and the ship in the trees later in *Aguirre, the Wrath of God*, that is, anti-social affronts to social order and logic existing in the landscape as a sign of hope for those who would see them. Aguirre values the river as a path to El Dorado; "Who follows me and the river wins untold riches." But he does so at the expense of appreciating the fact that its course still remains bounded, contained, within the killing landscape of the jungle. In Herzog's universal scheme society's grip on the individual may be broken, but not nature's. An Indian tells Ursua's wife that "there is no way out of the jungle." And the river itself is fraught with its own perils: rapids, stretches that becalm the quest, flooded areas that isolate the raft from shore, and whirlpools. As a basis for some sort of transcendent salvation the river is literally a dead end; it carries Aguirre to a whirlpool, which is where the film leaves him.

Such a conclusion is, in fact, "anticipated" in *Signs of Life*. For it should be recalled that the chicken immobilized by the line drawn in front of its eyes suggests a connection between lines, distraction and stasis. Stroszek's rebellion, too, had succeeded in breaking the structures that contained him. But his linear departure on the road, and his madness, were not an escape. Instead, they effectively removed him as a presence in the social and natural landscape; he disappeared. Similarly, Aguirre breaks the "circle" of civilization, only to end up in a mad confrontation with nature.[7]

In both films the rebellion of the hero is fated to fail. "Like those of his kind he was bound to fail," the postscript voice-over narration of *Signs of Life* dispassionately comments. And (for those viewers not already aware of the mythic status of cities of gold) the written preface of *Aguirre, the Wrath of God* identifies the story of El Dorado as a myth invented by the vanquished Indians, implicitly as revenge on their Spanish conquerors. So the object of Spain's and Aguirre's quests is non-existent. In addition, early in the film Aguirre himself, at least momentarily, recognizes that the river can lead only to his death. But despite the futility of the rebel heroes' actions both films attribute nobility to their efforts. The crown on the mountainside is *Signs of Life*'s symbol of resistance and the gypsy king is one of Stroszek's kindred spirits on the island. Aguirre is noble by birth and part of history's honored tradition of heroes. In these capacities, both men serve as exemplars for others, whether those bearing immediate witness (in *Signs of Life*), or those of later generations (in *Aguirre, the Wrath of God*) who will respond to the fame and glory of the endeavor of the quest. The rebels' actions, consequently, are signals to others, not just private acts.

If the marking of authorial attitudes in the textual system of a narrative film is most apparent in the textual subsystem of narration (excepting, perhaps, in the case of ironists such as Ophüls and Rohmer), then it must be concluded that Herzog's ideas underwent a substantial shift between *Signs of Life* and *Aguirre, the Wrath of God*. For there is significant difference in the two films' narrational description and evaluation of the heroes' rebellions.

As has been discussed above, the very nature of visionary resistance is altered in *Aguirre, the Wrath of God* by virtue of its separation of nature and society into separate oppressive existential realities impinging upon the individual. Such a differentiation is latent in *Signs of Life*, in the war narrative's identification of a specifically social sphere of power contested by the Germans and the Greek partisans. But the minimal attention (and eventfulness) paid to this matter confirms the narrational assumption that the significant forms of social life on the island are untouched by such historical contestations of political power. In *Aguirre, the Wrath of God* nature and society are more clearly demarcated, and the power of the latter is considerably more fallible. Thus, the possible emergence and effectivity of individual rebellion is dramatically expanded. In *Signs of Life* culture is as entrenched as nature. So the act of resistance can only have momentary significance – the duration of a fireworks display, the time it will take for the dust to settle in the wake of the truck carrying Stroszek away, the alteration of the universe by the loss of one chair and one donkey. However brief, the spectacle of the fireworks honors Stroszek's struggle (and is echoed in the cannonfire, and the night gunfire of the crazed men on the raft in *Aguirre, the Wrath of God*). But regardless of his vision and heroism in daring to act, the world is indifferent and quickly oblivious; signs of Stroszek's revolt are fleeting or quickly dispensed with (he and the donkey are taken away) and, ultimately, insignificant. While continuing to acknowledge the enduring indifference of nature, *Aguirre, the Wrath of God* has made society more malleable. Specifically, history (and narrative) can preserve traces of heroic vision. And in such historical effectivity the literal moment of failure and mortality can be transcended. Heroic example is no longer fated to be ephemeral and manifest only in the immediate spectacle of performance. Despite his demise, "like others of his kind," Aguirre is not left dwarfed by his world at the end of *Aguirre, the Wrath of God.*

Accompanying the conceptual differences of the two films is an affective change on the part of Herzog. The thematic pessimism of *Signs of Life* is matched by a narrational tone, literally and stylistically, which is restrained and unrelieved by the humor which usually punctuates Herzog's films (with the possible exception of brief occasions of absurd irony, for example, in the visual and voice-over treatment of the chair and the donkey). Generally, the narrator's voice and commentary are straightforward and, arguably, sympathetically reserved in their descriptions of Stroszek. This, despite evaluatively observing that his defeat was better than no responsive action at all. Logically, then, the closing, summary, narrational perspective is apart from Stroszek, in the "god's-eye" distance of high-angle extreme long shot. It is as if the hero's quixotic undertaking and its implications are so hopeless that Herzog finds it best to seek the emotional detachment of "objectivity." (There is a bit of irony in this, too, since Herzog appears as one of the stretcher-bearers who carry Stroszek into the film in the first place.)

In contrast, the narrational perspective of *Aguirre, the Wrath of God* responds to, and affirms, the power of Aguirre by fulfilling his vision in two ways. First, the film representationally constructs an end to Aguirre's revolt which is beyond his narrative grasp as a mortal. In an act of pure narrational authority the camera circles Aguirre and the raft in the last shot, effectively restructuring the relationship between nature and individual which Aguirre has madly insisted upon. Not only does this last shot forego the earlier film's objectivity of extreme long shot, by shifting to closer distance, but also, its circling movement scales the shot to Aguirre as an anchoring center. In this concluding image landscape loses its fixity and is destabilized relative to Aguirre. This image carries Herzog past mere narrational attachment to full identification with Aguirre's madness itself; the image is structured by his world view, not the narrator's view of him. In this situation the valorizing spectacle of rebellion attaches not to material effects but to the individual himself.

The second task performed by Herzog on behalf of Aguirre's vision is to make history of him (where others might simply have produced movies). Citing the evidence of an existing journal, Herzog's film labors to retell its story of Aguirre, assisted by the journal's documentation (the frequent citation of entry dates), but in such a way as to see around and reverse civilization's judgment of Aguirre and grant him, instead, the fame he anticipates from his actions. In service to this task Pizarro becomes a supporting character, timid in heroic comparison. Through the logic of Old and New Worlds already discussed above, the film champions the example of Aguirre and his quest, regardless of its literal outcome. In fact, though, the film, through the gold ornament worn by the Indian/jaguar even grants some credence to the myth. But, more significantly, the literal truth of traditional history ceases to matter. The film's prefacing disclaimer concerning El Dorado momentarily strikes the same note of detached objectivity (relative to Aguirre's subjectivity, and belief in El Dorado) which had concluded *Signs of Life.* But in this case, the rhetorical movement of the film toward the exhilarated fascination with Aguirre in the final shot plays against, and undermines, the opening "civilized" view of history by critiquing its materialist bias toward results (as Aguirre despises his men who measure riches only in terms of gold) and asserting the transcendent value of subjectivity.

Late in the film, unmotivated (and unsuspected) by character glance, the narration of *Aguirre, the Wrath of God* directs its attention to a shot of the calm river reflecting the (gold) light of the sun. In this image, mysteriously but undeniably, nature, sun, gold, and the quest are synthesized. Only Werner Herzog would dare show us El Dorado in a travelogue image.

Notes

1   This chapter is a revised version of an article published in *Movietone News*, no. 56 (November 1977).
2   Herzog himself has repeatedly resisted attempts to portray him as self-absorbed. To a Berkeley audience in 1976 he stated, "I make personal films. I say personal, not private."
3   For those unfamiliar with *Signs of Life,* its narrative centers on a young German soldier named Stroszek wounded (in the head)

not a word on 'fascism' — its cult of nature
Indians success in jungle previously

during World War II and sent to a Greek island to recuperate. Except for a crown drawn on a mountainside during the night by partisans, the war is far removed from the island's tranquil reality – a way of life that has lasted centuries. Stroszek, his Greek wife, and two other soldiers are assigned to occupy an abandoned harborside fortress and mount guard over its antiquated munitions supply. The first portion of the film observes their routines, which do little more than provide a way of passing time. This daily monotony is punctuated by chance encounters with children, villagers, a wandering gypsy king, and the island itself. There is a "found" quality to the film – in its use of non-actors, in its episodic narrative events, and in its almost random inclusiveness of incidents, anecdotes and persons that must simply have struck the director's fancy (one old man was a friend of Herzog's grandfather years before). Tranquility and inactivity come to index entrapment for Stroszek. He rebels. He locks himself in the fort and besieges the city with home-made fireworks, any of which could set off the munitions. As his rebellion continues his madness grows. Eventually, inevitably, he is overpowered and taken away.

4 The topic of subjectivity which exists in isolation from conventional means of self-expression is movingly explored by Herzog in a documentary format as well, in *Land of Silence and Darkness*.

5 This dichotomy between narrative and narration is underwritten, in large part, by the frequent representational tension between the fictive content of shots and the documentary "feel" of Herzog's styles of shooting and editing his films. In *Aguirre, the Wrath of God*, for example, images are occasionally "flawed" by water on the lens or less than perfect focus. Much of the shooting on the rafts is hand-held and seems improvised in its movements. On other occasions the film suggests a hospitality to "found" footage, for example, when the narrative seems interrupted by, and therefore momentarily made subordinate to, footage of the river, a butterfly on a finger, a mouse moving its young, etc. When the Indian, "Hombrecito," plays his pipes, the very long take (with one cut-away) breaks the preceding narrative rhythm in favor of (documentary) fidelity to the event of the immediate moment, an event which has some narrative import (in Aguirre's attentiveness) but not enough, seemingly, to justify the shot's duration on screen.

6 This feature of Herzog's films, not to mention its inversion of the opening of *Triumph of the Will*, would seem to invite further, Kracauer-style, analysis.

7 There is a beguiling romantic logic in Aguirre's claims of power.
   Nature dominates culture (the earthquakes and ruins of *Signs of Life*
   testify to this fact, for example). Aguirre has defied civilization ("I
   am the great traitor"). Therefore, he asserts an equivalence between
   nature and rebel.

7 Signs of literary life (*The Mystery of Kaspar Hauser*)

7

Literature and writing in the films of Werner Herzog

Brigitte Peucker

Werner Herzog has often said that his films have their origin in images; repeatedly – and with justification – he has asserted the supremacy of the visual over the verbal in his films (Cott, 1976, 54; O'Toole, 1979, 42; Bachmann, 1977, 7–8). The dominance of the image, Herzog claims, begins with the moment of the film's conception: one central image will generate a cluster of visual moments, until Herzog, like Hitchcock in this respect, is able to "see" the entire film before him. Herzog also acknowledges music as a source of inspiration in his filmmaking; Baudelaire's *Correspondances* between the musical and the visual hold true for Herzog as well. When he speaks of film as the "art of illiterates," Herzog implies that the visual code, inspired as it may be by music or by an image, should predominate over the narrative code in cinema (Kent, 1977, 19 and 30). Herzog's assertion that film is the "art of illiterates" also has certain implications for the role of the movie audience; it affirms the necessity of "seeing" a film, an act which for Herzog is defined by its immediacy, its capacity to evoke an emotional or spiritual response, as opposed to "reading" a film, or responding in an analytic, and hence mediated, way. More importantly, in claiming "illiteracy" for himself as a filmmaker, Herzog denies the significance of reading and of writing for his art of the film, thus in effect denying the relevance of literary sources and models to his work.

In this chapter, then, I shall take up the implications of "illiteracy" as they are treated formally and thematically in Herzog's films, especially in *Every Man for Himself and God Against All: The Mystery of Kaspar Hauser*, and also take up what is denied by the notion of "illiteracy," the question of Herzog's literary indebtedness.

Herzog asserts rightly that his cinema is not primarily a narrative cinema. Naturally, most of his films depend upon a plot for coherence, but even at their most story-oriented, they tend to fall into a series of loosely connected episodes. *Fata Morgana,* the one film that has no plot at all, is itself the visual fantasy to which its title refers. In this extreme case, voice-over narration completely replaces narrative, and dialogue is reduced to monologue in an obliquely connected series of interview situations. The film appears at first to rely upon the voice-over narrations for its cohesiveness, but after these have begun promisingly with a creation myth, they then disintegrate into a string of Dada-like nonsense phrases, only some of which bear any relation to what we see on the screen. In fact, it is clear from the beginning of the film, when we *hear* about the Creation and *see* only images of death and decay, that Herzog is setting up a counterpoint between image and narration. Where disjunction between the two occurs, it is the image which we are to "believe." In *Fata Morgana,* narration is conceived as the "literary," and hence deceptive, component of the film.

Aguirre, the Wrath of God, another feature film in which Herzog uses narration nearly throughout, exhibits a similar, though less obvious, disjunction between the voice-over narration and the cinematic narrative that unfolds on the screen. The former, which consists of entries from the narrator's diary, a written text, provides the audience with names, dates, major events – that is, with the "significant facts" of the narrative. The camera, on the other hand, tends to focus on the visual detail which evokes mood and functions as commentary, rather than on event, even in the midst of the most action-oriented scenes. When, for example, the explorers "attack" the cannibals' burning village, the camera lingers on images of a dog nursing her young, of pigs, an abandoned boot, and a charred human head, thus both interrupting the narrative flow of events and commenting upon the narrator's spoken text.

A still more striking instance of the disjunction between this text and what we see – "reality" as it is conveyed by the camera – occurs in *Aguirre.* The Spaniards treat history itself as though it were a text to be written; events are less often *recorded* after the fact than *proclaimed* or decreed. "We are forging History," they say as they write yet another "document," for nothing has significance for the explorers until it moves from the moment of its occurrence in the present into the timeless realm of history – until it is mediated and authenticated by the text. Herzog shows us the absurdity of such thinking, for what is proclaimed and what is "true" are often presented as being at odds: the

House of Hapsburg is simply decreed out of existence in one written proclamation, and "possession" is taken of the land to the left and right of the river, land on which the explorers no longer dare even to set foot. Like the narrator's diary, the Spanish documents are texts which bear almost no relation to the actual state of things as revealed by the camera; and yet these texts acquire a reality for the explorers which their very arrow wounds, ascribed by them to feverish hallucination, do not have for them.

Although in *Signs of Life*, his first feature film, Herzog does not play upon the disjunction of voice-over narration and image (perhaps because the narration is not conceived as being based upon a text), the issue of writing is nevertheless present. Becker, one of the three soldiers who are consigned to an isolated existence in an old citadel on the Greek island of Kos, struggles against anomie by studying hieroglyphs on ancient tablets which lie strewn about the fortress. These tablets and fragments of statuary were uncovered by an earthquake, the narrator tells us; nature has regurgitated what it once swallowed – the signs of an ancient culture – but flowers and grasses, the signs of nature, are already beginning to re-cover these traces. Significantly, Becker, who becomes obsessed with the secrets which the tablets and their writings may have to impart, is a philologist; Herzog presents him as someone for whom the decoding of hieroglyphs, of the text, is equivalent to decoding the mysteries of existence. Not only, however, is Becker quite unable to do anything of the sort, but he cannot even decode the writing; his academic training – his literacy – is not, after all, a sufficient preparation. Not only Herzog but the very statuary itself seems to be mocking Becker's futile and misguided efforts, as when the camera focuses upon a stone foot, complete with toes, which projects from a ruined wall. Herzog suggests that the hieroglyphs are not signs of life, but signs which belong to the texts of a dead culture. Being therefore at two removes from life, they are doubly empty.

Even though he understands these signs to be indications of man's unceasing attempt to mediate between himself and the external world, for Herzog this attempt is characterized by its futility. How can this be otherwise when for Herzog language itself is secondary and cannot express the essence of existence? *Signs of Life* includes, for example, a shot of a little boy who says to the camera: "Now that I can talk, what shall I say?" In another episode a little peasant girl, who has not yet learned to understand language, is forced by her father to recite a poem which is utterly meaningless to her. When a pianist plays Chopin and then delivers a lecture about the composer to Stroszek, the film's central character who comprises his audience, the listener does not understand the connection between the music and the lecture, between the direct emotion and the desiccation of the words, and responds to the pianist with a long – pained and painful – silence.

When this same character, Stroszek, is confronted with 10,000 turning windmills whose movement resembles that of the minnows he has watched swimming in circles, he feels as though the landscape were mocking him and he responds by going mad. He challenges the sun with fireworks, believing that "one can only counteract light with light"; as long as it is dark, Stroszek's fireworks, his signs of life and of rebellion, seem to have conquered. But then the dawn outshines his fire. As futile as it is titanic, Stroszek's challenge is an attempt to meet nature upon its own terms, to "speak the language of nature," to come to terms with it by means of immediate, natural signs rather than the arbitrary signs of writing, like those of Becker's tablets. Stroszek wants to "fight fire with fire," or, like the romantic artist, to create as nature does. Herzog devotes a surprising amount of footage to the blazing nighttime sky, recalling the naive delight with which the German directors of the 1920s indulged in protracted shots of darkened skies illuminated with fireworks, amusement parks, or city lights – as in *Variety, Sunrise,* and *The Last Laugh.* The fact that Herzog's sky is a filmic echo, then, and the fact that *Signs of Life* was originally to have been called *Fire Signs,* reinforce the idea that Stroszek's fireworks, his personal *son et lumière* show, which oppose the arbitrary signs of writing, are meant ultimately to suggest the contrast of visual signs with verbal signs, of film with literature.

The complexity of Herzog's juxtaposition of image with text, or film with literature, is perhaps best expressed in *The Mystery of Kaspar Hauser.* The word *Schreiben,* or writing, is the first word that Kaspar Hauser hears in the film, and with this word difference or otherness is introduced into his previously hermetic existence. *Schreiben* is not, of course, the first word that Kaspar *speaks*; that is *Ross,* horse, a sound he learns to connect with the wooden horse with which he has hitherto existed, not in a subject-object relation, but in a state of animistic identification. This identification is so close that it encourages Kaspar, for instance, to dress the horse as he himself is dressed. At first, both speech and writing are only conditioned reflexes for Kaspar, actions emptied of significance, just as he himself is still blank, a *tabula rasa*: the next word he speaks, we recall, is *leer,* empty.[1] As yet writing is merely tracing for him, even though the words he learns to trace are those of his own name. Kaspar first learns that words signify when a child uses a mirror to help him identify the parts of his own body; thus he falls into self-consciousness and learns the concept of meaning at one and the same time. It is hardly surprising that in this film about the imagination and its modes of expression, Herzog would once more affirm the immediacy of the visual imagination and of music over what he considers to be the secondary, mediated expression of the imagination through the written word.

Herzog deflects this theme in its more radical form into a minor character in the film, "the young Mozart." We are told by a side-show barker that "the young Mozart," one of the "Four Riddles of the Spheres" (each of which must be decoded, incidentally, if one is to understand the film as a whole), was once a prodigy who asked for nothing but to hear the music of the real Mozart, and who knew all the Mozart scores. But when "the young Mozart" was required to learn to read and write, the barker's story continues, the "whiteness of the page blinded him," and from that day he lost the power of speech. He then fell into a trance, seeking darkness, staring into wells and holes in the ground, fascinated by underground caves and water courses. There is a connection between this response of "the young Mozart" and that of Stroszek in *Signs of Life*, who was struck dumb, again, by his inability to connect Chopin's music with the words spoken about the composer by the pianist. The prodigy in *Kaspar Hauser,* whose whole life has been music, is alienated by the secondariness of writing to such a degree that he consequently refuses the realm of language and difference altogether. It is precisely the "whiteness of the page," that is, the pretense to clarity or enlightenment in the written text, that is the source of "the young Mozart's" alienation, knowing music as he does without the necessity of mediating signs. In seeking darkness, he seeks an ambiguity that is without pretense, the opposite of what society claims to be the enlightenment provided by the written word.

But if the "whiteness of the page" – so bright that it blurs the marks of the text printed upon it – has blinded "the young Mozart," surely this baffling of sight is an effect which it must share with the darkness the child subsequently seeks. But "the young Mozart's" attitude as he stares into the model "well" of the side-show is not at all frustrated; it is that of Rodin's thinker, an attitude of contemplation. We should remind ourselves again that this character illuminates and absorbs some of the themes which Herzog wishes to articulate in the figure of Kaspar. The prodigy does not reject language until he has already been introduced to the idea of difference or otherness. Possibly he seeks out wells not only because he perceives water to be an organic and primal medium, but also because, like Kaspar, he sees his own reflection therein. The perception of difference is the basis of self-consciousness, and perhaps it is his image that motivates "the young Mozart's" crippling preoccupation with water; unlike Kaspar, he does not attempt to "erase" it; in the very purity of his genius, with its continued lofty ignorance of difference, he has succumbed to the artist's besetting weakness, narcissism.

It is significant that "the young Mozart" turns to nature – to the earth or ground and to water – for the resolution of his conflict. As so often in Herzog, we can cite the preoccupations of romanticism for a gloss on this "riddle." A passage from Northrop Frye's "The Romantic Myth" is particularly apropos:

> In Romanticism the main direction of the quest of identity tends increasingly to be downward and inward, toward a hidden basis or ground of identity between man and nature. It is in a hidden region, often described in images of underground caves and streams ... that the final unity between man and his nature is most often achieved. The word "dark" is thematically very important in Romanticism, especially in Germany, and it usually refers to the seeping of an identity with nature into the hidden and inner parts of the mind. (Frye, 1968, 33)

But with the introduction of self-consciousness, no resolution – no identity or union – is possible from Herzog's point of view, despite "the young Mozart's" refusal of language and of writing; from now on even music itself can only be the dim echo of that irretrievable harmony.

For Herzog there is a kind of ideal state – a *Präexistenz*, as Hofmannsthal would call it – in which the faculty of the imagination lies dormant, and in which there is no need for its development. This is a condition of at-oneness more complete even than that of Schiller's naive poet; it is an oceanic state, a state of identification with all things, like that of Kaspar with his toy horse. In this state even dreaming itself is impossible, because there is nothing to dream *of*. The act of dreaming itself is founded on the loss of unity, and furthermore it requires a grammar of images which is at first unavailable to Kaspar. Once Kaspar is on his way to self-consciousness, he begins to dream, although at first, like Heinrich von Ofterdingen of whom Novalis says "Es träumte ihm" ("it dreamed unto him"), Kaspar sees himself as the passive recipient of his dreams: "Es träumte mir" ("it dreamed unto me"). Years pass before Kaspar can distinguish between dream and reality, and even when he comes to do so, he finds that he can envision and recount the dream of the Sahara, for example, only as long as it is restricted to the mythical territory of a desert in which reality and reverie, wisdom and clairvoyance, remain one. Kaspar can no longer envision the caravan as soon as it leaves the mythical realm of the desert to enter the "real" or social world of the city.

Like Herzog's films, Kaspar's dreams begin with images of land-scapes, although in Kaspar's case the images are of landscapes he has never seen. (It is worth noting, though, that Herzog had not seen the Amazon before filming *Aguirre*, but still claimed that the actual land-scape turned out to be precisely what he had imagined [Cott, 1976, 54].) Kaspar had been *told* about the Sahara and, as he says, "Das geht mir nicht aus dem Kopf" ("That refuses to leave my head"); he converts and subverts verbal representation, as Herzog often does, into visual images. In another dream vision, that of the Caucasus, Kaspar creates a mythical landscape with golden temples for which there has been no equivalent in his experience. In this instance, Kaspar is creating *ex nihilo* and in natural signs, just as the romantic artist wishes to create. Like Stroszek's fireworks, Kaspar's image-oriented dreams are akin to the art of the cinema, and, like the images of film, according to Herzog, they are "archaeological," "anthropological," or "archetypal" (Bach-mann, 1977, 7; O'Toole, 1979, 46; de le Viseur and Schmidmaier, 1977).

Herzog presents his visions on the screen for his audience to see, but, as we have said, they do not necessarily declare themselves in narrative terms. It is significant that the meaning and even the point of view of the sequence which constitutes the primary, central image of the film – the swan sequence – remain ambiguous: is it one of Kaspar's visions, or is it part of the narrative? It is certainly the centerpiece of the film, anticipated as it is by the opening scene, a romantic idyll which contains many of its elements. Just before the swan sequence, there is a shot of Kaspar lying in bed with tears running down his face, a shot which signals the coming of interiority and reverie. Yet, unlike the other dream sequences, this one is not accompanied by Kaspar's voice-over narration. Later, Kaspar implies that he has been boating, mysteriously recalling the fact that one of the images of this sequence is of two men in a rowboat. Yet one still feels that the scene is not part of the narrative, but remains a vision so personal and so enigmatic that it is beyond the reach of words, and can be encompassed only by Albinoni's music.

The Albinoni Adagio connects the swan sequence with the one that follows it: Kaspar in the garden writing a letter to Daumer in which he describes the moment of the most acute joy he has ever experienced. He describes how he has sown his name in cress seeds and how they have sprung up and created an organic, vital embodiment of his name. He has attempted, in other words, to convert the arbitrary signs of writing into natural signs, and has managed to bring about a union of language with nature. There is an analogy to be drawn, I think, between Kaspar's cress words and the swan sequence which precedes them. The swan appears in a nighttime scene involving a tree-lined pond across which two men glide in a rowboat; there is a medieval tower at the left side of the frame. The scene is, in short, a gathering of romantic images taken not so directly from romantic *painting* as from the language of romantic *lyric* – from poems by Eichendorff, Mörike, Lenau and Heine. The swan itself, of course, symbol of *poésie pure*, will find its strongest imagistic resonance in the poetry of Mallarmé, Yeats and Rilke, but its origin, too, is in romanticism. Whereas the rolling green hills dotted with villages and church steeples which form the background of an earlier scene represent the "romantic landscape" *per se,* this composite image gives visual expression to the interior landscape of the romantic imagination. Like Kaspar, who subverts writing by giving it organic form, Herzog converts the specifically *verbal* images of romanticism into the quasi-natural signs which C. S. Peirce calls icons. Herzog does so, I would argue, in order to subvert writing, to assert his preference for the visual over the literary and, in so doing, to suppress his literary indebtedness. It should be borne in mind that Herzog spent his childhood not at the cinema, but reading; it is no superficial background for which his filmmaking substitutes itself.

Unlike "the young Mozart," Kaspar takes to writing quite happily: he learns to accommodate himself to a society which equates verbalization with verification when he writes his autobiography. It is at this point in the film, I believe, that the bilingual pun on *Reiter*/"writer" in Kaspar's first sentence – "Ich möcht ein solchner Reiter werden, wie mein Vater einer gewe'n ist" ("I want to become the kind of rider that my father was") – is confirmed for us. This pun, if we accept it, explains the connection between the first two words that Kaspar hears, *Schreiben* (writing) and *Ross* (horse). Kaspar, who had formerly existed in a state of animistic identification with the horse, now follows the optative of his first sentence, patterns himself after his "father" or keeper, who teaches him to write his name, and therefore identifies no longer with the horse but with the rider – or writer. Both rider and writer harness and curb the vitality of nature. Earlier, one of Herzog's typically protracted images, that of the monkey in the posture of a rider on a horse's back, helps to confirm this connection. Rider and writer are mimic men, apes of nature.

Herzog's bitter invective against writing in *Kaspar Hauser* includes his portrait of the notary, whose obsession with recording the details of what he takes to be "reality" reflects the sort of naturalist aesthetics that equates painstaking representation with truth. Kaspar adopts something of this attitude in writing his autobiography, for he hopes to understand experience in the writing of it. It is perhaps for this reason, too, that he informs Daumer of the destruction of the cress writing in a letter, rather than telling him about it directly; Kaspar's response to the event is so deep and so emotional that writing about it gives him the distance from the experience that he needs. Kaspar will allow no one to read his autobiography until he has learned more words; in imitation of society (again like Heinrich von Ofterdingen) Kaspar believes that in knowing more words he will possess greater knowledge (Novalis, 1963, 90). In this scene Herzog portrays Kaspar as having fallen victim to the misguided teachings of society. This becomes particularly apparent when Herzog cuts repeatedly from the scene of Kaspar's painstaking writing of his autobiography to that of Daumer's reading aloud from the obituary page of the newspaper. The reduction of life and experience to the meager facts recorded in the obituaries – which Daumer reads – is paralleled by Kaspar's attenuation of his experience, the circumscription of his being and spirit by his writing.

And yet the relative immediacy with which Kaspar responds to experience cannot be wholly subverted by society and by writing. Kaspar calls his autobiography a *Lebensbeschreibung* (a description of his life), and the fact that his entries are *descriptions* partly redeems his fondness for writing in Herzog's eyes. Description is the language which most typically suits Kaspar's visual mode of perception; we recall his encounter with the professor of logic in which the professor dismisses Kaspar's solution to his riddle as "mere description," rather than logical deduction. The professor maintains that logicians "do not learn to understand, but to deduce." But Kaspar has understood, in Herzog's terms, as is clear from the nature of his solution to the riddle, which has recourse not to a trick of syntax or logic but to the organic image of a tree-frog.

As I have suggested and will now attempt to demonstrate, Herzog is never wholly friendly toward writing because his films must channel and surmount a rich literary heritage. One of the first titles of *Kaspar Hauser* – "Hören Sie denn nicht die entsetzliche Stimme, die um den ganzen Horizont schreit und die man gewöhnlich die Stille heißt"

("Don't you hear that horrifying voice that screams across the entire horizon and is usually called silence") – is quoted from Büchner's *Lenz*. And when Kaspar, still in a relatively early stage of his linguistic development, varies his original sentence ("Ich möcht ein solchner Reiter werden, wie mein Vater einer gewe'n ist" ["I want to become the kind of rider that my father was"]), romantic poet that he is, he is "unconsciously" quoting Eichendorff when he says "Ich möcht als Reiter fliegen/Wohl in die blutige Schlacht" ("I want to fly as a rider into the bloody battle"). This is not a spontaneous linguistic permutation like those of Peter Handke's Kaspar. These are lines taken verbatim from "Das zerbrochene Ringlein" ("The Broken Ring"), and in the context of the poem they are by no means as alogical or naive as Herzog intends them to appear to be in this scene. Although both the Büchner and the Eichendorff quotations are unaltered, they are unacknowledged and fit so effortlessly into Herzog's material that they are lost as quotations. Herzog's use of music, by contrast, calls attention to itself: the passage from Mozart's *Magic Flute*, for example, frames the film and the importance of its meaning is unconcealed: it is Tamino's aria of act I which includes the phrase "this something I cannot name," and reinforces the importance of unmediated experience in the film as a whole. Herzog's use of literary quotations, on the other hand, seems to remain as designedly unselfconscious as possible under the several circumstances in which it appears.

Herzog owes a debt to Büchner – this time to *Woyzeck* – for yet another scene of *Kaspar Hauser,* the fair. The animals – the horse and monkey – which are the main attraction of the announcer's "show" in Büchner's *Woyzeck* are relegated to the periphery of Herzog's fair in *Kaspar Hauser,* where they function emblematically, as I have mentioned. Büchner's announcer says of the monkey: "Sehen Sie die Kreatur, wie Gott sie gemacht: nix, gar nix. Sehn Sie jetzt die Kunst; geht aufrecht, hat Rock und Hosen, hat ein Säbel" ("Look at the creatures, the way that God made them: nothing, simply nothing. Now look at art; walks upright, has a coat and pants, has a sword") (Büchner, 1965, 117). But of the horse he says: "Beschäme die Société. Sehn Sie, das Vieh ist noch Natur, uNideale Natur" ("Shame the society. You see, the beast is still nature, unideal nature") (Büchner, 1965, 118). These two quotations articulate the polarity of the social and the natural, which Büchner never quite resolves. For Herzog, however, the polarity is clearly resolved in favor of nature, the horse, whereas its rider, the clothed monkey, is a figure of scorn. While these images are at the periphery of *Kaspar Hauser*, the issues they raise are of central importance in the film.

There are other echoes of Büchner's *Woyzeck* in *Kaspar Hauser* as well: in the general negative attitude toward science, for instance, which treats Kaspar – as Woyzeck is treated – like an experimental animal, and which culminates in his autopsy. It hardly seems necessary to cite Herzog's 1979 adaptation of *Woyzeck* in support of my assertion that Büchner exerts an important influence on Herzog, and that *Woyzeck* has an important place in the literary subtext which underlies *Kaspar Hauser*. I might add, however, that Herzog has said of Büchner's *Woyzeck* that "it's really the most remarkable and probably the strongest drama-text that has ever been written in the German language" (Walsh/Ebert, 1979, 11–12). He has also said that when he wrote the screenplay for yet another film, *Stroszek,* he wanted "something with the basic feeling of *Woyzeck* [the play] in it. And so I wrote *Stroszek,* although *Woyzeck* was still on my mind and it kept bothering me" (Walsh/Ebert, 1979, 12). It will be clear by this time that this kind of admission is a serious one for Herzog to make. It is certain in any case from *Kaspar Hauser,* the earliest of these three films, that Büchner's *Woyzeck* was already "bothering" Herzog long before he wrote *Stroszek* or adapted *Woyzeck.* Indeed, two images in Herzog's *Woyzeck* are in fact based on similar images from *Kaspar Hauser.* One image, ironically, derives from the field of windblown wheat over which Herzog placed his quotation from Büchner's *Lenz* in *Kaspar Hauser,* almost as though he were metonymically, by means of *his* image, "returning" what was borrowed: this image is the waving field of poppy pods in which Herzog's Woyzeck hears the voices from nature. The other, like the swan sequence in the former film, must certainly be one of the central images from which the film emerged. It, too, is a shot of a pond at night, melodramatically illuminated as though to simulate moonlight, and bordered on its far edge by a large weeping willow tree. Never described by Büchner, who simply calls it *Teich,* pond, and leaves it at that, in the film this scene derives its appearance from romantic lyric.

One might name literary sources for other images in Herzog's films: the genre scenes representing peasant life in *Heart of Glass* lean heavily upon the portrait of the mountain people in Büchner's *Lenz;* in *Stroszek,* the scene that shows two armed farmers riding by one another on their tractors, glaring their hatred, is taken from the opening of Gottfried Keller's *Romeo und Julia auf dem Dorfe* ("Romeo and

Juliet in the Village"), while another scene in this film, which centers on mesmerism or "animal magnetism," echoes this theme in the work of E. T. A. Hoffmann; *Fata Morgana* is also a title of a poem by Eichendorff which addresses a "Pilger im Wüstensande" ("Pilgrim in the desert sands"); *La Soufrière* recalls Kleist's *Erdbeben in Chili (Earthquake in Chile)* insofar as the eruption – or the threatened eruption – of a volcano inverts the very laws of nature; a gypsy violinist, who has prototypes in Keller and Mann, among others, functions emblematically in *Nosferatu*. *Signs of Life* is based very loosely on Arnim's *Troller Invalide auf dem Fort Ratonneau* ("Mad Invalid in the Fort Ratonneau"), and somewhere behind *Nosferatu* there lurks Bram Stoker's *Dracula*. It should be added, however, that the issue of literary borrowing with which I am concerned in this essay is best kept separate from that of the cinematic adaptation of a literary text, which, if it is to produce a successful film, should involve the development of an independent mode of narrative. What is at issue here is not only that certain narrative moments in Herzog's films derive from literature, but also that he has actually taken central images, the primary constituents of his cinema, from a medium he scorns – or claims to scorn – for its secondariness. In other words, Herzog's images are not only taken from nature – ordinarily from landscape – and inspired by music, but often additionally manifest signs of literary life that are covered over by the polemical stance of "illiteracy," Herzog's relentless denial of reading and of writing as aspects of the art of film.

Notes

1   "It can hardly be an accident that, while both the wild child and Helen Keller learn to ask first for what is contained in their cups, Herzog's Kaspar learns the word *empty* first when his cup is drained." David Overbey on Truffaut's *L'enfant sauvage*, Penn's *The Miracle Worker,* and Herzog's *Kaspar Hauser*. David Overbey (1975) "Every Man for Himself," *Sight and Sound,* 44, no. 2 (Spring) 74.

Works cited

Bachmann, Gideon (1977) "The Man on the Volcano: a portrait of Werner Herzog," *Film Quarterly*, 31, no. 1 (Fall).
Büchner, Georg (1965) *Woyzeck,* in *Werke und Briefe*, Munich, DTV.
Cott, Jonathan (1976) "Signs of Life," *Rolling Stone* (November 18).

Frye, Northrop (1968) "The Romantic Myth," *A Study of English Romanticism*, New York, Random House.

Kent, Leticia (1977) "Werner Herzog: Film Is Not the Art of Scholars, But of Illiterates," *The New York Times* (September 11), section II.

Novalis (1963) *Heinrich von Ofterdingen* in E. Grassi (ed.) *Klassiker der deutschen Literatur*, vol. 11, Hamburg, Rowohlt.

O'Toole, Lawrence (1979) "I Feel That I'm Close to the Center of Things," *Film Comment*, 15, no. 6 (November–December).

Overbey, David (1975) "Every Man for Himself," *Sight and Sound*, 44, no. 2 (Spring).

Viseur, Raimund de le and Werner Schmidmaier (1977) *"Playboy* Interview: Werner Herzog," *Playboy* (German edition), no. 1 (January).

Walsh, Gene (ed.) (1979) " 'Images at the Horizon': a workshop with Werner Herzog," conducted by Roger Ebert, Chicago, Facets Multimedia Center (April) (pamphlet; no publisher).

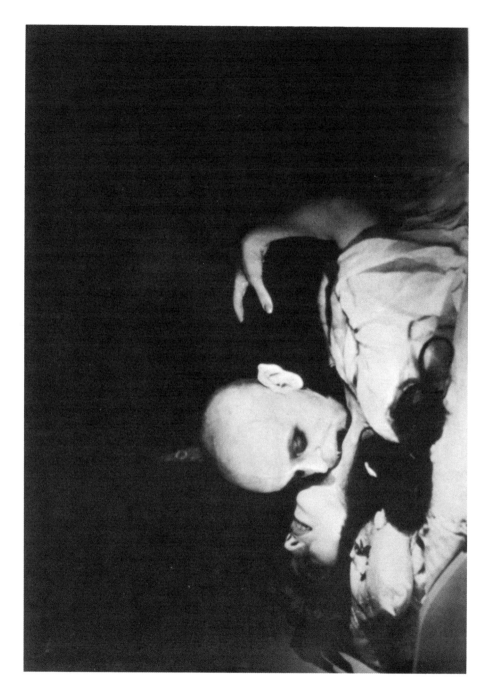

8 Rereading Murnau in order to rediscover Stoker (*Nosferatu, the Vampire*)

8

Herzog, Murnau, and the vampire

Judith Mayne

Lotte Eisner described Friedrich Murnau as "the greatest film-director the Germans have ever known" (Eisner, 1973a, 97). Werner Herzog's 1979 film *Nosferatu*, in many ways an homage to Murnau, seems to confirm the relevance of Eisner's judgment to the New German Cinema. Murnau's 1922 version of the Dracula legend is surely one of the best-known and most successful films of the silent German cinema. Herzog's self-described goal in retelling Murnau's cinematic tale is to affirm a kind of spiritual bond between the contemporary German cinema and the past: "We are trying in our films to build a thin bridge back to that time, to legitimize our own cinema and culture. We are not remaking *Nosferatu*, but bringing it to new life and new character for a new age" (Andrews, 1978, 33). How appropriate that Lotte Eisner should affirm Herzog's "rebirth" of *Nosferatu*, declaring that "the film is not being remade, it is being reborn" (Andrews, 1978, 33).

The "rebirth" of *Nosferatu* suggests that just as Murnau and screen-play author Henrik Galeen read and transformed the vampire legend as presented in Bram Stoker's 1897 novel, *Dracula*, so Herzog undertook a similar process of revision, this time with the Murnau film as his source. (As we shall see, Herzog's retelling of Murnau's film also involves a return to Stoker's novel.) To consider Herzog's film in relation to the Murnau source runs the risk of a facile adaptation analysis, now between two film texts rather than the more common comparison of literary source and cinematic adaptation. But if it is understood from the outset that "adaptation" is always a process of reading and interpretation (and not the simple transposition of a narrative from one medium to another), then an analysis of Herzog's

Nosferatu as an adaptation of Murnau raises some key questions of film narrative.

Perhaps the most obvious of these questions is the relationship between the classics of the cinematic tradition and the present. Herzog himself offers a Kracauer-like reading of his project: "Murnau's *Nosferatu* . . . prophesied the rise of nazism by showing the invasion of Germany by Dracula and his plague-bearing rats. And it gave a legitimacy to German cinema that was lost in the Hitler era" (Andrews, 1978, 33). Certainly the persistence of expressionism and its wide array of cinematic and narrative devices in the contemporary cinema in general, and the New German Cinema in particular, is a fascinating area of inquiry. However, Herzog's description of Murnau's film, suggesting the interface between the two Nosferatu's as the pre-fascist prophecy and the post-fascist rebirth, is misleading. True, both Herzog and Murnau represent their vampires as obstructive forces in the staid middle-class environments of Delft and Bremen, respectively. But despite the claim that he is transposing a pre-fascist film to contemporary circumstances, Herzog initiates a dialogue with Murnau that has little to do with the political metaphor of vampirism. Rather, Herzog's *Nosferatu* uses Murnau's film to explore questions of authorship, sexuality, and narrative voice.

The plot and structure of Herzog's film follow directly from Murnau. Herzog changes the names of many of his protagonists to conform to the cast of characters in Stoker's novel. Bruno Ganz as Jonathan Harker (Thomas Hutter in Murnau's film) is sent by his employer, Renfield (Knock in Murnau's film) on a real-estate venture to Count Dracula's castle in Transylvania. Isabella Adjani portrays Jonathan's wife Lucy (Ellen Hutter in Murnau's film, although here Herzog takes the name of another female character from Stoker's novel, rather than calling Jonathan's wife Mina Harker, as Stoker does) who senses impending disaster and begs her husband not to leave. A long journey takes Jonathan to the vampire's castle. As in Murnau's film, the vampire (portrayed by Klaus Kinski) attacks Jonathan, but cross-cutting in both films suggests that Jonathan's wife is closely identified with the vampire (when the vampire attacks the husband, it is the wife's reaction we see). Nosferatu voyages by boat to Delft, bringing with him plague-infested rats; while Jonathan, stricken, returns on horseback. Murnau quickly leaves Jonathan in the wings to focus on the encounter between the vampire and the woman, whereas Herzog gives Jonathan a more central role. Jonathan's fever has left him without memory, and when he returns to Delft he does not recognize his wife. In both films, however, it is the woman's task to confront the vampire, and both Lucy (in Herzog's film) and Ellen (in Murnau's) acquire their sense of duty from the book of the vampires which informs them that the vampire will perish if a woman "pure of heart" spends the night with him. Herzog's Lucy prepares for her task in a setting considerably more spectacular than what surrounds Murnau's heroine, for the spread of the plague in Delft creates a carnivalesque environment of death, frenzy, and celebration – a scene common to many of Herzog's films. Indeed, the scene where Lucy wanders through the town square and encounters a population in the grips of a kind of collective madness is the most obvious departure from Murnau in *Nosferatu*, for this representation of the plague is pure Herzog.

The conclusion of Herzog's *Nosferatu* also departs from Murnau's film. Lucy sleeps with the vampire, and, as in Murnau's film, both she and Nosferatu die when the sun rises. Herzog adds two final touches: Dr Van Helsing, the inefficient and somewhat bumbling voice of science and reason, expresses regret that he had never listened to Lucy, and asks for a hammer and stake to destroy (somewhat belatedly) the vampire. Jonathan, huddled in a corner and surrounded by crushed communion wafers placed by Lucy to protect him from the vampire, calls for the arrest of Van Helsing and orders a servant to sweep away the wafers. Now sporting the characteristic fangs and fingernails of a vampire, and saying he "has much to do," Jonathan rides off into the horizon on horseback in the final image of the film.

The narrative framework taken directly from the 1922 *Nosferatu* is Herzog's most direct homage to Murnau. It is as if the film's plot represents a convention, a structure, inherited from the past and within which the contemporary filmmaker demonstrates his own vision. Herzog also gives us direct quotations from Murnau's film, that is, images which are drawn directly from the 1922 film. Just before the Count's departure for Delft, Jonathan observes as the vampire loads coffins onto a cart. A striking point-of-view shot in Murnau's film shows Nosferatu from a bird's-eye view, in extreme long shot, suggesting both Jonathan's perspective from inside the castle looking out, and a detached, distant perspective perched in a kind of no man's land. Herzog uses a similar image in his film when Jonathan watches the identical scene, but with a sharp difference in angle. The image evokes Murnau, yet reminds us simultaneously of another authorial presence, one that leans decidedly toward the implications of a point of view located in a hypothetical "no man's land."

This particular use of quotation is demonstrated more strikingly early in Herzog's film. The interior of the Harker house is presented to us in close-up shots of two kittens playing with a miniature of Lucy. A cut to another image shows the bright, orderly interior of the house where Lucy and Jonathan are eating breakfast. Jonathan picks up the miniature as he leaves to go to work.

The miniature of Lucy and the kittens refer us to two specific moments in Murnau's film. When the couple is introduced in Murnau's *Nosferatu,* the man is portrayed in front of a mirror, with a window at his side, and as he gazes through the window, we cut to a close-up of his wife, who is seen through a window pane, playing with a kitten. The introduction to the man and woman also introduces us to the use of cross-cutting, which is the primary means by which Murnau establishes different forms of identification between Nosferatu and other characters in the film. If the kittens in Herzog's film evoke the introduction to the heroine of Murnau's film, there is also a difference in emphasis. Nature, as it is represented at the beginning of Murnau's *Nosferatu*, is tranquil, domesticated, and definitely subservient to the human order. But in Herzog's film it is not Lucy who plays with the kittens, but rather the kittens who play with an image of Lucy, suggesting from the outset a conflict between vitality of a human and an animal kind. To be sure, the natural tranquility with which Murnau's *Nosferatu* begins will be challenged by the encounter with the vampire. But whereas such a conflict is gradually introduced in Murnau's film, it is a given in Herzog's.

By introducing the miniature of Lucy at the beginning of the film, Herzog foreshadows a reference to another famous scene in Murnau's film. When Hutter shows his miniature of Ellen to Nosferatu, the vampire exclaims lasciviously that the woman has a lovely throat. Herzog repeats the scene, but there is a significant difference in emphasis and context. In Murnau's film, the display of the miniature exemplifies both the increasing identification of Ellen with the vampire, and Hutter's failure to recognize or comprehend what is going on. Just before Hutter shows Nosferatu the image, he examines his throat in a pocket mirror, and then writes to Ellen of the puncture wounds he has found on his throat. But Hutter has an extremely limited imagination, and can only laugh about this peculiar development. When Herzog's Nosferatu comments on Lucy's lovely throat, it is in the context of a discussion with Jonathan during which Nosferatu speaks of his fondness for the shadows, of time as an abyss, and of death. When Murnau's Nosferatu sees the picture of Ellen, it marks the decreasing importance of Hutter; however, in Herzog's film, Jonathan and Lucy are just as equally designated as under the vampire's spell.

The most obvious references to Murnau's film serve to evoke the original, yet indicate a difference in focus and emphasis at the same time. In other ways, however, Herzog's evocations of Murnau suggest that some of the most quintessentially Herzog themes have their spiritual and cinematic roots in Murnau. Murnau's film is concerned with journey and passage, and a large amount of screen time is devoted to the voyage from one culture and one set of values to another. Murnau shows us Hutter's voyage to the count's castle as a frightening rite of passage between the known and the unknown. The sheer amount of screen time devoted to the vampire's journey to Bremen suggests that the movement of passage is central to Murnau's reading of the vampire legend. In this sense, Herzog is perhaps Murnau's most appropriate heir. As Jonathan embarks on his journey, Herzog shows us the vast expanses of landscape in which Jonathan is a fragile, tiny figure. The protagonists of other journeys – Fitzcarraldo, Aguirre, Kaspar Hauser – come to mind as readily as Murnau's original.[1]

I would argue, however, that in spite of these similarities in appearance, the voyage has profoundly different implications in the two films. Murnau's preoccupation with passage is a preoccupation with the space between the points of voyage, a hypothetically ambivalent space where one is neither native nor foreigner. Where Murnau is concerned with voyage as a kind of tightrope walk, Herzog shows us the journey as a definitive crossing-over of boundaries. In Herzog's journey, one leaves the "self" behind to embrace an identity founded on "otherness." Jonathan's destiny, seen from this perspective, is less of a trick ending and more of a logical conclusion of the implications of Herzog's narrative structure. For we are shown, from the moment of Jonathan's arrival at the vampire's castle, two diametrically opposed views of the count's home: a ruined castle, perched on a mountain, and the furnished rooms in which Jonathan is a guest. The gypsies at the inn where Jonathan spends the first night of the voyage warn him that if he ventures too far into the "land of the phantoms," he will be lost. Jonathan does indeed lose his way, in the sense that his leap into this "land of the phantoms" is definitive. There is no possibility, in the universe Herzog depicts, of the kind of hypothetical space Murnau creates in his film, for this is a world where the lines between dream and waking, between passion and reason, between mysticism and materialism, are absolutely drawn.

Thus, however much Herzog seems to have found a soul-mate in Murnau, and however much both directors are preoccupied, even obsessed, with voyage and passage, the narrative visions of the two men are distinctly different. In Murnau's film, the constant preoccupation is the space between opposing terms, in what I have described elsewhere as a "twilight" area (Mayne, 1986). Like Bram Stoker in his novel *Dracula,* Murnau treats the vampire legend as a study in contrasts – the west versus the east, bourgeois domesticity versus the wild and threatening nature associated with the vampire, reason versus passion. In Stoker's novel, the forces of reason prevail in the end. It is the vampire's function, in the novel, to upset the prevailing pattern of dualistic oppositions, but it is the function of the scientist, Van Helsing, and the group of men assisting him, to meet the challenge of the vampire and to conquer him. In Stoker's novel, the central conflict is between Van Helsing and the vampire. If Murnau restages the conflict to pit the woman against the vampire, it is in part to accentuate the sexual conflict in Stoker's novel, and in part to suggest that the Van Helsings of the world are as incapable of conquering the threat of the vampire as they are of providing a satisfactory narrative resolution. Whereas Stoker's novel leads toward conflict and resolution, Murnau's film is intent upon exploring the ambivalent space between opposing terms.

Murnau reads Stoker's novel against the grain, and his reading focuses on the role of woman and the role of the scientist. Even though there are many "changes" between the novelistic source and the film, the functions of Ellen and Dr Bulwer in the film allude to their very different roles (Mina and Van Helsing) in the novel. The character of Dr Van Helsing in the novel might have been eliminated from the film; instead, he is presented almost as an aside, when the city scribe whose diary provides the overall narrative perspective of the film suddenly introduces Dr Bulwer giving a lecture on carnivorous plants. Van Helsing is thus given a metaphoric function, and as images of his lecture alternate with Knock's escape from the mental institution, he serves as a decorative analogy. Dr Bulwer is again referred to at the conclusion of the film, when Ellen, prior to summoning the vampire to her bed, tells Jonathan to call the doctor.

Murnau virtually does away with all women in the novel except for Jonathan's wife. In Stoker's novel, Mina's fate contrasts with that of Lucy, her friend, who becomes a vampire after being attacked by the count. Murnau, however, eliminates all traces of female vampirism in his film. Women in Stoker's novel are presented according to the familiar dichotomy of good and evil, chaste and pure versus sexual and contaminated. While Ellen in Murnau's film is certainly a stereotype, her identification with the vampire speaks to a fundamental affinity that transcends the stereotypical dichotomy of Stoker's women.

In his retelling of *Nosferatu,* Herzog also focuses on Mina (now Lucy) and Van Helsing as points of transformation. It is interesting that Herzog's reading of the functions of these two characters brings him closer to the Stoker novel. True, Dr Van Helsing as presented in Herzog's film is a caricature, somewhat like Murnau's version of the doctor. But his function in Herzog's film is structurally similar to his function in the Stoker novel. Herzog even gives back to Van Helsing the task of vampire killing, although here it is a mere decorative appendage to Lucy's sacrifice. Like Stoker's Van Helsing, this character represents the forces of science and reason, and he is constantly brought forth at the moments when the threat of the vampire is the greatest. Whereas science confronts the embodiment of passion and irrationality in Stoker's novel, in Herzog's film it merely runs away and protects itself with platitudes about superstition. Herzog and Stoker may give the scientist completely opposing roles, but Herzog's universe is just as divided as Bram Stoker's. Unlike *Dracula,* where Van Helsing represents the triumphant forces of reason and the Western world, in Herzog it is the realm of what Van Helsing would call "superstition" that triumphs.

The fate of Lucy, as Herzog's sole female character (there is a minor female character in both Murnau's and Herzog's films; in Herzog's film she is called "Mina," thus reversing the names of the women in Stoker's novel) is somewhat more complex. Herzog's vision of where the scientists of the world belong is clear; as for women, there seems to be a bit more ambiguity. Herzog chose the name of Lucy for his female protagonist, thus suggesting the woman in Stoker's novel who does succumb, as it were, to the advances of Dracula, and who becomes a terrifying vampire in her own right. It would appear that Herzog is attempting to complicate somewhat the facility of the virgin-whore dichotomy. Herzog's Lucy has none of the horrifying proportions of female vampirism in Stoker's novel, but her sexual identification with the vampire is nonetheless more emphatically drawn than in Murnau's film. For when Lucy shares her bed with the vampire, she draws the vampire to her in a gesture that speaks her desire as much as his. Indeed, throughout most of Herzog's film, Isabelle Adjani's performance of Lucy emphasizes variations on the single theme of fear. Her final scene suggests that these various manifestations of fear have been so many stages on the route to sexual desire.

Unlike Murnau's *Nosferatu,* where the woman's relationship to the vampire is actually produced and created in the course of the film, the identification of Lucy with the vampire is a constant in Herzog's film. Lucy's identification with the vampire *is* her identity, the basis of a kind of female essence. Immediately following the credit images of the film is a shot of Lucy, suddenly sitting up in her bed, screaming as a bat enters her room. Her husband tries to comfort her. Lucy's shriek abruptly stops the music that accompanied the credits. If Lucy's destiny in the film is her sexual identification with the vampire, she serves as well to underscore the link between sexuality and death. Lucy appears to occupy center stage, at least alongside the vampire, and in the opening passage just described, Lucy possesses a tentative narrative authority, her consciousness a focal point of the film. And more so than in either Stoker's novel or Murnau's film, Lucy actually attempts to do something, whether by attempting to convince Dr Van Helsing of the seriousness of the vampire's threat, or to convince the townspeople of the real cause of the plague. Janet Todd dispels any illusion there might be about a possible feminist impulse in Herzog's film: "this is no feminist statement and female failure remains constant. In Stoker's novel the woman is saved through the man; in Herzog's film the woman's act cannot save the man" (1981, 203). I agree with Todd's assessment, but for somewhat different reasons. The capacity to act counts for very little in Herzog's film. Rather, narrative authority here is measured by the power to mesmerize – a power that is uniquely the vampire's. Put another way, the vampire is a kind of master narrator in Herzog's film. That power is conveyed in a variety of ways, and there is a marked difference between how that power is demonstrated in relationship to Jonathan and to Lucy. During the first conversation between Jonathan and the vampire at the castle, Jonathan is portrayed in close-up, the surroundings of the room clearly visible. Reverse shots of the vampire, however, portray him in such obscurity that only his white face is visible. There is certainly a radical difference between the two men, and Nosferatu is given a certain power of omniscience, given the literal "no man's land" he inhabits in the image. Yet this is an encounter for which the conventional means of shot-reverse shot is adequate. No such encounter is possible between Lucy and the vampire, a point that is strikingly made when she actually encounters Nosferatu for the first time: seated in front of a mirror, Lucy gasps as the door opens. Nosferatu enters her room, but there is no image of him reflected in the mirror. Lucy's gasp, then, is initially directed, not toward Nosferatu, but toward her own reflection in the mirror. The narrative web of identification is ultimately one in which Lucy is nothing more than an empty space.

Lucy can be described in other terms as well. There are in Herzog's film a number of figures who function as witnesses: they have no real role in the immediate plot, but serve rather as bystanders. The gypsies who warn Jonathan of the dangers of his voyage are witnesses, as is the boy playing a violin whom we see at two moments during Jonathan's stay at the vampire's castle. Such witnesses are not necessarily living characters. The film opens with images of statues of human figures, all of which evoke death and agony, and the haunting effect is underscored by the musical soundtrack, a mournful chant. These images have no immediate relationship to the film, but they serve to emphasize a mythos of death, an overarching perspective of a cinematic archeology, of sorts. These witness-figures expand the contours of Herzog's narrative, suggesting the all-encompassing nature of the vampire legend. Ultimately, Lucy exemplifies the role of these witness figures. For her function is to be a decorative prop that facilitates the primary encounter of the film, between Jonathan and the vampire.

In Murnau's film, the transformation of the conflict between Van Helsing and the vampire in Stoker's novel, to the conflict between Mina and Nosferatu, has to do primarily with the overall preoccupation, in Murnau's reading of the vampire legend, with the space between opposing terms. Casting the two opposites of Mina and the vampire in conflict serves to question dualistic opposition. This is not to say that Murnau's image of woman is necessarily more noble than Herzog's, but that the end that image serves is a complex attempt to open up narrative opposition and resolution.

In contrast, there is no such opening up in Herzog's film. True, Herzog gives us an interesting alternative to either the shadowy conclusion of Murnau's film or the pat resolution of Stoker's novel. Jonathan's vampirism suggests that the vampire's power cannot be conquered by either the sacrifice of a woman "pure in heart" or the sudden conversion of the scientist. Ultimately, however, there is little substantive difference between the narrative vision of Stoker's novel and Herzog's film. Both texts affirm a dualistic hierarchy, with the only difference being which side of the hierarchy triumphs. Herzog rereads Murnau in order to rediscover Stoker, and if the conclusion of Stoker's novel is clearly ideological – men protect women, science triumphs over passion, the western world dominates its "others" – so too is the finale of Herzog's film. But the ideology in question here is not just a simple reversal, with the vampire now representing the positive side of the scale. Certainly Herzog's quasi-mystical, visionary celebration of the irrational and the absurd is at odds with the dominant middle-class order, but it is a vision which relies on such a traditional sexual division of the universe that any challenge to familiar dualistic patterns of thought is effectively denied. Both Lucy and Jonathan are mesmerized by the vampire, but in radically different ways: for the woman, identification with the vampire can only lead to death, whereas for the man, identification leads to a kind of mastery. Herzog's very choice of subject matter dramatizes his own contradictory stance, for the vampire legend, and particularly as it is told in Bram Stoker's novel, is a tale of men and women as well as fathers and sons. In Stoker's novel, Van Helsing is a figure of patriarchal authority, and the younger men who work with him to conquer Dracula are his spiritual and intellectual heirs. For Herzog, the lineage is irresistible, and the relationship between Nosferatu and Jonathan reverses the relationship of Van Helsing and his followers in the novel.

One senses that for Herzog, the vampire legend is equally appealing as a myth of authorship. However different their narrative visions, there is a convincing stylistic affinity between Herzog and Murnau. But the more profound affinity may lie elsewhere, for it is perhaps toward Nosferatu himself that Herzog is drawn as a fitting image of cinematic authorship. In Murnau's film, Nosferatu becomes a central narrating figure. It is the function of Nosferatu to be both mirror and window to all the characters who dare look at him – that is, Nosferatu functions as both self and other, at one moment a foetus-like version of one's former self, at another a horrifying vision of otherness. Nosferatu is the exact opposite, narratively speaking, of the city scribe whose diary forms the narrative framework of Murnau's film. For the city scribe is a literal, one-dimensional voice of "truth" – the truth of recorded and uninsightful observations. Nosferatu occupies and opens up the space of narration between that observing individual and the reality so unproblematically observed.

Nosferatu in Herzog's film also reflects all those characters who are drawn to him. But unlike Murnau's film, there is no real contrasting narrative perspective. Instead, there is a kind of overarching narration of which Nosferatu is the supreme instance. The tension between different narrative perspectives that informs the development of Murnau's film has been eliminated in Herzog's film, where we have one single, all-encompassing perspective that links the opening images of death-like statues to Lucy's scream, or that punctuates the film with images of a bat swooping in slow motion.

Murnau's *Nosferatu* thus becomes, for Herzog, a way of exploring certain questions of cinematic narrative, and of affirming certain myths of authorship. Herzog reads Murnau in order to return, in various ways, to Bram Stoker. There remains, however, another dimension to Herzog's reading of Murnau. That Murnau was gay is one of those well-known facts of film history that has had little more than anecdotal impact on what most critics have actually had to say about Murnau's films. Lotte Eisner's references to Murnau's "homosexual tendencies" notwithstanding (1973b), Murnau's gay sexuality has by and large not been taken up in any sustained way as a perspective for reading his films.[2] Could Herzog's film, with its designation of Jonathan and the vampire as central protagonists, thus be read as a gesture of bringing Murnau's film out of the closet, as it were? Luce Irigaray, writing on the symbolic economy of patriarchal societies, distinguishes between two kinds of homosexuality. "The trade that organizes patriarchal societies takes place exclusively among men," she writes. Hence: "Homosexuality is the law that regulates the socio-cultural order." Now lest Irigaray's remarks be taken as homophobic, the homosexual laws to which she refers are laws of the symbolic order, and gay male sexuality threatens those laws, which "cannot be practiced in any other way but in language without provoking a general crisis." If Herzog's homage to Murnau acknowledges a homosexual impulse, it is homosexual according to Irigaray's definition of the prevailing social order. Murnau's *Nosferatu* is in no way an openly gay film, to be sure; but Murnau's inquiry into the dualities of sexual and narrative identity is a much more radical gesture than Herzog's vision of male bonding, for which the death of the female protagonist is required. Irigaray says that if gay male sexuality *were* practiced outside of the conventional symbolic order, "[a] certain symbolic order would come to an end" (Irigaray, 1980, 107). Herzog's vision of cinematic authorship has too much invested in that symbolic order to engage in the kind of inquiry that informs Murnau's *Nosferatu*.

Notes

Research for this essay was made possible by a grant from the Ohio Arts Council.

1 As Janet Todd (1981, 206) points out, the vampire's sea voyage is reminiscent of Herzog's *Aguirre*: "the boat with its sails a dried blood color sits on a smooth blue sea while the camera circles round (as it did with the doomed raft in *Aguirre*) to heighten the isolation and futility."
2 Notable exceptions are Robin Wood's writings on Murnau (1979, 1983).

Works cited

Andrews, Nigel (1978) "Dracula in Delft," *American Film*, 4 (1), 32–8.
Eisner, Lotte (1973a) *The Haunted Screen*, Berkeley CA, University of California Press.
Eisner, Lotte (1973b) *Murnau*, London, Martin Secker & Warburg.
Irigaray, Luce (1980) "When the Goods Get Together," in Elaine Marks and Isabelle de Courtivron (eds), *New French Feminisms*, Amherst MA, University of Massachusetts Press, 107–10.
Mayne, Judith (1986) "Murnau's *Nosferatu*: Dracula in the twilight," in Eric Rentschler (ed.), *German Literature and Film: Adaptations and Transformations*, New York/London, Methuen.
Todd, Janet (1981) "The Classic Vampire," in Michael Klein and Gillian Parker (eds), *The English Novel and the Movies*, New York, Ungar, 197–210.
Wood, Robin (1979) "The Dark Mirror: Murnau's *Nosferatu*," in Richard Lippe and Robin Wood (eds), *The American Nightmare*, Ottawa.
Wood, Robin (1983) "Burying the Undead: The Use and Obsolescence of Count Dracula," *Mosaic*, 16 (1–2), 175–87.

9 A blocking of the all-too-ready transparency of signification (*Where the Green Ants Dream*)

9

An anthropologist's eye:
Where the Green Ants Dream

Thomas Elsaesser

Herzog the international auteur

Ever since the success of *Aguirre* in 1972 and of *Kaspar Hauser* in 1974, the mold of Herzog's cinema has been cast. Graduate students in film classes learnt constructing a Herzog scenario more quickly than they recognized the structural rules of a Gene Kelly musical. It is an indication of success, but also a danger that as an auteur, he is to his audiences a known quantity, a definite set of associations, of remembered and anticipated images, just as surely as to another kind of audience a new special-effects extravaganza promises pleasures already experienced many times before. Indeed, the pleasure may consist of nothing other than the recognition of the same beneath the difference of the referent. *Where the Green Ants Dream* is both a recapitulation and an attempt to break the mold.

[handwritten margin note: Recognition of the same beneath the difference of the Referent]

First, however, a related question: how did Herzog attain such a high recognition factor, and become not only a media star and personality in his own right, but a one-man cinematic genre? Mainly by becoming totally identified with his films and creating out of this a persona (for a self-made, self-promotion filmmaker not only a useful but a necessary accomplishment). He is his films and they are him; *Was ich bin sind meine Filme,* as the title of a German TV documentary has it (Keusch and Weisenborn, 1978). To accomplish this symbiosis, more was needed than traveling and giving interviews: Herzog is one of the rare filmmakers who with only a handful of films has created two exemplary heroes, even icons. Not only is there a blurring of the boundaries between actor and role (Klaus Kinski, the trained actor, and Bruno S., the "natural," have become permanently identified with the parts they played in Herzog's films). But there is also a secret unity between the meaning of their archetypes. Although apparently worlds apart as eternal underdog and eternal overreacher, Bruno S. and Klaus Kinski are the two sides of Kaspar Hauser: one the child abandoned by the father, the other the child abandoning the father to preempt being abandoned. Two aspects of the same crisis of patriarchal society, of failed submission to and failed rebellion against the symbolic order: these roles therefore refer to a single figure, pointing to Herzog himself as the author who is subtly living this dialectic, not as a key to his life, but as the image of his filmmaking.

For at a time when even the American cinema can no longer claim to be by itself a self-sustaining, self-referring universe without recycling its own past ever more rapidly, an independent filmmaker practically shoulders with each film the burden of reinventing not, as Herzog is fond of saying, film history but the film industry. The preparations for his films resemble a military campaign, but also cast him as a victim. The very real anachronism of independent filmmaking in the age of fully capitalized media imperialism is one of the buried themes of Herzog's work. Not the least of the many ironies involved in his championing of those individuals or groups who eke out their existence on the margins of the capitalist world is that the symbolic opposition between the weak and the strong, the underdogs and the overreachers, splits Herzog himself: the filmmaker has a foot in either camp, and often David is difficult to tell from Goliath. *Where the Green Ants Dream* is no exception: behind the Aborigines' resistance to the mining company determined to drill for minerals stands Herzog's determination to make a film about this resistance. One can see this, Herzog might argue, as his "athletic" concept of filmmaking: that it is a physical activity, and so his films are on the side of those whose contact with the world is above all physical. But one can also see it thematizing another kind of dilemma. Is Herzog not doing battle on his heroes' backs? Are they not inevitably the foot-soldiers thanks to whom the machinery of his own filmmaking can fight it out with the juggernauts of the commercial film industry? In having a boat moved over a mountain by hundreds of Indians in *Fitzcarraldo*, Herzog conceived of a perfect metaphor for his own filmmaking, as well as of the cinema: an obsolete technology with a human face. "Herzog makes films, he turns himself into an instrument- – the man disappears. The instrument is what is necessary to run the machine that constructs the film" (Greenberg *et al.*, 1976, 39).

Usually, Herzog's pre-production (like any Hollywood blockbuster) makes headlines and is good copy, not only on the arts pages. The fact that Werner Herzog had taken a camera crew to Guadeloupe in order to film the eruption of a volcano was reported with bated breath: although *La Soufrière* failed to deliver, Herzog did. *Fitzcarraldo* was political news because it started a minor civil war in Peru, in a scenario only half written by Herzog himself. It also engendered two films about the filming (*Burden of Dreams, Land of Bitterness and Pride*). The production and its difficulties somehow became the real event of which the film when it finally appeared seemed in a sense merely the record: that, too, is a danger when the cinema becomes infatuated with the reality of its own making, even though by giving full publicity to this reality Herzog might be said merely to have endorsed the situation facing a "media-person," that reality is never as real as when it is "cinema."

Is there a law of diminishing returns at work in the effort of the author to be true to himself: does what is meant to shock, shake up or surprise, end up by merely wearying? This fine line between the pleasure of recognition and the tedium of repetition is, in the cinema, often a matter of genre. In Herzog, in particular, it becomes the question of whether the fiction, the solidity of the story, is strong enough to carry not only the fantastic nature of the reality he has discovered, but also a truth beyond the anecdote, as any durable film-genre does. The doubt that lingers over Herzog's films, in other words, is to what extent they are real myths or, more properly, variants on a private mythology. Is he a fiction-maker loyal to his subjects as only a documentary filmmaker can be, or a documentarist too impatient with reality not to want to shape it to his own fictions? Perhaps the heroes he has created are more lasting than the stories they appear in.

If genre cinema has always turned pro-filmic reality into the terms of its own system, an author's film necessarily operates on its own material a further mise-en-abyme, where each film not only refers back to the genre it helps to sustain, but to the myth its author is all the while propagating about his activity. Herzog's films have become over the years unmistakably part of an *oeuvre*: success invariably means rewriting the past in order to enable a future. The more films he makes, the more subtle can be the interplay of cross-references, echoes and recurrent motifs. Though taking place in Australia, and telling a story that might have made ten lines on the back page of any newspaper with an interest in the temporary and local setbacks of multinational capitalism, *Where the Green Ants Dream* is part of another landscape, only fortuitously located in the Australian bush and otherwise a fully charted map to an already existing territory of obsessions and *idées fixes,* visual jokes and eccentric characters, paradoxically familiar for all their strangeness and deadpan acceptance of the bizarre. Many spectators must have been uneasy about yet another exploration of vanishing tribes and exemplary types in order to exploit them as heroes of a pseudo-mythology. After all, what they and the green ants dream seem no more than Herzog's usual anti-civilization fantasies. Even the mute eloquence, the awkward but moving grace of the tribal elders as they speak up for their sacred objects and sacred places, owe more to the romantic conception of the noble savage, and Karl May fiction for boys, than to the anthropology of Margaret Mead and Lévi-Strauss, or the politics of Greenpeace. Herzog states:

> I don't see it as an environmental film, it's on a much deeper level: how people are dealing with this earth. It would be awful to see this film only as a film on ecology. It has a common borderline with that [but] it's also a film on a strange mythology, the green ants mythology. It's a movie, that's the first thing. (Mizrahi, 1984)

The opening shot of *Where the Green Ants Dream,* a long aerial traveling across a desert landscape spotty with hundreds of small white pyramids – like the camp of an army turned to stone – is reminiscent of the Cretan Valley of the Ten Thousand Windmills in *Signs of Life.* The carcasses of burnt-out cars, buses or heavy industrial machinery recall the airplane wrecks covered in sand from *Fata Morgana*; the impressive sequence of a tornado – a dark funnel sweeping the ground like a giant vacuum cleaner – has the same grainy texture and somnambulist remoteness as the dreams that Kaspar Hauser tells on his death-bed; the biologist, studying green ants and obsessed with magnetic fields, combines single-minded devotion to one of nature's more eccentric creatures (like the lizard and turtle specialist in *Fata Morgana*) with the anachronistic crankiness of an amateur inventor (like Herr Scheitz and his animal magnetism in *Stroszek*). Also close to the world of *Stroszek* is the tragi-comic clash of civilization and its rejects, when the tribal elders shop in Melbourne for nylon anoraks and digital watches, before having a lunch date in an ethnic Greek restaurant. Miliritbi and Dayipu, the two leaders, sitting in the cockpit of their newly acquired Australian Airforce plane, look as grimly determined as do Herr Scheitz and Stroszek peering through the windscreen of their second-hand Buick on the New Jersey turnpike, headed for Railroad Flats, Wisconsin.

In this sense, a line of development becomes visible in Herzog's work. Not toward (modernist) self-realization, but toward its in-escapable reference point: the international film industry and the Holly-wood intertext. *Where the Green Ants Dream,* his first fiction film to be shot entirely in English, is certainly conscious of the challenge of addressing two types of audience: one to which a well-constructed script is a betrayal of cinema, and one to which a film without one is not cinema at all. This may be the cause for some of the interference in the signals to Herzog's habitual audiences, and why it not only failed to become a financial success (not all of Herzog's films were, or needed to be, given the funding system of films in West Germany), but also failed to attach to itself the sort of "narrative image" which his other films – from *Aguirre* to *Fitzcarraldo,* via *Kaspar Hauser, Nosferatu, Woyzeck* and *Stroszek* – achieved so seemingly without effort in the public mind. The titles themselves might give a clue: all of Herzog's successes are centered on a single hero, are stories of exceptional or excessive individuals, a fact which further encourages the transfer to filmmaker from protagonist, and vice versa. Is his Australian film, then, a hybrid of Hollywood and the New German Cinema, two films in one, or a synthesis?

[handwritten margin note: All of Herzogs successes are centered on a single Hero, are stories of exceptional or excessive individuals]

The question of heroism

The plot of *Where the Green Ants Dream,* if it holds few surprises and disdains suspense, develops the main conflict almost in the manner of a classical narrative; after less than ten minutes, the issues are clear, there is no doubt about the rights and wrongs and who is in the middle. The geologist Lance Hackett, charged with supervising the exploratory drills of the Ayers Mining Company, finds himself challenged by an Aborigine tribe, who refuse to vacate the site, on the grounds that the land is not only the home of their ancestors and thus sacred, but the place where the green ants dream. To disturb them might entail disaster of cosmic proportions. The company treats the Aborigines' protest as no more than a minor irritation, but is sufficiently concerned about adverse publicity to offer bribes in the form of compensation and an old airforce plane. An unequal battle of will-power and wit ensues, which ends in the courts. They decide predict-ably, in favor of the mining company. As the tribal leaders hold a vigil in the plane, an ex-pilot, half-white, half-Aborigine, joins them, and flies them over the mountains, never to return.

The question posing itself is therefore not who is protagonist and who antagonist, but who is the hero? This, it seems to me, determines how one reads *Where the Green Ants Dream*. Is it the Aborigines? Then why is so much attention focused on Hackett? And what if he is the hero? Hackett is a Hollywood character, ordinary, unheroic, nice. Although his job puts him in a position of power vis-à-vis the tribe, his youth makes him too much of a liberal to identify with the covert racism of his fellow whites; and although he is legally on the right side, the Aborigines' stubborn refusal to have their land destroyed convinces him that morally he is in the wrong. Little satisfaction for him in the company's victory before the courts, or comfort in the judge's regret that colonialism should still be the law of the land. He finally has the courage of his convictions and joins a disenchanted academic gone native, Arnold, who is already encamped in the desert.

Hackett is no Herzog figure, no mythical rebel, nor even a militant protester, like the ecological "punks" that fill the back benches at the Supreme Court hearing. The case of the Riratjingu tribe is not his own, however much the green ants' dream turns him into a speculative philosopher about the universe's curved spaces, black holes and planetary collision courses. The desert does not seduce him into madness and titanic revolt, as the Valley of the Windmills in *Signs of Life* did the original Stroszek, whom Hackett resembles in his ordinariness. Nor has he internalized the values of his masters, while secretly in sympathy with the inmates' anarchic revolt, as was the director of the institution in *Even Dwarfs Started Small,* immobilized in a gesture of frantic impotence. Hackett is altogether too resigned a participant to be suddenly seized by the "wrath of God" or the madness within, to be affected by anything stronger than self-doubt and the general malaise of losing faith in western civilization. All that remains is to exchange his company-owned trailer home – another reference to *Stroszek* – for a corner in Arnold's corrugated shack. But the radical, lapsed anthropologist who practices his belief by living with an Aborigine wife and raising her children, directs Hackett to an abandoned water tank, possibly an ironic allusion to the Eureka experiences in bath tubs and water barrels among the ancient Greek philosopher-engineers.

Hackett, therefore, is the hero of *Where the Green Ants Dream* only in the limited (and classical) sense of motivating the progress of the narrative, serving as intermediary between the film's opposing factions and as mediator of the audience's sympathies. This is another source of interference: although he is a stand-in for the spectator, he is not the object of ambiguous, masochistic identification one would have expected from a Herzog film (Dawson, 1977, 57).

Herzog and Wenders

In fact, a quite different intertext opens up when one compares Hackett not to the gallery of Herzog's "titans who perish miserably," but to the heroes of his compatriot and competitor on the international scene, Wim Wenders. Hackett is a loner, much given to sitting on the floor at night, with a cassette recorder playing rock music, cradling a telephone, especially after futile attempts to establish communication with an unnamed and invisible woman somewhere amidst dinner parties and going to the movies. Although perhaps not quite the writer-hero of *Alice in the Cities* or *Wrong Movement* strayed into the Australian outback from the wastes of Middle America or West Germany, it is as if Herzog, out of commercial considerations of what sort of hero (apart from Klaus Kinski and Bruno S.) connotes the New German Cinema to the world, or in order to have a different perspective on his own themes, had decided to make Hackett – "melancholy Hackett," as he calls himself – an ironic pastiche of the Wenders protagonist and his Hamlet-ish indecision. When Arnold tells Hackett that he is "like somebody on a train that is going so fast toward its doom that all you have time to do is run through to the rear compartment," Herzog might be providing a doomwatch gloss to the scene from *The American Friend* where Bruno Ganz, after helping Dennis Hopper dispose of the murdered bodyguards, walks to the rear of the train and leans his head out of the cockpit-shaped window.

Mentioning Wenders is perhaps not as incongruous as it might at first seem. Both directors are concerned with temporality, a specifically European, non-Hollywood emphasis on *temps mort*, the passage of time when it is not consumed by action. And yet, their approach to its filmic forms is quite distinct. Perhaps the difference has to do with the importance each director attaches to narrative as a basic cinematic structure. Herzog has often professed a lack of interest in narrative: "Personally, I don't think the cinema ought to subject itself to the imperatives of narration. In *Fata Morgana* or *Heart of Glass,* narrative is less important than the visions or the prophecies. It's a deliberate choice" (Mizrahi, 1984). Only in his later films – from *Stroszek* onward, under the impact of addressing American audiences – does he seem to compromise and develop something like a story-line. Yet even then, by Hollywood standards, the scripting is slack. Wenders, whose stories are episodic and loosely scripted in quite another way, has always been preoccupied with the mechanics of narrative, and the creation of a specifically filmic sense of time, of which the presence of characters is merely the convenient embodiment (as evidenced by his avant-garde films from the mid-1960s: *Same Player Shoots Again* and *Silver City*).

In the case of Herzog, one senses that an interest in character usually overrides the exigencies and possibilities of narrative. One can venture that his exploration of the significance of body and gesture in relation to space or environment (here indeed is a direct affinity with German expressionism) ultimately conflicts with the logic of narrative, because what is important to Herzog – the dialectic of the physical irreducibility of gesture and its equally inescapable sign character – is not compatible with psychological motivation or causality, because of the different density which gesture inscribes in the movement and rhythm of a film.

Where the Green Ants Dream is interesting insofar as Herzog juxtaposes the professional movie acting of Bruce Spence as Hackett with the almost ceremonial role-playing of his Aborigine characters, who can put on dignity along with a suit when appearing in court, stay obstinate or merely silent when faced with a flood of abuse from a racist foreman, play innocents abroad in front of the mining company director, or be devastatingly tongue-in-cheek when talking to an intrigued but inexperienced Hackett. In earlier Herzog films, only Klaus Kinski and Bruno S. transmit their body language to the mise-en-scène. *Heart of Glass* is such a hybrid not least because the characters are never more than a gallery of Bavarian gargoyles and grotesques, whose torpid or surreal gyrations slow down the narrative and make each actor a sort of carved wooden prop in an Oberammergau puppet play.

Where his Aborigine film is different is in the way Herzog has succeeded in constructing scenes to work mainly through subtly nuanced contrasts or bold clashes in performance and acting styles. They determine the pace and rhythm of the film, and give substance to the conflict of different temporal orders: dreamtime and progress, the patience of the land against the impatience of profit, or a feeling of loyalty against quick-fire anger, whether righteous or merely resentful. In the same way, the episode of the old lady dressed in Victorian tea-party clothes, imploring Hackett to help find her dog, and waiting patiently at the mouth of the tunnel into which he is supposed to have strayed, acts as a temporal as well as gestural counterweight to the otherwise so symmetrical opposition between mining interest and ecology. With the Aborigines, the camera dwells a lot on faces, which one might attribute to Herzog's documentary touch, until the long shots reveal it as a device for generating low-key comedy: Hackett is well over a foot taller than everyone else, a fact which makes his performance seem awkward and him something of a freak (echoes of the inverted perspective in the *Dwarfs* film). Yet it yields comic effects simply because no one in the film seems to be aware of it.

Wenders, too, disdains psychological motivation, or so it would seem, since his protagonists generally like nothing more than to drift aimlessly and haphazardly through their environment. One only has to see what happens to the *film noir* topos of the "gangster on the run" in *Summer in the Cities* (1971), to realize that the mise-en-scène not so much parodies the genre as turns it inside out, by removing the motivational core. In actual fact, the reasons for doing so derive from a much more conceptual attitude than Herzog's interest in hypnotic states and mythological time. Wenders simply tries to let conventional generic motives (toward action, conflict, progress and resolution) shrink to a kind of zero degree, in order to focus on *process*: on what takes over (in the narrative, in film) when the motor of motive is turned off. The result is a form of foregrounding; spectator attention and involvement are directed to other aspects of the film, or to the "empty" compositions and to the passage of time giving substance to space. Wenders is a minimalist of motivation, because for him the film itself develops its own orders of causality and intermittence, which have nothing to do with historical time, and little with psychological time. But whereas his characters are often chosen with an eye to making their presence the most effective vehicle for the transmission of the gaze, Herzog's characters have a quality of bodily resistance to both narrative progress and the direct translation of thought into action.

Narrative and motivation

Classical narrative, conceived as conflict and resolution, implies a conception of history: Herzog's anti-narrative perspective seems to suggest that he, too, does not believe in history. A lack of interest in causality, for instance, is evidenced by the way he handles transitions from frame to frame, as well as from scene to scene. Instead of the narrative building up from dramatic sequences, Herzog works in isolated units. The cut is merely a way of reaching another situational block, to move to another place or another space. Individual scenes tend to have what could be called a downward movement. For Herzog an event is never open toward development or a future: it has its end inscribed in its beginning, for the first shot already tells it all, and there is very little suspense or dramatic tension between characters. Herzog's concern is with a different kind of intensity, a negative one that makes it difficult for him to think of narrative as anything other than an accumulation of isolated moments, running their course, in fact, running down like clockwork and being succeeded by others.

Such an attitude not only implies a pessimistic view of history, it also entails a fundamentally tragic view of human endeavor, which in turn is focused on the isolated, single hero, whose inwardness consumes whatever world surrounds it: Herzog's experience of time is that of an apocalypse that never arrives, of transitional states, of boredom and degradation. The situation of *La Soufrière* corresponds perfectly to the basic condition of all his films: "an inevitable catastrophe that did not happen." His narratives grind themselves into a situation which is itself sustained only by circularity, and his characters experience time oppressively and with impatience. The hero of *Signs of Life* goes mad, the dwarfs revolt by throwing furniture and plates on a driverless car going round a courtyard in interminable circles, Kaspar Hauser's life is a "terrible fall," and Stroszek shoots himself on a circular scenic railway: all expressions of the painful experience of a time that is irredeemable.

In this, as in other respects, *Where the Green Ants Dream* offers a different perspective. On the face of it, it is a film about history as destructive and progress as utterly futile. The mining company wins, and as news comes of the disappearance of the plane, the rumble of underground explosions can be heard in the distance. After having been dramatically stopped in the opening sequence, destruction resumes: the narrative is closed, in classical fashion, by a return to the status quo. But Hackett has been unable to help the Aborigines, or ultimately himself. As with most Herzog films, *Where the Green Ants Dream* ends with the character threads of the narrative not tied up, but undone. At some level, the plot and its trajectory resolve themselves, but the protagonists are refused any kind of transcendence.

Although, therefore, in one sense the Aborigines are Herzog's predictable victims, the gaze that falls on them, and more importantly their gaze on the narrative, is significantly different from that of Herzog's earlier heroes. This has to do, first of all, with the presence of Hackett, the "Hollywood" intertext. Through him, not only are there psychological motives and a linearity of an almost classical type; his presence is underlined cinematically by point-of-view shots and a psychological perspective. Nonetheless, he is by no means the gravitational centre of the film: had this been an unambiguously "Hollywood" film, Hackett would, among the resisting Aborigines, have found a love interest, and defection from his job would have led to the formation of a couple. As it is, Arnold, the lapsed anthropologist, acts as Hackett's surrogate in this respect.

This ambiguity – that it is not Hackett's perspective moving the narrative – makes the Aborigines seem neither victims nor victimized heroes, neither overreachers nor underdogs. Between Miliritbi and Dayipu, the two tribal leaders, it is difficult to decide who is Klaus Kinski and who Bruno S.: each has elements of both, and yet they are defined differently, because of a different relation to time, and therefore to the narrative in which they figure. Heroism in Herzog is a combination of futile revolt or stoical acceptance, but in each case, against an ineluctably deteriorating, self-degrading situation. The Aborigines' stoicism is of a different order, as is their resistance, because they are concerned with a different time scale to that of Hackett, or the mining company, or Herzog's other heroes. Stasis, indifferentiation, and the negation of time which causes the Herzog hero the anxiety that leads to revolt or suicide, is for the Riratjingu tribe, living outside historical time, a natural state. The Aborigines are stoically persistent, single-minded, immovable, but they are not tragic. Because they experience the whites as pure opposition, their subjectivity is undivided, unlike that of any other Herzog heroes. It is this which ultimately frees them from both narrative and history: "You white men are lost. You don't understand the land. Too many silly questions. Your presence on this earth will come to an end. You have no sense, no purpose, no direction."

Thus, while Hackett seems to be divided morally in his allegiance and ideological choices, he is too remote from the Aborigines in physical stature, body language and in the way the plot positions him, to split the narrative in the style of, say, Kinski in *Fitzcarraldo*, who is both on the side of the natives and exploiting them. He, too, therefore is not tragic, but seems to drift on the narrative, gradually moving to the periphery not only of the conflict between the mining company and the Aborigines, but of the spectator's interest: Arnold's abusiveness as he sends him to the water tank for a home almost seems to spell Herzog's own lack of interest in a form of dramaturgy which relies for its mediation of conflict on a middle-of-the-road hero.

Subjectivity and motivation

Especially in his early films, instead of explaining the startling or extravagant behavior of his protagonists, Herzog suppressed whatever might be interpreted as a psychological clue to their inner states and motives. Aguirre's relation to his daughter, for instance, is never made explicit. As Andrea Simon has noted:

> Herzog's energy, like Aguirre's, does not proceed to a goal ... [his camera] drifts along the river bank or over the impenetrable planes of an Indian's face, the very intensity of certain images seeming to render their narrative context incidental (Aguirre awkwardly clutching his velvet-gowned daughter to his waist: she is dying, but that is not the point of the shot). (Simon, 1975, 26)

Discontinuities in the narrative, and images such as these in excess of their diegetic function, are the hallmarks of his style: they give the illusion of some unmediated presence of the real, heightened and powerfully suggestive. At the same time, they are usually read as signifiers of a subjectivity too intense or idiosyncratic to manifest itself in discourse or action. Hence the impression that Herzog's heroes are visionaries, madmen, dreamers and holy fools: all of them solitary or solipsistic existences, whose inner life remains impenetrable, intuited rather than understood. Subjectivity in Herzog is in fact nothing other than the effect of a resistance to signification, and especially to language as transparency. Communication in his films is impersonal: more like lifting luggage onto a train than exchanging information. The lines, in Simon's apt phrase, are "as opaque and grammatically over-explicit as a sentence from Wittgenstein" (Simon, 1975, 26). Excessive clarity empties language both of connection to objects and of relevance to the speaking subject.

Thus, rather than the shifts in motivation foregrounding the filmic processes, as they do in Wenders, attention goes to an enigmatic inner life of the protagonists, whose signs must be read as a symptomatology: of verbal and physical gestures, behavioral mannerisms or idiosyncractic tics. "I'm interested in human beings in the manner of an anthropologist, not a psychologist," Herzog has explained. "I hate psychology: it's an impotent science, like medicine during the centuries where it had the same cure for everything: it put leeches on you, whether it was for a migraine or pneumonia" (Mizrahi, 1984).

In the earlier films this meant the spectator had to scan the image for clues, or see in the bizarre detail metaphoric connotations: in *Signs of Life,* for instance, the clay feet buried in the wall of a house, the donkey in the village square or a smoldering chair became indices of Stroszek's inner life; in *Kaspar Hauser,* wheat buffeted by a gust of wind, or a cow ruminating while tethered to a tree, transferred meaning to the blankly expressionless hero. Reticence on the level of denotation is ironically overcompensated by a play of apparently incongruous connotation, and the logic of a given sequence of shots relativized by the verbal or musical commentary: in *Fata Morgana,* the Peruvian Myth of Creation which Lotte Eisner reads in a voice meant to sound the way parched earth feels, like Herzog's own texts, is a deliberately excessive way of motivating the sequence of images, because it is fortuitously appropriate but also ludicrously or pompously inappropriate. Discontinuity of word and image becomes a means not of underscoring the autonomy of the signifier, as in Godard or avant-garde films, but of redeeming the signified, indeed celebrating its resistance to imposed meaning. *Fata Morgana,* for instance, sets out to parody the cultural documentary which always already knows the human significance of what it shows, by a ruthless and even sadistic subjection of the image to the metaphoric constructions of language, and then glorying in the images that "got away," like the heat haze in which a tourist bus is caught, or the musicians wearing goggles.

Where the Green Ants Dream has few moments not integrated into the overall fiction that frames even the *temps mort*. The play of insufficiency and overexplicitness between image and commentary in the documentaries has been replaced by the many incongruities and incompatibilities between the Aborigines and their chief sympathizer, Hackett. But since Hackett is never interesting enough to engage the audience, the spectator often switches perspective to look at Hackett through the Aborigines' eyes, inverting the anthropological binoculars, as it were.

TEMPS MORT [handwritten annotation]

The anthropologist's eye

Herzog has often stated his detestation of cinéma vérité, and yet his cinema is unthinkable without the documentary element against which the fiction, as it were, rebels, but to which it also always submits. He notes:

> Around 1973, at the Perth Film Festival … I read about Len Wright's battle of some Aborigines against a mining company that did bauxite mining in the north-west of Australia. And I learned that many such struggles took place. It intrigued me and I wrote a story which was already entitled *Where the Green Ants Dream*. Then a few years later I saw some documentaries by a young Australian filmmaker, Michael Edols, and I became very intrigued by the leading character in the film *Lalai Dreamtime,* who was called Sam Woolagoocha. (Mizrahi, 1984)

Setting his flights of poetic fancy on the solid ground of an actual event or a person has always been typical of Herzog: he first came across Bruno S., for instance, in a Berlin film school documentary, Lutz Eisholz's *Bruno der Schwarze*. But the weaving of fact into fiction is also another example of wanting to rescue the referent: going on location to a faraway place, employing untrained or semi-professional players, and other ways of signaling what Herzog, somewhat rashly, proclaims as the "authenticity" of his films, is also meant to put a limit on metaphor. To use a term of Roland Barthes', which seems more appropriate, Herzog's cinema makes itself at certain points "obtuse" (Barthes, 1977, 54 ff.) by trying to develop the narrative out of an irreducible materiality of the image, though this also brings it to a standstill:

A voice in ecstasy about a goal that was scored by Argentina ... and a child holding a stone in her hand and not knowing what to do ... an image like that is probably as important as the whole story. And that's why I want to make films ... I want to show things that are inexplicable somehow. (Mizrahi, 1984)

This could either be a stupid or a sublime image, and the possibility of their coexistence is what Barthes' reflection about the "third meaning" helps one to grasp. Herzog has been called a visionary filmmaker, mainly because he contrives so often to suggest this possibility of·a relation between different elements of the pro-filmic, often between a solitary human being and an object or a landscape, where the images are not framed by any narrative perspective, and no causal chain explains their place in the fiction.

The stance of the anthropologist which Herzog would attribute to himself to counter any suggestion of a psychological perspective, implies an idea of detachment which, however, is in direct contrast to such a visionary cinema. Herzog's interest in his characters is external in the sense indicated above, that he pretends to read their behavior as symbolic action, making only their bodies and gestures speak, and treating language as a mere reification of such gestures. What inner life of theirs he gives access to, is either a fantasy concoction of his own making, or exhausts itself in the physiological-anthropological affinity the heroes are supposed to entertain with their environment:

Aborigines *are* the rocks you have to move away. They understand themselves as a part of the earth.... That's why a man like Sam Woolagoocha said to me one day: "They have ravaged the earth and don't they see they have ravaged my body?" That explains everything ... they are the rocks, they are the trees and you'd have to shoot them first, or blast them, before they would move. It has nothing to do with modern "sit in" techniques. (Mizrahi, 1984)

Herzog's films are obsessed by the impossible dream of immediacy and transparency; they are haunted by the desire to achieve a direct communication between human beings, by experiences which are existential and which cut through social and historical forms of mediation, in order to reach an always intimated but never accomplished fusion. Many of Herzog's admirers are not fully aware of the ambiguity hidden in this relationship; consuming beautiful images as if in a trance, they want to climb into these pictures and abandon themselves to their seductiveness, their strangeness, their power. And insofar as his films are often associated with landscapes, Herzog might be thought of as in essence a "cultural" documentarist: many of his early films came out of his own experiences of travel which he (as much a child of the 1960s as more self-conscious filmmakers on the road) undertook in order to have a vantage-point on his own country and its history – a subject he has encompassed as no other German filmmaker. He traveled to the Sudan and West Africa, to Greece and the United States, to Ireland and the Canary Islands; there is a curious and altogether typical mixture of uncivilized, primitive places, and the by now traditional holiday spots of affluent West Germans (islands in Greece or off the coast of Africa, the Sahara Desert, Yugoslav or Czech mountain ranges, the Bavarian or Swiss Alps, or a rocky shore in Ireland). His landscapes are thus of an ambiguous other-worldliness, and of that all too easily reproduced painterly sense, which made critics refer to Caspar David Friedrich in his *Kaspar Hauser,* and of the grandiose panoramas one remembers from romantic poetry.

Hence the charge of irrationalism and the naive confusion of the imaginary effects of cinematic representation with immediacy. But this would be to overlook that the price for seeing these visions is always indicated in the fate of the protagonists; they go mad, they fail, they perish miserably. If in his films Herzog has elaborated a whole mythology of exceptional vision, his heroes do not interact with the landscape nor project themselves and their action into it; they remain in opposition, cut off from it.

The paradox, it seems to me, lies elsewhere than in Herzog's romanticism: it is that in order to convey both the desire and its failure, Herzog has to go to the most deprived and victimized and make a biological or social muteness become the sign of a new language, outside the conventional symbolic systems of exchange. Yet one could argue that via a growing awareness of the political implications of the search for immediacy – achieved invariably through identification with an imaginary "Other" – Herzog becomes a semiologist almost in spite of himself, and the special status of *Where the Green Ants Dream*, coming after *Fitzcarraldo,* can best be located in its different solution to the problem of filmic enunciation, as it places both the spectator and the referent.

The status of the referent

Herzog distrusts narrative not only because of its contamination with "psychology"; his hatred has itself to do with the question of significa-tion in the cinema, and the extent to which any logic of the signifier – whether narrative, causal, psychological or formal – dematerializes the image on the side of the referent, while effectively excluding the subject from discourse. The irruption of the unmotivated in his films, the search for contrast and bizarre juxtapositions, is a way of preserving the "thereness" of the physical object and to mark that exclusion of the human subject as a certain inviolability.

Kaja Silverman has criticized Herzog for what she sees in *Kaspar Hauser* as, finally, failing to confront the issue of signification as necessary separation from desire:

> When a voice asks us, at the beginning of the film: "Don't you hear that screaming all around us, that screaming men call silence?" we are being alerted to the existence of everything that language separates us from – to the censorship of signification. Kaspar attempts to undo that censorship and to reassure his own relation-ship with an inarticulate real. However, the strategy to which Kaspar resorts does not in fact constitute an alternative. Herzog's text un-questionably maintains the opposition ... between being and meaning; between full self-presence and the loss of that presence in signification. The critique which he levels is therefore a critique from within, one which merely shifts the privilege from one term to another – i.e. from meaning to being in an interdependent and mutually signifying set. (Silverman, 1981/2, 91–2)

Silverman's critique of the "romantic" Herzog is partly based on not conceding that his filmmaking in certain instances breaks explicitly, as well as implicitly, with the transparency of the filmic signifier and classical cinematic enunciation. There is, however, a contradiction in most of his films (least so perhaps, in *Kaspar Hauser*, with its art-film production values). While it is true that, considered as an ideological discourse, his films (and his own commentary on them) are all on the side of "being" as an unmediated presence, Herzog seems prepared to manipulate his actors and the pro-filmic in general, precisely in order to convey these qualities of inviolability and presence. This manipulation, it can be argued, is always a constituent part of his mise-en-scène, and as such represented in the enunciative process: it is in fact what causes most spectators a certain unease in their political response to his films.

Jan Dawson, in a review of *La Soufrière,* wrote about Herzog that "gratuitousness [is] the single value he consistently celebrates," referring to the director's admiration for those who remained on the island threatened by a volcano, because rescue to them would only have meant another cycle of the exploitation that made up their lives.

> [T]hey have nothing to live for and hence no fear of dying. It is here that the disquieting moral ambivalence of all of Herzog's work comes most sharply into focus: the old man, stretched out with his cat to die on the grassy mountainside, is offered at once as an object for emulation and for indignation. By staying gratuitously, he becomes not a martyr but a hero. (Dawson, 1977, 58)

But if one can call gratuitous those acts of stubbornness and resistance that attract Herzog, one has to see them as a kind of blocking of the all-too-ready transparency of signification which the television discourse especially brings to news, disasters and current events, where in a single image camera and commentary try to condense the meaning of an entire news-story. Gratuitousness would therefore itself be a sort of zero degree of motivation, or rather the cancellation of motive would be a refusal to accept the availability of images for signification.

Where the Green Ants Dream is in one sense an extension of *La Soufrière.* In both films the poorest of the poor, the most deprived of western civilization, possess strength of resistance directly proportional to the degree to which they are dispossessed. Is the spiritual freedom that Herzog seems to grant them a mere consolation prize for material rights that no one is prepared to concede, perhaps not even Herzog who moves the Aborigines before his camera in much the same way as the mining company threatens to have them moved by the police? This question Herzog does not disguise any more than he did in *La Soufrière,* which quite clearly not only depends on the presence of a voyeuristic-exhibitionist axis, but actually makes this its main subject. The distance Herzog keeps from his subjects lets him appear like a

documentarist, but one whose method is itself a protest against the construction of the referent as a mere adjunct to the ideological or informational discourse of television reporting. The freedom he necessarily takes with the pro-filmic (after all, his leading players among the Aborigines are actors) and the fact that *Where the Green Ants Dream* is a fiction film, make it inevitable that the resistance of the Aborigines is itself a metaphoric-fictional representation of Herzog's larger project: to dramatize in his films the resistance of the signified, in relation to the cinematic signifier.

Herzog often seeks out landscapes that look as if they existed prior to man, and in a certain sense seem indifferent to man. Nonetheless, his films are committed to an animistic view: when human beings appear, it is either as visionaries or natives that they can inhabit the land, or rather, be inhabited by it: many take on the shape and texture of the environment that surrounds them. Their appearance and behavior give the spectator the illusion of intimacy which is based on reading their environment as an expression – if not of their psychology, then of their "soul" and inward state. So although, as Andrea Simon put it, Herzog "in distinct contrast to the more typical procedure of exotic or rugged location films [does not] make the vegetable world a silent accessory to the values discussed by the plot" (Simon, 1975, 26), he does establish metonymic relationships between characters and settings. In *Aguirre,* for instance, we are invited to understand Aguirre's mad behavior by looking at a cannon plunging down a ravine, a torrential river, and a jungle bristling with sounds. To an impenetrable jungle corresponds a mad conquistador, as if every landscape for Herzog demanded a response, and as if most of his landscapes demanded a demented response. The outer world as inner world as outer world: in *Stroszek,* when Bruno S. tries to explain to Eva Mattes what it looks like inside him, he does it with the aid of junked car parts.

In the so-called documentaries (*The Flying Doctors of West Africa, Impeded Future, Land of Silence and Darkness*) the distrust of signification is more a matter of blocking (apart from psychological explanation) any easy interpretation of the stories and images as sociological case studies, a refusal to have the handicapped, the blind or the sick become subsumed under the discourses of institutionalized medicine, charitable religion or the welfare worker, before they have a chance to appear first and foremost as human beings. Instrumentalized politics is rejected by Herzog in the name of human dignity, or (if one takes Jan Dawson's use of "gratuitous" as a critique of Herzog's idea of freedom) in favor of existential, surrealist "convulsive beauty."

The more narrative films which also have a documentary dimension (*Stroszek, Where the Green Ants Dream*) not only take up clearly social and political issues (a life spent in institutional care unable to cope with "freedom", and the genocidal politics of international finance capitalism, with its ecological disasters) but conduct themselves as an apparently ever more openly political discourse. His documentary about the Miskito Indians waging guerrilla war against the Sandinista Government, *Ballad of the Little Soldier,* is a good example of how far Herzog has ventured into political and ideological controversy. As if to make amends to the Jivaro Indians he had offended in Peru over *Fitzcarraldo,* Herzog seems to give over his film to the Indians' self-representation (much in the way that *Where the Green Ants Dream* could be understood as a self-representation of the Aborigines), knowing that he will offend the western Left, sympathizing with the Sandinistas. Although the film does not say so, Herzog might well detect in western Third World politics an overabused and vulgarized fascination with the imaginary "Other" at too little cost to their own comfort and moral security. As a specialist in cultural and social "Others," Herzog has always insisted on the risks involved, and thus he is, even in his recent work, once again more interested in dramatizing the act of self-representation as one which escapes the speaking subject's control (foregrounding the role of his camera and its sympathetic intervention), than in passing judgment. What is politically ambiguous, on the other hand, is the extent to which Herzog is prepared to read as a resistance to the regime of signs and thus as a resistance to social deformation precisely those signs that speak most clearly of the hold that western civilization has even on the bodies of those it marginalizes and rejects.

Where the Green Ants Dream could itself be seen as conducting a denunciatory discourse: earth-moving bulldozers carry before them mounds of red dirt and dust, dumping them almost on top of the squatting tribespeople. The implied visual poetry of the enormous machines, around which the protesters dance and chant and play the didgeridoo, or the symbolism of the Airforce plane looking like a giant green ant out of a 1950s mutant movie, are neither bizarre nor innocent enough to modify or nuance the heavily thematized contrasts between machine and man, naked force versus naked humanity, sophisticated technology versus Stone Age mythology. It is no longer a question of displacing motivation, but of too stark and bald an opposition confining signification to a rhetorical operation of moral reflexes.

In an effort to close off one kind of transparency (that which classical narrative gives), a structure of meaning imposes itself on Herzog's images that can only be called manichean: if the level on which the film is meant to work is cosmic, then the issue he chooses is too politically urgent, and the case too specific, for the metaphysical fiction to become convincing, especially with Hackett as a concession to conventional film dramaturgy acting as the story's (inadequate) central consciousness. If on the other hand, Herzog documents, even in reconstructed form, an actual case, then the fantastic anthropology of the green ants seems an unnecessary and irritating intrusion. The reverse side of Herzog's attempt to subvert the narrative cinema's inherent discursiveness by recourse to a documentary style becomes itself a form of discursiveness, an accumulation of assertions about his material, chief among which is that his characters are unknowable. Yet at the very point where Herzog's discussion of the referent as unassailable to the operations of signification and sense seems most ideological, it is necessary to look more closely at his own forms of cinematic enunciation.

Enacting a self-alienating discourse

He surrounds himself with people, primitive, innocent, or slightly mad (on whom the pressure of a deformed life becomes visible), so long as their behavior, their use of language, their reactions and gestures indicate, unconsciously and by default, a certain kind of reification. Through them he can represent in action processes of alienation, dehumanization and exclusion which society imposes on them. But what is this society? Sometimes it seems that Herzog, for the sake of his films, makes himself into the instrument of this society, in order to simulate the conditions he set out to document. There is, in other words, a poetry even of social anomie and alienation which Herzog's cinema cannot but recognize as an aesthetic value and with which it colludes. It is a technique even for representing an ultimately purely filmic, that is to say imaginary, authenticity: "[My characters'] actions are somehow oblivious, it seems, to themselves" (Greenberg *et al.*, 1976, 122); "there is a strong sense of not being able to know and of becoming more real because of that" (Fricke *et al.*, 1968, 177).

Herzog's attitude to his heroes is both unrelenting and tender: if his camera observes them from a distance, it also never lets them go. In *Land of Silence and Darkness* a deaf, dumb and blind man who has escaped into the orchard of his institution gingerly explores a tree. For what seems like an eternity, a hand-held camera frames him in middle distance, only slightly panning to accommodate his movements. Such detachment connotes respect and loyalty, but one wonders whether Herzog's protective, fatherly care does not also resemble that of the botanist for his specimen, for the raw material of his experiments in which he has invested time and labor: he treats them with gentleness because he knows how fragile they are. Others, more robust, he is prepared to put on the rack. The power that the media, the film industry, the world of the movies, gives him he uses like a mask, to approach his actors. In front of the camera they can be seen to react to this monster that provokes them, a monster they fear but also seem to love, because it plays on their exhibitionism as much as on their reticence.

> A lot of my scenes only emerge during shooting. I put obstacles in the way of my actors, especially non-professionals, so that the obstacle leads them to reveal their personality and how they cope.... The fact that I manipulate my characters and locations doesn't contradict their reality, I have simply pushed things a little further, so they reveal their essence. (Fricke *et al.*, 1968, 177)

Such a direction of actors aims at an immediacy and directness which it elicits by way of reaction as much as from acting, and can imply an element of provocation, anger and aggression. But before concluding Herzog's sadism from this, or accusing him of exploitation, what is it that this strategy is meant to reveal? The different ways of manipulating proximity and distance are attempts at finding an alternative, on the level of enunciation, to the suturing process of classical narrative, and its form of cinematic identification. Herzog does not want the spectator to "get inside" his characters, at least not in the conventional sense. There is thus a dilemma, which in a sense becomes more urgent with each successive Herzog film: in *Signs of Life, Aguirre, Kaspar Hauser*, the mystery created around the central character deflects psychological identification away from the person, in order to intensify identification with the setting, the objects and places. Likewise, the parables and riddles, the dreams, the myths, the mystifications and pseudo-scientific discourses which the tribal elders, the entomologist and even Hackett on one occasion offer as explanations or self-revelations in *Where the Green Ants Dream* must be understood as so many ways of imposing a moral and an emotional distance from the characters in order to direct the spectators' attention elsewhere, or so as to split word from image. Positing his characters as enigmas, Herzog constructs a perspective for the spectator which marks as impenetrable the space that separates the spectator's space from that of the characters. Even though some of this is undercut by Herzog's empathetic and subjectivizing use of music (usually choral, or the solo voice of an aria or of a *Lied*), the subjectivity connoted by such moments, their combination of intimacy and remoteness, constitutes them as separate registers. They remain distinct because rarely if ever are they motivated by a diegetic point of view, a character perspective. As spectators we are never really inside the film, but neither are we outside.

This is above all a matter of not conceiving the diegetic action around the point-of-view shot and its inevitably psychologizing structure of inference. One might say that Herzog's mise-en-scène seeks to create a point of view, without the point-of-view shot as its basis. What substitutes for fictional empathy in the early films is precisely this ambiguous shift between aggressive provocation and experimental curiosity: there is never any sense of the camera *not* being present, indeed one might say in a film like *Last Words* or *Fata Morgana*, Herzog not only made his players acknowledge the camera but provoked them into dramatizing this relationship, underlining its exhibitionist dimension, by marking very strongly the space occupied by the director behind and the actors in front, as distinct from the space the camera shares with the audience. With this, however, Herzog was able to enact, indeed to mimic and parody, the "castrating" function of the cinematic discourse. In Germany, Herzog's films were attacked for a sort of technical incompetence, a vagueness and imprecision in the means of his mise-en-scène. In contrast to, say, Jean-Marie Straub, there seems no beauty in Herzog's editing, no clarity to his framing, no reason why one image should follow another. For certain writers this meant that the beauty of the images was bogus, fake and kitsch, because of a basic inability or refusal to engage with film as a specific formal discourse (Gansera, 1975, 518).

Yet as a filmmaker emerging in the 1960s, self-trained and unteachable, Herzog rejected classical Hollywood narrative as much as the classically purist avant-garde traditions. Instead he went to those "wild" forms of the avant-garde which stretched from Stan Brakhage to Buñuel's early documentary.

In the event, it was the documentaries he made that were crucial in terms of Herzog's development as a fiction director, for in them he could push the discrepancy between the perspective of the protagonists and that of the audience to an extreme. Herzog eliminated the traditional forms of cinematic mediation, scene dissection or classic construction of space, any variation of axis or angle in the editing to distinguish between extra-diegetic shots and diegetic ones, or to modify the imbalance between the characters' look and that of the camera. Reverting to a pseudo-primitive frontality created a stance halfway between pathos and pure aggression emanating from the pro-filmic, while producing a impression of stasis and immobility for the spectator: a sense of physical effort in the subjects communicated itself to the viewer which in turn became the principle of his fictional narratives.

Herzog: a comic director?

Where the Green Ants Dream is clearly not primitive in this sense. It is technically competent in a way recognizable to Hollywood, and to that extent, marked by the impersonality of the cinematic institution. But it retains what is fundamental to Herzog's filmmaking: the question of the body and its resistance to discourse. Herzog's admiration for courage, for physical prowess, goes hand in hand with his perception of another kind of courage, that of physical and emotional weakness and vulner-ability. His characters persevere in the knowledge of failure, and this stoical heroism is no vitalist version of the superman, but a more flamboyant expression of that concern with the "obtuse" already noted in his idea of filmic signification. Whenever the films have inscribed a human temporality, the overreachers and underdogs complement each other. Against a background of temporal decay, Herzog's view of history has always been tragic: he sees the flawed nature of his characters' rebellion, the radical innocence of their deformation, the resilience and perseverance they oppose to their situation.

Even when "victims of society" they are engaged in a resistance and an effort in the same way as his inspired madmen. But when the temporality is of a different order, as it seems to be in *Where the Green Ants Dream*, the question of the body is differently posed. What is effort and resistance in the early heroes becomes a form of theater in the Aborigines. Their subjectivity does not have to be rescued from dis-course. *Where the Green Ants Dream* is therefore not quite as didactic as the simplicity of the fable suggests. In contrast to the mining company, which has to call in the bulldozers to back up its own persistence, and the law to break up a "mob," the tribesmen show the kind of mental agility that in a stalemate such as exists from the outset, becomes a definite form of wit: they may be doomed as a tribe, but they survive every concrete situation, like heroes in the comic-picaresque tradition. They adjust to their opponents while not ceding their position. In *Where the Green Ants Dream*, the Aborigines look at us, the white spectators, and seem to be looking through us. Even more than the mining company, they can bide their time. Outside time as history, Herzog can afford to be both an essentialist and let his characters let us know that they perform, and that their performance has the gravity beyond tragedy.

Not unlike the Riratjingu leaders, Herzog has, without ceding on principle, found that his narratives of circularity and of time as degradation carry the seeds of transcendence into comedy; resistance, survival, heroism in *Where the Green Ants Dream* is ultimately, perhaps, a matter more of comic than of cosmic perspective. The comedy is not only directed at the spectator who, like Hackett, always enjoys a good story of a last stand; it is also directed against himself, the filmmaker whose last stand is always to turn himself into a myth; unless, like the Aborigines, you choose silence, exile and cunning.

Works cited

Barthes, R. (1977) "The Third Meaning," in Stephen Heath (ed.) *Image/Music/Text*, New York, Hill & Wang, 52–68.

Dawson, Jan (1977) "Herzog's Magic Mountain," *Sight and Sound*, 47 (Winter), 57–8.

Fricke, F. *et al.* (1968) "Werner Herzog," *Filmkritik* (March), 177.

Gansera, R. (1975) "Kaspar Hauser," *Filmkritik* (November), 518.

Greenberg, A., H. Achternbusch and W. Herzog (1976) *Heart of Glass*, Munich, Skellig.

Keusch, E. and C. Weisenborn (1978) *Was ich bin sind meine Filme* (German TV documentary).

Mizrahi, S. (1984) "Interview with Werner Herzog," production handout (no page numbers).

Silverman, K. (1981/2) "Kaspar Hauser's 'Terrible Fall' into Narrative," *New German Critique*, nos 24–5 (Fall/Winter), 73–93.

Simon, A. (1975) "Werner Herzog's *Aguirre, the Wrath of God*," *Monogram*, no. 6, 26.

IV

ARGUMENTS

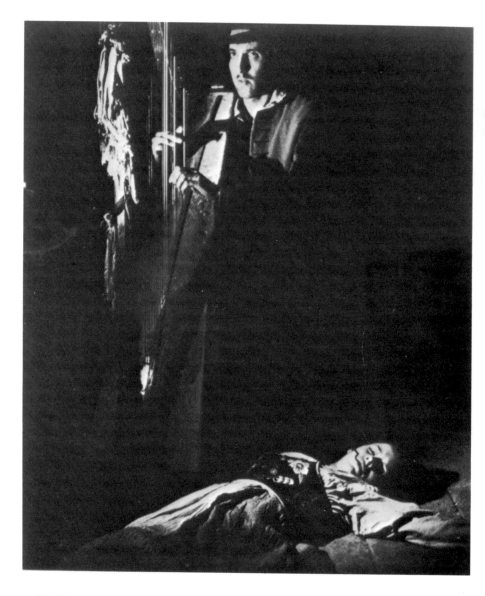

10 The cabinet of Werner Herzog (*Heart of Glass*)

10

The politics of vision:
Herzog's *Heart of Glass*

Eric Rentschler

We do not deform, we stylize for the sake of a new perspective.
                        Werner Herzog (Greenberg *et al.*, 1976, 18)

It's not only my dreams. My belief is that all these dreams ... are
yours as well. And the only distinction between me and you is that
I can articulate them.
                        Werner Herzog (Blank and Bogan, 1984, 61)

Modernism was not a movement exclusively of the political Left or
Right. Its central legend was of the free creative spirit at war with
the bourgeoisie who refuses to accept any limits and who
advocates what Daniel Bell has called the "megalomania of
self-infinitization," the impulse to reach "beyond: beyond
morality, tragedy, culture." From Nietzsche to Jünger and then
Goebbels, the modernist credo was the triumph of spirit and will
over reason and the subsequent fusion of this will to an aesthetic
mode. If aesthetic experience alone justifies life, morality is
suspended and desire has no limits.
                        Jeffrey Herf (1984, 12)

I

In *Heart of Glass* Werner Herzog assumed the role of a hypnotist,
putting his actors (all but the male lead, Sepp Bierbichler) under a
spell in the hopes of portraying "people on the screen as we have never
seen them before" (Greenberg *et al.*, 1976, 14–15). The work, a crucial
and telling one in the director's cinema, marks a decisive point in the

filmmaker's development, the juncture at which Herzog first manifested troubling evidence of an instrumentalism that would increasingly become more apparent both on- and off-screen. Casting himself as a benevolent Caligari, he lorded over a host of daunted Cesares and Janes, characters we see in the film looking frenzied, disembodied, afflicted. He saw himself more as a facilitator than a manipulator, claiming his interventions set free the flow of fantasy rather than controlled it:

> Hypnosis has nothing to do with demonical power (will power) that is given the hypnotist (even if hypnotists at county fairs would have us believe that), but, rather, it deals generally with self-hypnosis, to which the hypnotists give aid by way of fixations of the mind and speech rituals. (Greenberg *et al.*, 1976, 15)

Maintaining that his work in this vein was unprecedented in film history,[1] Herzog oddly overlooked a native legacy clear to anyone concerned with German cinema.

This, of course, is that infamous heritage under discussion in Siegfried Kracauer's *From Caligari to Hitler*, the procession of fictional mesmerists (the mountebank of the title, the diabolical Mabuse, the malevolent Nosferatu, among many others) which presaged the ascent of totalitarian leadership over a spellbound nation. Weimar films in fact display a marked predilection for hypnosis and hypnoid states, suggesting an affinity between these phenomena and the gripping potential of the cinematic medium itself. Such metareflection, though, is anathema to Herzog. His disavowal of the past and tradition comes as a typical gesture for someone vehemently convinced that his visions transcend history and circumvent the known. *Heart of Glass* exercises a profoundly enthralling hold on many of its viewers and this is as the director intended. Nonetheless, we need not so readily surrender to Herzog's commands, lest we – as he likewise intended – lapse into a comatose state in which we dream someone else's dreams, losing the orientation of time and space, becoming utterly subservient to another person's designs.

Herzog's earlier films abound with images of hypnosis and transfixed beings: delirious chickens, the unblinking stare of Kaspar Hauser, the other-worldly hallucinations of Aguirre and his crew. In *Heart of Glass* Herzog sought a higher degree of stylization, one he believed would allow "a new perspective" (Greenberg *et al.*, 1976, 15). His treatment of actors catalyzed much discussion. (One detractor wondered whether the director planned to nail his players to trees in future productions

[Achternbusch, 1978, 266].) Almost every account of the film speaks of the collective hypnosis, seeing it as an expression of a "restless need to experiment which often pushes Herzog to eccentricity" (Forbes, 1977, 255). Less often noted is Herzog's equally strong desire to hypnotize his audiences as well, an ambition voiced by the director on numerous occasions (Walsh/Ebert, 1979, 19, Wiedemann, 1976, 27). This consonance of intended effect on actors and audience was apparent during the casting of *Heart of Glass.* The future participants in the film received a preparation for the initial hypnosis, a screening of *Fata Morgana*, a film Herzog claimed would be "unlike anything they had seen before. It would be an exquisite, magical vision of life, they were informed, with music rare and beautiful" (Greenberg *et al.*, 1976, 22). The response of the players-to-be could not but please the director of the experimental documentary: "In the first row, a housewife gasped in awe. She clasped her hands to her breast as if in prayer. Further back, a young man from Iran strained wide-eyed, leaning forward, trying to get inside" (Greenberg *et al.*, 1976, 22).

Provoking acts of religious devotion, ones in which the faithful seek to erase the distance between their own world and the screen world before them – quite literally trying to crawl into the film – Herzog sought to involve the spectator every bit as strongly as his actors in the work's diegesis. Like so many of his New German colleagues, the director has a pronounced awareness of film's reception dynamics. The medium does not only live on the screen, but above all in the minds of spectators: "Films do not exist per se: you have to have an audience that completes the film" (O'Toole, 1979, 42). His ideal audience is a sympathetic one, open to his images and his unique vantage point.[2] Unlike so many of his distantiation-minded peers, directors like Fassbinder, Kluge, and Syberberg, Herzog eschews Brechtian ploys, ironic reserve, and critical strategies meant to engender a thinking spectator. He disdains those who respond to his films intellectually, arguing that such viewers impose foreign meaning on his films and thereby denigrate primal simplicity and direct appeal, the very strengths of his work.[3] Herzog insists on a transfixed audience without categories of its own or conceptual frameworks gained elsewhere. His pristine landscapes and bizarre denizens push us to a more encompassing notion of the real.[4] They can best be appreciated by equally uncluttered and unprejudiced minds: "What I often regret about film audiences is that they don't simply look at the screen" (de le Viseur and Schmidmaier, 1977). The implied viewer should enter the cinema without predispositions. Ideally there is a *tabula rasa* on both projection spaces, on the cinematic screen and in the spectator's head. The Cabinet of Werner Herzog demands a captive audience.

Quite systematically, Herzog has endeavored to control response to his films; no other title in his canon, though, so dramatically demonstrates this predilection as *Heart of Glass*. This stretches from his authority over actors and technicians to audiences and, indeed, critics and scholars. It is quite fitting that the printed script version of the film contains not only the scenario but also the report of a Herzog acolyte who followed the production, an individual who refers to himself as "the witness."[5] The screenplay thus incorporates a series of fictional scenes, but likewise an array of reverent responses to the director, unquestioning acceptance of his every whim, enthusiastic recordings of even the most trivial detail of the artist's daily routine, undying attention – in the manner of Hitler's table talks – to crackpot speculations, a document lacking all irony or distance. The tone smacks of the most devout Führer-worship:

> "Herzog peoples emptiness," thought the witness, tearing off a shard of vegetation clinging to a rock, "and this is his proof: he uses forms according to the life, not according to the form." (Greenberg *et al.*, 1976, 44)

The observation is followed by a description of the script girl Regina, how she first met Herzog at a retrospective of his films in Vienna. At the end of the program, she approached the master:

> Regina knew for sure what she must devote her life to. She begged Herzog then and there for a position on his production team. He was taken by the intensity of her plea.
>
> "Walk from Vienna to Munich," he said, somewhat seriously. "That will tell me how much you want the job." (Greenberg *et al.*, 1976, 45)

Herzog has found a cultish fervor among film critics as well. Some of the notices of *Heart of Glass* unconditionally laud the film; as if obeying the director's decree against interpretation, one celebrates the artist's creative power and denies historical actuality:

> Herzog's *Heart of Glass* is a masterful, heartbreakingly beautiful movie. It is primarily a visual experience, but the emphasis on color, line and imagery is never arty or artificial; the visuals are the vision, the very stuff – the obsession – of the movie itself. The plot is secondary, as is characterization or "acting." Something grander, more important is at stake. . . .
>
> What *happens* throughout the film is never as important as the

overall vibration, the drift and movement in time and space. (Baker, 1977)

Prose extolling the film's "mesmerizing beauty" (Corliss, 1977) honors the director's intention to captivate and engross. Actors, audience, and critics are reduced to unquestioning followers: the immediacy of the aesthetic experience obviates any possible route of access to the text other than that of the artist's own imaginary. This is not a generous film in the vein of Kluge, a work with empty spaces, gaps, and disjunctures which leave room for free response and reflection. *Heart of Glass* does not disturb and provoke the viewer with its subversion of generic expectations as do Fassbinder's recycled melodramas, his reheated potboilers. Herzog's is a cinema aiming to resist accepted patterns of thinking and seeing. As Noël Carroll extols the work, these films have an auratic way about them, exuding a sense of ultimate presence and not readily lending themselves "to satisfying descriptions or explanations in terms of narration, psychology, and sometimes even physics" (Carroll, 1985, 30). Such pronouncements indicate how, even in sophisticated scholarly corners, Herzog has also succeeded in hypnotizing the onlooker, finding further disciples.

Clearly, not everyone has been as willing to surrender to Herzog's demagoguery, least of all Herbert Achternbusch, author of the film's script (cf. Achternbusch, 1978, 262–8). In a bitter and sarcastic attack, he lashed out at his former friend Herzog, complaining that the film-maker had betrayed the vision, sucking all vitality and vigor from the original conception for the sake of a screwball experiment:

> This ceremonial aura framed by hypnosis! Unfortunately the master of ceremonies remains behind the camera, so that the male lead and prophet Sepp Bierbichler does not have much else to do besides seeing and talking; once he slices himself a piece of bread and eats it, in the inn he doesn't even take a drink, and he walks around in a coat taken from Orff's idea of peasant theater. (Achternbusch, 1978, 267)

Herzog's films, according to Timothy Corrigan, are framed by an intelligence who "would engage the spectator's eye not in the titillating fashion of Hollywood cinema where voyeuristic distance maintains the spectacle but as an exploration and hypnotic participation in the energies of space" (Corrigan, 1983, 139). This challenge to the dominant cinema, however, does not liberate. If anything, it *heightens* the absorbing effect of classical narrative, striving to make the spectator capitulate unconditionally to the vision on the screen, the product of the hypnotizing force who shaped these images. In other words, Herzog espouses a cinema that utterly engages the viewer in the trance-like state described by Christian Metz, moving him or her

> to perceive as true and external the events and the heroes of the fiction rather than the images and sounds belonging purely to the screening process (which is, nonetheless, the only real agency): a tendency, in short, to perceive as real the represented and not the representer (the technological medium of the representation), to pass over the latter without seeing it for what it is, to press on blindly. (Metz, 1982, 115)

Rather than couch our discussion of Herzog's *Heart of Glass* in terms of his own imaginary, it would behoove us to move beyond his trans-fixions, to demystify his mystifications. This does not mean forsaking the film and imposing foreign meaning on it, but instead looking at it carefully and taking it even more seriously than the director might like, as a formal entity, as part of a larger body of work, and, finally, as an historical artifact and a product of – no matter how much Herzog would deny this – certain traditions and legacies of considerable interest to any student of twentieth-century Germany.

II

Heart of Glass is not as narratively random or structurally chaotic as previous critics have claimed. This denial of plot logic and causality, in fact, provides a ready defense of the film as something situated in a no man's land outside of time and space, a result of artistic immediacy, not historical mediation. Herzog took the story-line of Achternbusch's script and framed it with a prologue and an epilogue containing the seer Hias's visions: an initial one of collapse and perdition out of which arises a new world, a closing one of hope and redemption. The embedded narrative remains faithful to the scenario insofar as it ensues along similar plot lines and uses most of the original dialogue. In a pre-industrial setting somewhere in the Bavarian Forest, a remarkable ruby glass is produced in a factory owned by an eccentric young nobleman who lives with his deranged and sickly father. When Mühlbeck, the sole bearer of the ruby glass formula, dies, the indus-trialist frantically takes measures to regain the secret that has followed the worker to his grave. He calls on employees to try their hands at reproducing the glass, plunders Mühlbeck's grave and home for traces of the formula, sends for the visionary Hias and seeks to ply him with money, finally succumbing to a madness that drives him to murder his servant girl (thinking the virgin's blood contains the missing ingredient) and burn down his factory. As the small village around the works comes unraveled, giving in to a general ambience of fear, insanity, and destruction, Hias, the shepherd who has come from the mountains, looks on, predicting ultimate perdition and also presaging the course of western history well into the twentieth century. The scenario ends with Hias in the woods, feasting on the roasted meat of a bear he has slain in hand-to-hand struggle.

Rather than a narrative gallimaufry with a systematically blurred point of view (cf. Forbes, 1977, 256), *Heart of Glass* possesses two distinct modalities corresponding quite clearly to Achternbusch's script and Herzog's elaborations centering around Hias and his visions. There are no unmotivated or random images in the entire film: the moments where Hias's pronouncements explode into images are clearly marked, indeed decidedly literal. In the prologue, for instance, he says, "The earth boils over, this is the sign," and we see a shot of bubbling lava. "I look into the cataract," he proclaims, and we glimpse a vast waterfall cascade. A second extended visionary sequence later in the film comes after another description of apocalypse, catastrophe that leaves the world nearly uninhabited. We cut from Hias (telling of a man running down a road, screaming, "Am I really the last one, the only one left?") to a series of unpeopled landscapes, the world after the cataclysm, a collection of images which essentializes his vision as well as anticipates the destruction in the village. A short glimpse of the Skellig Islands also points ahead to the epilogue. (It might be noted that this sequence contains stark similarities to parts of Herzog's *La Soufrière* as well as the opening passage of Achternbusch's *The Young Monk*.) At the end of the imagistic eruption, we cut back to Hias in the woods as he walks through the trees and back into the story proper.

In the actual narrative, Hias remains a spectator to a string of bizarre events involving the factory owner and the quest for ruby glass. These scenes unfold, to be sure, in an oblique and often disjunctive manner. The editing only minimally provides spatial orientation, at times leaping from one location to another without establishing points of reference. In our initial exposure to the village and its inhabitants, for example, we partake of the following series of elliptical tableaux, all single shots:

– the father seen straight on, staring at the camera while he sits in a dark corner, telling of death and the lost formula;

- the workers in the factory discussing Mühlbeck and the lack of a written description of the ruby glass;
- Mühlbeck's mother praying at her son's grave;
- an extended documentary-like tracking shot past the glass workers in the factory.

The narrative action blends a large number of different tonalities, a mix that leaves the spectator at the beck and call of the always partial and quite often inconclusive disclosures. These elements include: *Volksstück*-scenes (characters dressed in peasant garb, speaking a stylized Bavarian redolent of Achternbusch's cinema), low-lit interiors framed in claustrophobic compositions, long takes in which characters address the camera or speak to themselves seemingly oblivious to their onscreen audience, moments where doors close on the spectator so that one can only see part of the frame, in general a lack of establishing shots, clear transitions, and a decipherable narrative trajectory. Beyond this, it is not readily apparent how the framing sequences relate to the overall narrative, what Hias has to do with the factory owner, and how the larger visions of doom, destruction, and redemption accord to the downfall of the industrialist, his quest for the ruby glass, and the destruction of the factory and undoing of the village.

One reads typically that *Heart of Glass* "is not really a narrative film" (Forbes 1977, 256), that the "story told, the film remains disconcertingly 'about' something else" (Fell, 1979, 54). This sort of criticism privileges the visionary passages, glimpsing them as the dominant element in the film, rendering Hias as a stand-in for the poet-priest-seer Herzog (Forbes, 1977, 256), and leaving the film as a whole unaccounted for. Previous approaches to the film have come to a series of conclusions demanding closer scrutiny and rethinking:

1 Commentators have surrendered to Herzog's commands, denigrating plot and possible meaning for the sake of vision – or, conversely, less sympathetic viewers have denied the film completely, as ponderous, boring, and so perversely self-indulgent as to be unbearable.

2 Discussions have focused on Hias and maintained that his play with the future is the thing, reducing the rest of the film to a somewhat predictable demonstration of his apocalyptic pro-phecies. What one has overlooked, however, is the manner in which Hias interacts quite significantly with the industrialist, how the editing in fact renders them as doubles, figures whose

shadows melt into each other upon their first meeting in a stair-way, individuals who will join later in a dark cell, kindred spirits bound up in a larger design present in the film, one quite telling in its revelations about Herzog's art.

3 In general, critics in recent years have continually presented a hypostatized notion of Herzog's films and heroes, seeing them as compelling variations on a limited set of themes and motivations. One rarely distinguishes or differentiates:

> Whether Woyzeck or Stroszek, Aguirre, Fitzcarraldo, Nosferatu or Kaspar Hauser, these characters are moved by inner forces that for Herzog remain inexplicable, unnameable and undescribable. The inscrutability of the springs that move them erects a certain affective distance – a kind of obdurate clarity – between them and us. Such figures are virtually canonized by Herzog for the uniqueness and the inaccessibility of their passions and their inner life. (Carroll, 1985, 35–6).

The force that moves these characters is of course not such a deep secret: it is a filmmaker who has worked now for twenty years, producing a body of work which does have a certain logic *and* development to it, no matter how much people – quite in keeping with Herzog's desires – would like to deny process and evolution for the sake of artistic creation and the filmmaker's authority. In this regard, the double hero of *Heart of Glass* and the film's double discourse, as we shall see, mark a very singular juncture in the career of Werner Herzog.

4 Finally, one has tended to see this film outside of generic patterns and cultural history,[6] as further evidence of the director's originality, the work of someone who once claimed he made films as if there had been no film history (Walsh/Ebert, 1979, 6). Like-wise, critics at best broach the question of the film's deeper significance before lapsing into murky locutions. "Its political meaning," wrote one reviewer of *Heart of Glass*, "is a faint rumble in the distance; and it is held together by the power of its visions" (Forbes 1977, 256). Clearly, other powers have made an equally telling mark on Herzog's visions. *Heart of Glass* does not stand outside of tradition or beyond history, but rather harbors a curious and fateful discourse on the function of art in modernity. Only a witness overcome by Herzog's ministrations will fail to perceive the political rumblings in *Heart of Glass*.

III

Werner Herzog recognizes the power of generic convention and its hold on popular audiences. Hardly an enemy of genre films, he sees in them "the largest possibility for placing the spectator on secure ground in order to undertake explorations together with him" (Hopf, 1975). Although he claims, quite emphatically so, that he thinks outside of such categories, he has often voiced the wish to work in this vein on some future occasion. He knows well what sort of questions he would have to ask: "What is this particular genre about? What are its basic principles? How am I going to modify and develop this genre further?" (Walsh, 1979, 25). *Heart of Glass* bears some of the external trappings of a *Heimatfilm*, to be sure: the Bavarian Forest and the peasant milieu replete with dialect and local color. Nonetheless, Herzog does not mean to suggest the provincial *Heimatfilm* of the 1950s, those picture-postcard indulgences with titles like *Green is the Heather, Black Forest Girl,* and *To See the Homeland Once Again.*[7] "The locations have a more dismal atmosphere about them," he claimed (Greenberg *et al.,* 1976, 19). Herbert Achternbusch described a conversation with Herzog before the Munich première of their film. He told the director that he hoped the work would be the best *Heimatfilm* of all time. Herzog was not pleased with that prospect and "resisted, because his film had nothing in common with the *Heimatfilm*" (Achternbusch, 1978, 266).

The *Heimatfilm*, the German equivalent to the American western, has a long history, spanning the entirety of the nation's cinematic tradition, covering all the epochs, from the pre-World War I landscape panoramas, through the mountain films of the 1920s, blood-and-soil dramas from the Third Reich, the plethora of such ready-made productions during the Adenauer era, ersatz housing for a homeless nation still in the process of rebuilding, and, ultimately, the renovations of the genre by New German filmmakers, subversive refurbishings of the structure by critical young directors. More recently, of course, Edgar Reitz has provided a mammoth paean to the homeland, a stunning mix of affirmation and variation otherwise lacking the revisionist zeal of his colleagues, the 16-hour-long epos, *Heimat.* Where does Herzog, if at all, fit into this legacy?

Heart of Glass, unlike the *Heimatfilme* that abounded in the 1950s (virtually 20 per cent of West Germany's film production between 1947 and 1960), does not contain the earmarks we associate with postwar exercises along these lines. One finds no initial images of plenitude and equilibrium, a state of harmony called into question by some intrusion from the outside or threat from within, challenges to a pre-ordained and timeless order the narrative will ultimately serve to restore. The film lacks the lush images of flora and fauna, the nature worship, the sentimental songs and music, and the upbeat conservatism one associates with the popular genre. Herzog knows these films; he grew up with them. If he has learned anything from film history, he avers, it has been from negative examples, bad films. "German films of the fifties – they were the great educational experiences for me: how not to do things" (de le Viseur and Schmidmaier). Nevertheless, Herzog has not totally desisted from all traces of the homeland film and its iconography. The opening shot of the herdsman sitting in the fog minding cattle while Alpine choral music plays is at least a nod in this direction.

The first shot in the mist gives way to images of catastrophe and upheaval. The apparent calm is belied by Hias's presentiment of calamity: "I look into the distance to the end of the world. Before the day is over, the end will come. First, time will tumble and then the earth." A semblance of idyllic peace which suddenly turns into fierce disorder is a trait common to the so-called *Anti-Heimatfilme*, works like Reinhard Hauff's *Mathias Kneissl*, Uwe Brandner's *I Love You, I Kill You*, and Volker Schlöndorff's *The Sudden Wealth of the Poor People of Kombach*. These revisitations of the homeland reshaped the genre at the same time as their progressive directors sought to rewrite German history, to fashion images of the past with alternative information and a less affirmative view of native tradition. Herzog did not share in this project. He made no effort to reconstruct the historical past, taking recourse to documents like Schlöndorff and Hauff. The seer Hias may represent a figure well known in Bavarian lore; nonetheless, Herzog portrays the prophet as a mythic presence. The diegesis is not clearly fixed, either in time or space. The setting is a vague pre-industrial one; the images of the countryside combine a host of locations and landscapes.[8] Herzog's *Heimat* is a very synthetic one, hardly the site of nostalgia and organic community. Human agency all but fades against the backdrop of a world propelled by an inexorable destiny.

If the patterns of recognition at work in *Heart of Glass* do not have ready analogues in the recent past or near present, what happens when we look further back in time? The attempt to align Herzog with adherents of the Third Reich has above all stemmed from Nina Gladitz's shrill vendetta against the director. She has documented Herzog's putative abuses against landscapes and cultures in her book, *Der Fall Herzog*, and the film, *Land of Bitterness and Pride*.[9] Gladitz, also involved in a recent court battle against Leni Riefenstahl (see Enzensberger, 1985; also Mathes, 1985) has taken both Herzog and Riefenstahl to task for their mistaken understanding of artistic calling, the way in which they readily exploit people and situations for an art beyond good and evil. Unfortunately, Gladitz limits her investigations to production-related concerns, not delving into the films proper. It is clear that Herzog and Riefenstahl both have appropriated the romantic legacy. The question remains: how similar were these appropriations and did they lead to consonant filmic visions?

The Blue Light, Riefenstahl's directorial debut, and *Heart of Glass* bear striking resemblances, in a number of ways. Both films are dramas set in a pre-modern world of pastoral landscapes and sweeping mountains. The iconography in each case draws heavily on nineteenth-century German painting. Riefenstahl's film quite explicitly underlines this tradition by having an artist from Vienna journey to the Alpine location: an early shot in fact has him pose as Caspar David Friedrich's "Traveller Overlooking a Sea of Fog." The final sequence likewise borrows freely from Friedrich's work, especially as the painter strolls through the woods in the morning fog. Herzog just as strikingly evokes this painterly heritage: the scene of Hias in the mountain gorge calls to mind Friedrich's "Rocky Gorge in Elbesandsteingebirge." Similarly, the candle-lit interiors of the *Gasthaus* go back to Georges de la Tour in the same way that the views of the glass works, replete with luminescent colors commingling the industrial and the elemental, seem to refer to Adolph von Menzel's modulated interiors (cf. Wetzel, 1979, 121). Landscape for both filmmakers assumes evocative powers, becoming a realm whose immensity dwarfs the human, a space where one loses all individuality, an expanse whose endless horizons and vast cloud banks possess a mystical resonance. Both films feature compositions in which characters, with their backs to the camera, face into the distance, gazing at the inexorable reaches in front of them with a sense of awe. Riefenstahl, a student of Arnold Fanck and the *Bergfilm,* and Herzog both are able to direct clouds and elements in a way granting them a consuming sublimity, imparting to them a hypnotic immediacy.

Siegfried Kracauer viewed in the mountain film a primer for fascist sensibility, maintaining that these Alpine dramas functioned as allegories of self-sacrifice, where immature heroes succumbed to a religion of death and destiny (Kracauer, 1947, 110–12). The mountain enthusiasm means a desire to embrace the elemental, to die for a higher cause, dispositions that came to fruition in National Socialism. *The Blue Light,* although made in 1932, resorts to a romantic anti-

capitalism decidedly characteristic of Nazi ideology. At the same time, *Romantic*
however, it embraces the world of elemental nature and simultaneously *Anti-Capitalism*
seems to defend the harnessing of the natural – an odd collusion of *Decidedly*
romanticism and technology. Junta, a strange woman living in the *Characteristic of Nazi*
Alpine peaks above a Tyrolean village, has privileged access to a *Ideology*
crystal mountain that on full-moon nights lures fascinated boys to
seek out the source of its radiant blue light, a quest invariably ending in
death. A painter from Vienna befriends the outcast woman, becoming
her confidante, and ultimately learning her secret. He leads the townspeople to a grotto filled with valuable minerals, the source of the blue
light and Junta's private retreat. Armed with tools, the villagers mine the
cave and rejoice in their new fortune. Meanwhile, Junta, finding her
intimate space ravaged, despairs, and falls to her death. The rape is a
double one: the crystals are mined and Junta's intimate sphere is
penetrated. The minerals and Junta's image become objects of
exchange, things held up to tourists who come to the village. The
elemental becomes the ornamental through the incursion of the instrumental, a process ultimately – at least in part – condoned by the
narrative. Myth seems vanquished, the natural bespoiled, and the tale
of Junta becomes a legend contained in a book celebrating the village's
redemption. One mines the natural, transforms it into a commodity
(Junta literally is reduced to a kitsch art image sold to tourists), the
whole while defending any instrumentality in terms of the primeval
community's well-being.

Both *The Blue Light* and *Heart of Glass* speak a double discourse: on
the one hand, a despair over the incursion into nature and the robbing
of natural resources; on the other, though, an awareness that the
elemental has considerable use value, as the source and inspiration of
artistic vision, a source equally rich in its commercial potential. The
painter in *The Blue Light* captures the Alpine scapes as well as Junta
on his canvases; likewise, though, he encourages the villagers to put
the riches of the grotto to their use, which they do. The crystals, once
an object of enchantment and a cause of danger, become a means
to prosperity. Junta, viewed previously as a witch and an outsider,
becomes a local heroine, a figure incorporated in the village's lore,
serving to fascinate tourists and further spur the burg's economy. *Heart
of Glass* similarly involves the harnessing of nature and the capturing of
its secrets. The ruby glass serves both as the cornerstone of the industrialist's business and as the source of his intense reverence. The loss
of the formula therefore means more than just financial ruin. The
factory owner despairs without the aesthetic solace of the ruby glass

AURATIC
PoWeRS

and its auratic powers, feeling spiritually impoverished. We first gaze at him standing before a cabinet displaying the precious glass, a shrine of worship: "This splendor is now extinguished from the world," he laments. "What will protect me now from the evil of the universe?" The ruby glass alone can save him, he thinks. In the disorder of the firmament, only it provides sanctuary and peace.

If the artist in *The Blue Light* and the industrialist in *Heart of Glass* combine both aesthetic and pecuniary deliberations in their use of the elemental, what about the prophet Hias, the figure commonly viewed as Herzog's mouthpiece? The factory owner, we have seen, is someone more concerned with the aesthetics than the pragmatics of his livelihood. He, like Hias, is prescient, recognizing the ultimate catastrophe facing him and his like: "Will the future see the necessary fall of the factories, just as we see the ruined fortresses as a sign of inevitable change?" he queries, a foregone conclusion in the film, one echoing Hias's prophecies. Quite strikingly, the film's editing links the two through a series of matched cuts, an anomaly in a film otherwise so lacking in clear transitions.[10] In one shot we see Hias walking through the woods, disappearing behind a tree as the film cuts to a composition showing the industrialist similarly, his back facing us at the exact space in the frame. Later we glimpse Hias eating bread and cut to the industrialist at a table wiping his face with a napkin in a similar pose. More significantly, though, the initial meeting between the two takes place under an arched stairway. As Hias ascends the steps, his shadow blends with that of his double. Finally, we will last witness the factory owner and Hias together in a jail cell. The two are held responsible for the fire in the town, the former for setting the blaze, the latter for predicting it. The two come together in a remarkable way, imparting to the scene in the dark an eerie portance:

Hias: I don't see anymore! I want to go back to the woods! I want to see the woods! I want to see something again!

Factory Owner: And you don't want to see any people? I like you. You have a heart of glass.

The industrialist, who has just murdered a servant girl and endangered the lives of many others for the sake of his ruby glass, verbalizes a similar forsaking of the human in his counterpart. Herzog explains why this disregard for others is to be seen in a positive light:

*   If Hias does have this heart of glass, it means that he is translucent. It means that he cannot associate in such a warm way toward other

people because, as a prophet, or as one who looks over and through such things, he has to keep some distance from the people. And that makes him very lonely. He is very careful with his sentiments. He doesn't have many human relations with others. (Greenberg *et al.*, 1976, 57).

The meeting in the shadowy jail cell is not that of opposites, but rather of soul-mates, individuals whose visionary calling, be it as the priest of the ruby glass or the prophet of a new world, cause them to ignore human concerns. This exchange in the dark takes on symbolic importance when one views it in the light of Herzog's evolution as an artist. It becomes a psychodrama revolving around a creator whose triumph of willful vision increasingly comes at the price of ruthlessness and megalomania.

Both Riefenstahl's and Herzog's film, then, reflect on an art bought at a dire price. *The Blue Light* stylizes the rape of a landscape and a woman into a legend, providing an apologia for an ill-gotten prosperity. The crystals become money and Junta a popular story. The seemingly inexplicable is rendered as folk narrative, institutionalized as an object of spectacle and tourist fascination. *Heart of Glass* insists on art as a form of salvation in an excruciating world, be it the utterances of a poet-priest or the industrialist's fragile ruby glass. Both envision art as the sole possible redemption: Hias's poems not only foretell cataclysm, but also herald the birth of a new world. The factory owner sees the precious glass as a bulwark against the "disorder of the stars."

Both films contain a paradox: ostensibly anti-modernistic in their impetus, they nonetheless suggest images of a new order which leave behind the past. *The Blue Light,* as Kracauer has observed, laments the disenchantment of nature while at the same time championing the turn in the village's fortune. The "miraculous becomes merchandise"; a "rational solution" not completely undercut by the film, despite a lingering sense of melancholy at its conclusion (Kracauer, 1947, 259). *Heart of Glass* portrays the fall of factories as something inevitable, every bit as unavoidable as the collapse of feudalism once was. This, though, in no way accords to a dialectical view of history, but rather to a virulent fatalism, the feeling that an overarching destiny controls everything, one beyond all human intervention. (In this regard Hias's prophecies of the rise of Hitler and the holocaust make these events seem inevitable, natural cataclysms rather than historical phenomena – just as many postwar scholars in Germany couched their explanations of National Socialism in terms of natural rather than human catastrophe.) The seer, above all, looks ahead, to a new world, chastizing the villagers for their lack of foresight: "If nothing changes, you think it's a blessing." His final vision describes a man leaving the world of superstition for one of transcendence, breaking out with a crew to row to the end of the world to see if there really is an abyss. This is not a case where myth becomes enlightenment. The defiant act stands as one of will, not reason; it involves a reaching beyond, a heroism that may very well bring doom, for the dreamer and his crew.

Herzog and Riefenstahl share a romantic critique of the Enlightenment as a category-bound way of thinking which fetters experience, disenchants the world, vitiating rather than enriching. Both celebrate individual subjects in touch with a mysterious realm of the elemental, seeing them though as subservient to a larger destiny over which they have no ultimate control. In interviews (the directors spend a lot of time justifying their careers), Herzog and Riefenstahl both use the "jargon of authenticity" so incisively depicted by Adorno, an irrationalism valorizing certain absolutes and at the same time embedded in a discourse denying the powers of reason and explanation (cf. Herf, 1984, 13). Theirs is a cinematic art that puts aesthetics beyond morality and history. For this reason Riefenstahl has suffered the consequences of once placing her creative powers at the disposal of National Socialism, defending herself always in terms of an artistic vision she insists is utterly apolitical. Similarly, Herzog has frequently come under attack for allowing his personal fantasies to be realized at the risk of human life and limb. Denying the tools of modernity and his own instrumental aplomb, he encourages people to view him as a medieval artisan or, alternately, as an athlete with immense physical powers, underplaying the role of the apparatus with which he works as well as the highly technological character of his romanticism.

IV

Heart of Glass, for all its apparent elusiveness and seeming hypnotic appeal, operates along lines akin to what Jeffrey Herf has termed "reactionary modernism." It blends the rhetoric of nature and an embrace of the elemental characteristic of the romantic legacy with a forward-looking enthusiasm, a hope for a new order bringing purification and relief, a discourse quite prominent among conservative German intellectuals, poets, engineers, and politicians during the Weimar Republic and the Third Reich, a persuasion marked by what

Thomas Mann called "an affirmative stance toward progress combined with dreams of the past" (quoted in Herf, 1984, 2). No doubt, the visions of the future remain vague in *Heart of Glass* and do not fully coincide with the quite concrete utopia promulgated by National Socialism's powerful spokesman, Joseph Goebbels:

> We are all more or less romantics of a new German mood. The Reich of droning motors, grandiose industrial creations, an almost unlimited and unenclosed space which we must populate to preserve the best qualities of our *Volk* – is the Reich of our romanticism. (Herf, 1984, 196)

Heart of Glass proves to be a disturbing film, one in which Herzog leaves behind his Rousseau-tinged defense of untouched nature and his fanatic desire to combat the civilizing forces that ravage and pervert, imposing a *Gleichschaltung* on the heterogeneity of existence.

Hias may correspond to Herzog's preferred self-image. The seer, nevertheless, becomes indistinguishable from his double, the industrialist. If one looks closely (more closely than Herzog might like, no doubt), their merging betrays a larger development, the evolution of Herzog from someone whose art once allowed nature to speak its most expressive language while the filmmaker looked on sympathetically to a director who increasingly has intervened in the shaping of nature, manipulating landscapes and foreign populations for the sake of his films, no matter what the cost, an aesthetic mode beyond all normative considerations. Herzog clearly continues to cast himself in the role of the visionary speaking the language of metaphysical despair. The more apposite image, though, especially in light of his recent work, would be that of the young man possessed by his quest for the ruby glass, an individual who will stop at nothing to find the art that alone can justify existence and offer salvation.

Heart of Glass, then, stands at the middle of an evolution whose beginning can be best essentialized by the short *Precautions Against Fanatics* and whose ultimate consequences are borne out in *Fitzcarraldo.* The early short, anything but a simple lark without deeper meaning, shows horses being abused by various trainers. These race-track figures claim to have the animals' best interests in mind, but in fact they intrude on natural functions, forcing the creatures to walk in endless circles, to serve their keepers' selfish purposes, to swallow drugs and consume large amounts of garlic. An old man with one arm constantly invades the frame, declaring himself the true spokesman for the horses; he alone understands them. In the shots where he stands next to the animals, they do not register the uneasiness and anxiety we see when they appear next to their keepers. In essence, the film champions the natural against its tamers, preferring the fanaticism of the eccentric old man who speaks a broad Bavarian to the mercenary instrumentalism of the trainers. The self-proclaimed protector lashes out at a karate artist who shatters pieces of wood ("He's wrecking everything!"); in the same way Herzog eschews the partitioning of the natural. (He has always been an enemy of montage filmmaking and its fragmentations.) The film celebrates a directness that rather than shape or stylize reality allows it to exist unencumbered.

Increasingly, Herzog's films have moved from this regard for the special and the isolated, from a will to represent the marginal and the maltreated, a desire to explore the undisclosed and the suppressed. Instead he has come to intrude upon and often abuse those very tenuous and vulnerable entities he otherwise so readily used to champion. From the beginning of his career, there have been controversies about his treatment of filmic subjects, imbroglios about the midgets in *Even Dwarfs Started Small* and Bruno S. in *Every Man for Himself and God Against All*, protests from Dutch citizens, who once suffered German occupation troops, regarding Herzog's invasion of Delft during the making of *Nosferatu*. Repeatedly Herzog has told interviewers about moments during film production where he has confronted people who threatened the projects, promising anyone perdition if they got in the way, claiming that his film was more important than either of their lives. This triumph of aesthetics over all other considerations has thus far found its most chilling expression in the jungle drama, *Fitzcarraldo*.

Here there is no distinction between the visionary and the entrepreneur (just as is the case in the documentaries *God's Angry Man* and *Huie's Sermon* whose subjects combine a messianic calling with a mercenary zeal). Fitzcarraldo imagines bringing Caruso to the jungle, a dream he seeks to impose on a population with other more pressing needs, a design realized at the cost of exploiting nature, expropriating another culture's territory, and commanding native labor. Herzog valorizes this quest without reservation – just as his desire to risk "everything for new images" (Blank and Bogan, 1984, 51) took precedence over all other considerations. The director who has so consistently grieved over the ruin wreaked by western civilization on nature, the mourner of "embarrassed landscapes,"[11] virtually devastated a vast stretch of jungle for the sake of his "central metaphor," the transport of a ship "over a practically impossibly steep hill"

(Blank and Bogan, 1984, 51). Herzog and Fitzcarraldo became one and the same; the film spawned another film, the gripping documentary directed by Les Blank and Maureen Gosling, *Burden of Dreams,* as well as several books. The documentary chronicles the creator's battle with nature, his use of machines and technicians to overcome the challenges posed by the wild terrain. The protector of the elemental appears as a frenzied spirit who eschews the "obscenity" of the jungle – much as the industrialist in *Heart of Glass* could not bear the disorder of the firmament. Nature in the Amazon setting, claimed the director in a stunning confession, "is vile and base. I wouldn't see anything erotic here. I would see fornication and asphyxiation and choking and fighting for survival and growing and just rotting away" (Blank and Bogan, 1984, 56). Combatting nature itself, Herzog likewise endangered the lives of the natives hired to pull the boat over the hill, even despite the counsel of specialists and co-workers. In the words of Les Blank: "It's damned weird to have people risking their lives to fulfill a mad Bavarian's impossible fantasies" (Blank, 1984, 110).

In the end, Herzog's triumph (Fitzcarraldo's boat does make it over the hill) amounts to a victory of the instrumental over the elemental, one though that underplays the technical rationality that enabled the act – for we do not see the tractor whose skillful deployment allowed the feat; that, of course, would have been out of keeping with the film's historical setting. Herzog's romanticism relies strongly on modern technology. The "central metaphor" indeed depends on the "droning motors" Goebbels spoke of for its realization. The visionary as instrumental thinker: Herzog and his fictional stand-ins, Fitzcarraldo and the industrialist, sacrifice everything for the purposes of an obsessive aesthetics.

Heart of Glass presages the triumph of instrumental will in Herzog's romanticism, artistic vision bought at a dear price. The director has always privileged aesthetics over politics, setting himself aside from mundane temporality and staid tradition. Read carefully, *Heart of Glass* replicates, both in the film narrative and in the story of its making, a typical Herzogian situation where process and final product mirror each other and become inextricably bound – a paradigm outlined in Walter Benjamin's famous essay, "The Work of Art in the Age of Mechanical Reproducibility." When aesthetics become the ultimate standard, human beings are reduced to cult worshippers, the cinematic apparatus to a producer of ritual values. The fatal result of such a consummate "l'art pour l'art" persuasion is, of course, violence and destruction: the images of fire and murder in *Heart of Glass,* the endangered lives and embarrassed landscapes during the making of *Fitzcarraldo*. The creator's art is fueled by a "steely romanticism," one containing a depth of feeling and an equal hardness of being, a meeting of religious fervor and a brutal means-end rationality (cf. Herf, 1984, 195). The artist-leader demands total fealty from his subjects, seeking to transfix everyone around him, calling on people not only to partake of, but indeed to share, his vision. A psychoanalyst present on the set of *Heart of Glass* unwittingly summarized the dynamics at work here:

> Herzog makes films. He does that the only way he knows how. He turns himself into an instrument – the man disappears. This instrument is what is necessary to run the machine that constructs the film. It is all very plain to see. (Greenberg *et al.*, 1976, 39)

What is equally plain to see is how at times Herzog, for the sake of his films, has reduced others to cogs in a larger construction driven by a feverish instrumentalism.

Notes

I am grateful to the University of California Irvine Committee on Research whose generous grant in part provided the support enabling this essay to be written during early fall of 1985.

1 Herzog does mention two works with a related impulse, however: Morley Markson's *The Sad Story of Zeno, the Fool*, a film "shot with a theater group from a lunatic asylum in Canada," and Jean Rouch's *The Possessed Masters*, in which "some Africans in Ghana, after taking heavy hallucinogenic potions, act out in a mountain retreat the arrival of the English Governor and the Queen."
2 Herzog is moved by the sense of wonder O'Toole feels when he watches the director's films. "I'm glad that you say this, because you're some kind of audience that I have always wished for. I had always wished that things that touched me very deeply would come across somehow" (O'Toole, 1979, 41).
3 See O'Toole (1979, 41): "This kind of academic thinking and academic behavior that you find on campuses is so, so bad or horrifying because there's a profound absence of pain." See also Kent (1977).

4 Cf Jaspers, 1955, 51–2: "In order to see most clearly into what is true and real, into what is no longer fastened to any particular thing or colored by any particular atmosphere, we must push into the widest range of the possible. And then we experience the following: everything that is an object for us, even though it be the greatest, is still always within another, is not yet all. Wherever we arrive, the horizon which includes the attained itself goes further and forces us to give up any final rest. We can secure no standpoint from which a closed whole of Being would be surveyable, nor any sequence of standpoints through whose totality Being would be given even indirectly."

5 The volume, interestingly enough, only appeared in English, the language spoken by Herzog's most enthusiastic audiences.

6 The notable exceptions remain McCormick and Aufderheide.

7 The standard work on the *Heimatfilme* of the postwar era is Höfig.

8 The film's locations include the United States (Wyoming, Alaska, Utah), Bavaria, Switzerland, and Ireland.

9 *Der Fall Herzog,* a chronicle of Herzog's exchanges with Peruvian Indios during the pre-production phase of *Fitzcarraldo,* appeared as a special issue of the periodical, *Vierte Welt Aktuell,* a journal sponsored by the Society for Endangered Peoples, the German section of "Survival International."

10 Cf. Greenberg *et al.,* 1976, 69, where Herzog proclaims: "The rhythm of a film is never established in the editing room. The directors who rely on editing are cowards. Rhythm is made in the shooting – that is filmmaking. It is what you shoot, the images. Editing merely puts it altogether."

11 See O'Toole, 1979, 48: "What have we done to our landscapes? We have *embarrassed* landscapes." Cf. Blank and Bogan, 1984, 147, where Maureen Gosling expresses her amazement at Herzog's despoiling of the Amazon scape during the making of *Fitzcarraldo:* "I couldn't help but be appalled by the devastation of the clearing. The gray sky and drizzle made it feel even more depressing. It was a devastated area, a mess of felled trees and mud. It looked like the beginnings of a highway being built. All of my environmental consciousness surfaced, and I wondered if Werner himself had stopped to think when he was pre-planning the film what it really would look like and what such a project would require of the landscape."

Works cited

Achternbusch, Herbert (1978) *Die Atlantikschwimmer*, Frankfurt am Main, Suhrkamp.

Baker, Rob (1977) "Herzog vs. Truffaut," *Soho Weekly News* (November 13).

Blank, Les and James Bogan (eds) (1984) *Burden of Dreams: Screenplay, Journals, Photographs*, Berkeley CA, North Atlantic.

Carroll, Noël (1985) "Herzog, Presence, and Paradox," *Persistence of Vision*, 2 (Fall), 30–40.

Corliss, Richard (1977) "Cannes Quiz," *New Times* (June 24).

Corrigan, Timothy (1983) *New German Film: The Displaced Image*, Austin, University of Texas Press.

Enzensberger, Ulrich (1985) "KZ-Zigeuner tanz' mit mir," *Konkret* (February), 12–17.

Fell, John (1979) *"Heart of Glass,"* Film Quarterly, 32(3), 54–5.

Forbes, Jill (1977) *"Heart of Glass,"* Sight & Sound, 46(4), 255–6.

Greenberg, Alan, H. Achternbusch and W. Herzog (1976) *Heart of Glass*, Munich, Skellig.

Herf, Jeffrey (1984) *Reactionary Modernism: Technology, Culture, and Politics in Weimar and the Third Reich*, Cambridge, Cambridge University Press.

Höfig, Willi (1973) *Der deutsche Heimatfilm 1947–1960*, Stuttgart, Enke.

Hopf, Florian (1975) "Die Filme gehören zu dem, was unsere Mitte ausmacht," *Frankfurter Rundschau* (August 21).

Jaspers, Karl (1955) *Reason and Existence*, trans. William Earle, New York, Noonday.

Kent, Leticia (1977) "Werner Herzog: 'Film Is Not the Art of Scholars, But of Illiterates'," *New York Times* (September 11).

Kracauer, Siegfried (1947) *From Caligari to Hitler: A Psychological History of the German Film*, Princeton, Princeton University Press.

Mathes, Werner (1985) "Gesuch der alten Dame," *Stern* (March 21).

McCormick, Ruth and Pat Aufderheide (1978) "Werner Herzog's *Heart of Glass* – pro and contra," *Cineaste*, 8 (4), 32–4.

Metz, Christian (1982) *The Imaginary Signifier*, trans. Celia Britton *et al.*, Bloomington IN, Indiana University Press.

O'Toole, Lawrence (1979) "'I Feel That I'm Close to the Center of Things'," *Film Comment*, 15 (6), 34–9.

Viseur, Raimund de le and Werner Schmidmaier (1977) *"Playboy* Interview: Werner Herzog," *Playboy* (German edition) (January).

Walsh, Gene (ed.) (1979) *"'Images at the Horizon'*: a workshop with

Werner Herzog," conducted by Roger Ebert, Chicago, Facets Multimedia Center (pamphlet).

Wetzel, Kraft (1979) "Kommentierte Filmographie," in Peter W. Jansen and Wolfram Schütte (eds), *Werner Herzog,* Munich, Hanser, 87–144.

Wiedemann, Horst (1976) "Hypnose als Mittel der Stilisierung: Ein Interview mit Werner Herzog," *Medium,* 6 (12), 27–8.

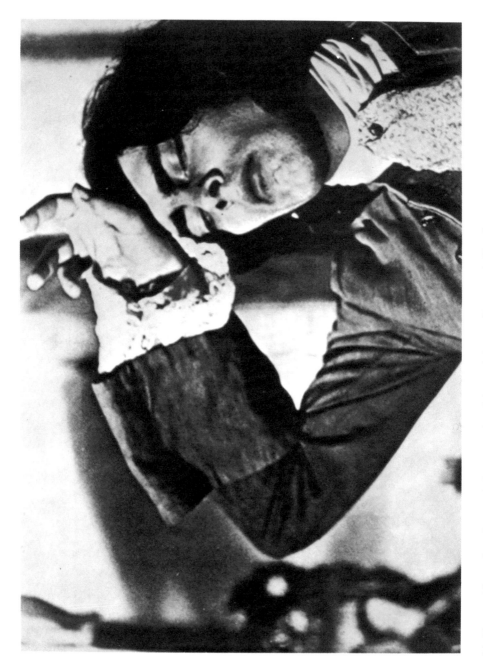

11 The artifice of reality and the tragedy of forgetfulness (*Heart of Glass*)

11

Comprehending appearances: Werner Herzog's ironic sublime

Alan Singer

I can't believe that God created everything out of nothing as you say.

Kaspar Hauser, in *The Mystery of Kaspar Hauser*

Bewildered by the spectacle of an infinitely diversified nature, Kaspar Hauser articulates the mystery of Werner Herzog's most enigmatic images. Like the mystery of Kaspar's God, Herzog's mise-en-scène presents the spectacle of a sumptuously particularized reality that, by its very exorbitance, seems to elude conceptualization and so to deny knowledge of its origins – the only knowledge that might anchor our faith in a world of appearances. The meaning of Herzog's images hovers, in each carefully composed particular, like the pantheist God. It gives the inference of a whole that is more than the multiplicity of its parts. Indeed, God, in the context of Kaspar's disbelief, is precisely the name of the desire for knowledge of origins that transcends the faculties of our desire and the world of sensuous mediations that desire inhabits. In the intellectual tradition of German idealism, Herzog's own inescapable cultural origin, this desire for the knowledge of super-sensible origins speaks definitively through the category of the sublime. Sublimity marks the limit of the human, and therefore the threshold of universality and transcendental immediacy. For this reason sublimity has been the irresistible categorical temptation of reviewers and critics alike who have sought to place Herzog securely in the tradition of German romanticism, heralding in his films a rebirth of the visionary imagination of Schiller, Goethe, even Heidegger, and thereby making of Herzog's otherwise anarchic mise-en-scène a time-honored certainty out of time.

And it is indeed tempting to see Herzog as the mystic seer of sublime intuitions, since his mise-en-scène is always most compelling insofar as it seems to represent more than it can show: a ravishing white water cataract is revealed to be a flow of clouds through Bavarian mountain valleys (*Heart of Glass*); a figure animated by heat waves teases the camera with a point of focus it can approach only as a distortion (*Fata Morgana*); a telephoto collapsing of space renders the descent of a line of Pizarro's soldiers from an Amazonian mountaintop as a static infinity of space (*Aguirre*). Such are the touchstones of Herzogian vision: images that must be seen through detours of perception.

Despite these mirage-like taunts of the representable, with all their promise of a transcendent point of view, I want to suggest that it is actually the threshold of sublimity itself that is the operative illusion of Herzog's filmic sleight of hand. For sublimity denotes a perspective that is too manifestly the inverse of the conditions of our viewing his films, no matter how much Herzog indulges it as the myth of our viewing. In other words, Herzog's mystic worlds finally always reveal the conditions of their viewing as their most oracular truth. We will see that Herzog is after all careful to particularize so elaborately what we see in his films that its adamant pretext of being something else never entirely escapes the immediate sensuous register. Perhaps only our longing for sublimity keeps us from seeking what is more obtrusively there as cinematic calculation and the refusal of unmediated vision. More importantly, I believe that the error of reading the text of the sublime into Herzog's films is that it would eclipse history from the screen. Despite the riddling imagery of his films, Herzog is emphatically not a transcendental philosopher but rather a narrative artist committed to history as a vital form of cultural production. History for Herzog is manifestly a condition to be reckoned with rationally, not a nightmare to be sweated out if we are truly to know our own mind with our own minds. This is not to say that Herzog's artistic practice is linear or empirical. On the contrary, his films are radically ambiguous in their temporal disjunctures and narrative ellipses. The montage opening of *Kaspar Hauser*, a cryptic juxtaposition of a face, a boat, a swan, deprives the viewer of the grammatical cues for ordering linear narrative priorities. The spatial elasticity of the desert landscape in *Fata Morgana* dislocates the viewer from the consoling authority of a static viewpoint. The dissociated images and affect of the actors in *Heart of*

Glass give the film an alienating disjointedness that threatens to engulf us in the characters' aphasic sensibility rather than securing the objectifying distance of curative analysis. Nevertheless, my point will be that these stylistic markers of Herzog's films are too simply read as a restless negation of time and its constraints (hence the threshold of sublimity), rather than as a critical perspective on the habits of human temporality. The thrust of this essay will be to show how these films justify the difficulties of inhabiting human time without the delusive idealism of sublimity that narrative tradition has fashioned as the audience's refuge from historical consequence.

I

Before I discuss the relevance of the sublime to the kind of history that Herzog makes with his films, it might prove most expedient to acknowledge that the sublime has its own history and briefly to rehearse the distinction between the Burkean and Kantian theories of the sublime that have shaped that history for the modern sensibility. I believe that it is a distinction in one sense without a difference. By emphasizing the similarity between Burke and Kant, I hope to reveal the difference between Herzog's mise-en-scène and that of more devoutly romantic artists.

Kant's most concise definition of the sublime is his most emphatic one: "an object [of nature] the representation of which determines the consciousness to think the unattainability of nature as a sensory representation of ideas" (Kant, 1968, 108). This definition establishes a fundamental principle: the sublime is the mind's limit, a threshold of transcendent knowledge. In the Kantian sublime, Nature inspires the faculty of imagination to image its own failure. Thus through failure does the mind discover its congruity with the law of its supersensible Nature. The failure of imagination is represented effectively as the overparticularization of Nature, taxing the image-making faculty into a frenzy of activity that causes it to reflect upon its sheer mathematical insufficiency to the manifold of sensuous existence. By contrast, the Burkean sublime posits a nature so vast and powerful in its manifestations that it is effectively departicularized, registered in the mind only as a cognitive vacuum and ultimately devolving to a transfigurative terror (Burke, 1958, 69). Despite their undeniable epistemological differences, in both cases the sublime postulates metaphysical need in a common representational mode, if only insofar as all representational modes are judged spectacularly inadequate to express the

[handwritten margin notes: "APHASIC SENSIBILITY"; "too easily READ AS A Restless Negation of time AND its CONSTRAINTS (Hence the threshold of sublimity) Rather than AS A CRITICAL perspective ON the HABITS of HUMAN temporality"; "Diff's BURKE + KANT's sublime"]

sublime. In both the Kantian and Burkean sublimes representation is a problem overcome by the mind surpassing its own faculties, dissolving the bonds of temporality in the discovery of a timeless unity that needs no representation because it needs no thought or image to animate it.

On the contrary, representation is the problematic not the problem of the filmmaker in general and of Herzog in particular. The mystique of Herzog's images is, I believe, clarified in the understanding that representation necessarily expresses the constraints of its own mediation in a Herzog film. If the Kantian sublime may be described as an overparticularization of the sensuous world and the Burkean sublime as a departicularization of the sensuous world – both convergent in the eliding of temporal contingencies – it may make sense to speak of the unique mise-en-scène of Herzog's films as constituting a reparticularization of the sensuous. Herzog's films present a reciprocal consciousness of temporal contingency as an artifact of mind and of mind as the conditionality of time. Such an aesthetic effectively vitiates the questions of the adequacy of mind to Nature (which the concept of the sublime was conceived to answer) by accepting the mediate status of all such reflections and thereby positing the inescapability of mediated vision as the proper scope of human will.

Nowhere is Herzog's grasp of time more inimical to the atemporality and ahistoricality of the sublime than in *Fata Morgana*. Here the myth of Genesis is read over the soundtrack by Lotte Eisner (herself a legendary embodiment of film history) as a lament for the history of a civilization that has lost touch with its timeless origins. Time is the proverbial curse of post-Edenic life. The spoken text gestures toward origins that have been betrayed by technological progress and indulges the romantic dream of revoking history in the access of a timeless universality. The intonation of the narrator's voice is poised regretfully over scenes of natural despoliation, the brutal superimposition of culture on nature. But this text, legitimating timeless Edenic beginnings, significantly gives way in the course of the film to two successive texts of beginning, self-evidently caught within the very snares of the temporal succession they belie. While the three voice-over texts announced in the prologue of the film as "Genesis," "Paradise," and "The Golden Age" adhere to a strict Christian teleology (the texts, all cognate forms of eschatology, are a mélange of pre-Colombian myths, Judeo-Christian scripture, and fictional tableaux devised by Herzog and his co-scenarist), it is a teleology without an end – in other words, an endless (because recurrent) beginning that makes a mockery of the nostalgia it provokes. It portends a ceaseless engagement with the very temporal order it professes to overthrow. The first frames of the film, showing an airplane land repeatedly, each time prevented by a subversive jump cut from touching ground, graphically belie the eschatology of the creation myth that would return us full circle to a timeless beginning. Ironically, the tedium of abortive montage is our most scrupulous awareness of the ineluctable passage of historical time.

In addition to turning beginnings into a self-conscious trope of beginnings, the film's scenes of cultural despoliation rendered in static long shots are conspicuously troped by the technology of the camera that produces them. The aerial tracking shots, which constitute a kind of formal armature for this film, transform the natural Saharan landscape into a man-made spectacle, imposing a motion and a shape that animate a mysterious life there. While the static long shot seems to obey a naturalistic imperative, the tracking shot possesses its own representational animus.

So the moving camera, in a sense, recapitulates the history that the voice-over text laments. At first we cannot be sure what we are viewing. Because initially the land, seen from above, is devoid of familiar earthly particulars, sifted into abstraction by the tracking motion of the camera, we are compelled to look beyond the strange surface the land presents for its meaning. Thus the natural becomes the pretext of metaphorical speculation. Perhaps the strangeness of the land represented by the tracking shots will reveal its coded resemblance to the lost particulars of the world imaged in long shots. But the obtrusive length of these tracking shots finally compels us to reconcile ourselves to the lost particulars of sand, rock, winding road, as irreducible blurs, radiating perspectives, and geometrical symmetries. There is no return to an original motionless moment wherein what we saw in static long shots and what we see in fluid tracking shots is recognizably the same thing. The earthly and the heavenly will be neither analogized nor allegorized to our satisfaction. Rather than reminding us of the static vistas of the land that precede them (and thus denying any metaphorical relation to them), the tracking shots finally represent merely tracking shots. The camera produces an apparent abstraction that concretizes in the pure technical autonomy of the medium, that is to say, in the mediations the camera constitutes as our perception. The camera thus assumes priority over what it records. It reparticularizes and anchors us in the transformations it performs, in the mechanisms of the technological history that is decried in each segment of narration. In *Fata Morgana* the tracking shot constrains all meaning to the mediational

contingencies of the desire for meaning instead of serving the exposi-
tional function of what is there to be seen. Form becomes desire.

It is of course nothing new for a filmmaker to use the camera as a
bricoleur would reassembling the sensuous particulars of nature to produce a second-order reality. But in *Fata Morgana*, where scenes of
native culture depict the recycling of technological hardware into primitive domestic shelters, the parallelism of tracking shots that "recycle"
the natural imagery of the desert into abstract geometry gives an ironic
lie to the narrator's nostalgic wish for a return to a moment of cultural
innocence. In the context of this visual logic we can no longer believe
that culture ever proffered immediate experience, that there ever was a
time before culture. The wish for a transcendent time is thus deflected
to its own too manifestly apparent means: the forms of filmic narrative.
In *Fata Morgana*, the land is neither departicularized in the abstraction
of nostalgic dreaming nor overparticularized in the literal vastness of
the desert horizon that would thereby be rendered unthinkable.
Herzog's vistas are deliberately not a release from the rigors of contemplation that is the seductive pleasure of the sublime, but are ever more
engrossing visual situations that compel attention to their unique
formal determinations. By contrast with the pleasure of sublimity, these
determinations might even be described as the exigencies of an
inescapable historical will/knowledge insofar as the traces of their
production are integral to their compositional order and intelligibility.
In *Fata Morgana* we are constrained to the order of human experiences
because we are bound to the forms of narrative time.

II

I do not wish to ignore the fact that Herzog's films extravagantly indulge
the wish for the transcendent vision so wistfully evoked by the voice-
over texts of *Fata Morgana*. Thematically, in one way or another all of
Herzog's films are quests after a redemptive cultural innocence: in
Stroszek the company of German pilgrims sets forth in pursuit of an
unspoiled America; in *Aguirre, The Wrath of God*, culture, humiliated
by nature, reverts to an animal innocence; in *Heart of Glass* the timeless lucidity of prognostication is the taunt behind the social disorder
of historical time; in *Nosferatu* an inhuman being suffers from its own
entanglement with the forms of human knowledge and desire as does a
beast in a cage. Nevertheless, a closer inspection will show how the
myths of transcendence proffered in each of these films are rendered
radically incongruous with the spectatorial position the films produce

All of Herzog's films are quests for a redemptive cultural innocence

in the viewing. It is the viewer's knowledge of the cultural apparatus of the production of meaning that becomes preeminent in Herzog's mise-en-scène, as though to see the film is first and foremost for Herzog to comprehend the contingencies of filmic vision.

So although each of the films thematically approaches the threshold of sublime knowledge, such knowledge proves to be too uncritical for the interpretive perspectives imposed by Herzog's exacting formalism. Inevitably the doom toward which the protagonists' aspirations for transcendence leads them devolves to a conceptual threat hanging over the aching heads of the audience who must struggle against the dream of mindlessly seductive images if they are to preserve a view of their own mind. The orchestration of this interpretive predicament in Herzog's films acknowledges a crisis of representation recurrent in modern art movements obsessed with the adequation of mind to world. But unlike the dream of sublimity, which excites our desire to go beyond human terms in order adequately to represent human desires, Herzog seems to presume a need for making desire itself the definitive limit of the human. This crisis of representation is faced by Herzog in his often-cited statement that "we live in a society that has no adequate images" (Walsh/Ebert, 1979, 143). For Herzog the possibility of representation is thwarted most belligerently by the impoverished knowledge of our own situation. Presuming the mystical trajectory of Herzog's films, it has been easy for critics to read this statement as a protest against the historical imposition of false cultural masks upon an organic human nature. Such is the legendary credo of the romantic artist who perennially decries the inadequacy of our ephemeral images to the eternal forms of existence symbolized in nature. But I believe that the sense of Herzog's statement, that we must construe from the formal imperatives of the films themselves, is that existence must be made adequate to our faculties for representing it in the first place. Thus Herzog's remarks constitute not a mournful lament for lost worlds but the pursuit of a more contented habitation of the mind that constructs them.

Indeed, Herzog's widely acknowledged debt to German expressionism might be said to express precisely his profound appreciation of the expression of the human in all manifest forms of life. Despite its alien look, expressionism most convincingly reveals how all our worldly forms are marked by human desire in the appropriative will of narrative representation. Expressionism after all was originally the work of designers (not theatrical directors or dramatists) like Hermann Warm, who believed that a film should be "a drawing come to life," as if to reestablish the aesthetic principles of the medium on grounds inimical to photographic realism. We can never forget that the objectivity of nature was the cinema's first pretext of truthfulness. But the truth of expressionism is the warp as well as the work of perspective. The ideal of the drawing come to life consecrates the habits of human perception canonized by the precursor art of painting, thus supplanting the pro-filmic with the purely filmic as the privileged representational register of the medium.

Certainly by contrast with expressionism, the aesthetic of the sublime would make a tawdry metaphor of human perspective by accepting with a transformative humility the limits of human will or desire as merely the inverse measure of a superhuman order, only apparent in excess of the powers of representation. Herzog vigorously combats any such vapid romanticism that would predicate the visionary upon the nullification of the faculties of imaginative vision. If Herzog is a romantic then he is a Coleridgean not a Kantian one, scrupulously sidestepping the conceptual abyss of sublimity in order to preserve the human animus of all sacred things that come out of the abyss as artifacts of imaginative activity. Coleridge's well-known bifurcation of imagination into primary and secondary aspects was of course a shrewd cooption of the transcendent idealism of Kantian sublimity within the pragmatic activity of mind that he called the "esemplastic" or combinatory power of imagination (Coleridge, 1907). So I would agree with Lotte Eisner when she says that German expressionism has its truest avatar in Werner Herzog. But mindful that the visionary rhetoric of expressionism is often mistaken for the threshold of transcendence, I will emphasize that its memory is consecrated in Herzog's films by a devotion to, not an abandonment of, the arc of human perspectives enclosing the world as hermetically as it encloses the sound-stage artifice of a film like *Caligari*. Herzog's expressionism is visionary, but it is a vision that meticulously limns the transformative agency of human imagination.

Indeed, Herzog is even more ambitious than his expressionist precursors. While the expressionism of *Caligari*, for example, was the privilege of the subjective point of view in a medium otherwise deeply invested in the objects of the physical world, Herzog makes the stylization of his films less a function of character point of view (as in the tradition of the later expressionists) than the expression of the viewer's own conditions of knowledge. Thus the artifice of reality is not excused thematically but remains an unapologetic formal element of the film, irreducible to the demands of objective verisimilitude or to the bias for the purely thematic film criticism that verisimilitude has served since André Bazin's famous purge of expressionist motives. The effect is less ornament and design than a scrupulous self-awareness of the historical character of all subjective descriptions. Insofar as artifice, more candidly than nature, discloses the conditions of its existence, the transparency with which Herzog's images reveal their own conceptual ground may be said to express their historical contingency. We will see that expressionism is thus made profoundly material and historical rather than spiritual and subjective in Herzog's films. Perhaps in this way Herzog escapes the fatal self-trivialization of the late expressionist directors, whose willingness to rationalize the excesses of self-conscious artifice as an allegory of psychological pathos quickly devolved to claustrophobic solipsism for the artist and arid formalism for the audience. But some examples are needed before we can take these claims much further.

Herzog's most passionate indictment of our impoverished image-bank occurs appropriately enough in the context of a discussion of his avowedly "experimental" film, *Heart of Glass*. In this film, Herzog directly confronts the question of human history that I have been arguing is an earnest subtext of all his work. Herzog himself explains that his designation of *Heart of Glass* as experimental entails the discipline of a rational self-knowledge rather than the mere promulgation of a new and virtuoso style:

> At the present time, I think that we do not know very much about the process of vision itself. We know so very little about it and with this kind of experimental work that I have been describing we might soon be able to learn a bit more. (Walsh/Ebert, 1979, 21)

If experimental film can be a self-education, a mode of self-production, it is in that way a striking analogue for the very historical awareness denied to the characters' consciousness in *Heart of Glass*. Their tragedy is their forgetfulness of the human dimensions of their lived reality, created as it is in the blood-hued image of their own mortal needs: the ruby glass.

In *Heart of Glass*, the crisis of the Bavarian mountain culture deprived of its livelihood in the glassworks is the crisis of all cultures cut off not from the natural genius of the organic world, the deity of the sublime, but from their own anthropological roots. Trapped within an historically uncaused universe they are the prisoners of a metaphysical faith. So, unable to re-create the glass that gave the semblance of substance to their world, they are obliged to transcend it. The young master of the glassworks accordingly exclaims that "the confusion of the stars makes my head ache." For him the pain of man is best explained by deflections from the consciousness that pricks him. Deprived of the secret of the ruby glass, all of the villagers in Herzog's film are deprived of their own history, of an origin and a fate.

Yet it will become clear that the viewer of Herzog's film is meticulously compelled to see that this is a ritual deprivation rather than an ordination of fate, as the villagers themselves must believe in order to solace their sense of hopelessness before the frowning god of ill fortune. After all, the secret of the glass has been deliberately made sacred by the consignment of the formula to the family of the works manager Mühlbeck. By removing the source of their cultural identity from their own consciousness, they have hallowed their existence with a spiritual aura and purchased belief at the price of historical existence. When the secret of the glass is deemed to be inaccessible through the devices of human rationality, through lived history, it is approached through that famous parody of rational history, rationalization, the familiar animus of all symbol, prognostication, and myth. Thus the seer Hias portends the fires of apocalypse in the flickering afterglow of the red glass. The master wants to divine the secret of the glass by dumping it in the lake and fostering its likeness as a watery mirror of his desire. In the end the master sacrifices the servant Ludmilla out of faith that the glass can be reconstituted in the likeness of the virgin's blood.

The distinctive mark of Herzog's conceptualization here, however, is that the characters' mythification of human circumstances comes, in the course of the film, to reflect the affinity rather than the difference between the worlds of reason and superstition, science and magic, the physical and the metaphysical, mocking any world view that is predicated on these abiding humanist dualisms. The underlying logic of the cultural predicament thus anatomized makes it inevitable that the gestures of compensatory mythmaking that express the pathology of the characters (their lack of rapport with the world of actuality) belie the natural order that they are seeking to redeem through myth. For the viewer, the myth and the historical fact of the glass are both made intelligible as emphatically human acts. The viewer sees how the glass has been deliberately enshrined by human forgetfulness: forgetfulness of the formula for making the glass and of the symbolic longing that the glass reflects in its mythification. Both forgetfulness and mythic remembrance manifestly express the same human desire for a synthesis of experience otherwise mired in a self-perpetuating dualism.

Like the paradox of the sublime, the cult of the ruby glass derives its power for the social community from making the limits of human knowledge in the physical world the vehicle for a displacement of human aspirations to a spiritual register – so that in the mythic world of apocalyptic fate, the inability to produce the glass may be redeemed as a superworldly knowledge, a transcendence of limits. The inhospitality of the one world is thus conquered in the displacement of desire to another. This is of course nothing more than the pattern of all metaphysical belief. Herzog's innovation in the exposition of this anthropological cliché is that the metaphysical leap of the characters is scrupulously denied to the film viewer. Herzog's visual compositions constitute a complex refusal of the supersensible realm aimed at by the mythic projections of his characters. Consequently, the non-narrative, ecstatically detailed images of natural spectacle that seem so vividly to adumbrate the fulfillment of mythic longing in this film resolutely return the viewer to contemplation of the representational devices that reveal them rather than to the putative world of visionary transcendence that would enfold them. Herzog makes such otherwise mystical images a tell-tale trace of human cognition rather than a release from the responsibilities of cognitive attention.

But this is perhaps not immediately clear. The irony of Herzog's film depends on its apparent complicity in the values it discredits. For both Burke and Kant, the most awesome testimonials of the sublime were manifest in those forces of nature that were too great to be compassed simultaneously by both sensuous and conceptual orders. Kant speaks of an incommensurability of the faculty of apprehension (anchoring us to sensuous spectacle) and the faculty of comprehension (which totalizes experience and conceptually frees the human from the natural):

> For when apprehension has gone so far that the partial representations of sensuous intuition at first apprehended begin to vanish in the imagination while this ever proceeds to the apprehension of others, then it loses as much on one side as it gains on the other; and in comprehension there is a maximum beyond which it cannot go. (Kant, 1951, 90)

In *Heart of Glass,* the forces of nature are conjured in ever more paradoxical spectacles of physical splendor. The episodic narrative action is organized around recurrent images of nature that by their excessively contradictory appearance elude immediate recognition: clouds appear as a torrent of water coursing through mountain gorges;

glacial hot springs shimmer with the unnatural vividness of a pastel color scheme; a view of coastal islands resembles the tracked puddles of a human pathway; waterfalls superimposed on a white matte surface are reminiscent of the painter's canvas. Each image seems to posit the incommensurability of appearance and meaning. In each case, then, there is an economy of gain and loss that evokes the sublime as our apprehension increasingly fails to satisfy our desire for narrative comprehension.

In effect, these images of "artificial nature" reproduce for the viewer the mind of the characters in the film, but significantly as an artifact for the viewer's scrutiny rather than as a reflection of the character's subjective viewpoint. The trance-like gaze of the characters in the film reflects their loss of a world that was in turn always only a reflection of their need for it. The characters in *Heart of Glass* are alienated through their reification of the glass world, which is only their forgetfulness of their complicity in its fragile order. By contrast it is precisely such forgetfulness that is precluded in the viewer by the insistent knowledge of how his or her own alienation from the cryptic non-narrative images is nonetheless continuous with an understanding of those images. This knowledge is articulated by the filmmaker's foregrounding of the very contextual ambiguities of imaging that complicates our perception of it. For example, the clouds seen as white water are a refraction of our habitual eye. The object we see is simply a product of a resemblance between water and clouds that is conjured by the camera through time-lapse photography. In this way, the subjectivity of the viewer's gaze is conspicuously constitutive of the object. Similarly, the image of glaciers emblazoned in "hot" colors that resemble sound-stage papier mâché taunts the cues of realism with an implausible reality. The image of cascading waterfalls conspicuously presented as a substitute for paint on canvas, by virtue of the white matte over which they are projected, further blurs the boundary between representation and its object. In every case, what we see is revealed to be a product of the contingency of our enabling perspectives.

I have alleged that the sensuous details of Herzog's nature imagery constitute something like a reparticularization (rather than a departicularization or an overparticularization) in their representation of nature as artifactual. As Herzog's most impressive images are revelatory of the mediations that disclose them, they are made emphatically textual, constructively implicated in the temporality of the viewer. The image in *Heart of Glass* that is perhaps most unequivocally a textual unfolding of the audience's contemplative relation to the characters is carefully composed so that the seer Hias, who stares blankly at the audience from the foreground of the frame, is contrasted with a crowd of villagers shrunken into frail mortality by the background perspective. They are soliciting his visionary wisdom. Ironically, they explain that they fear that the death of Mühlbeck and the resultant mystification of the glass portend the return of the age of giants. While their invocation of the mythic time of giants signifies the characters' loss of rapport with the physical space that encloses them, the age of giants is nonetheless vividly obtruded in the physical perspective of the shot in such a way that the entire mise-en-scène poses the dramatic equivalent of a rhetorical question: does the age of giants exist as a human construction of those who feel lost in the space of the physical world? The age of giants is apprehended in this shot, as in Rousseau's famous anecdote from the *Essay on the Origin of Languages*, in the rationalizing space of human comprehension that is more congruent with its own narrative exigencies than with the spurious dimensions of a physical world.

Similarly, Herzog's hypnotism of the actors in *Heart of Glass* and the mirror surface they present deny the viewer access to the metaphysical depths of character that human faces conventionally endow in movies, rendering the characters' faces more vividly an artifact of the audience's gaze than an independent illusion. Just as the physical stature of the gigantic Hias limns a perspective that is incommensurable with the character's reality, the materiality of the facial image and hence the temporality of viewing it become the most rigorous constraints of meaning. We might be led to believe that by this upstaging of narrative plot and foregrounding of static artifice Herzog declares his freedom from narrative exigency in general. But as we have seen in the other examples, Herzog's aesthetic does not so much articulate a refusal of narrative as it reorders narrative priorities, stressing the status of narrative as an act of mind rather than as the vehicle of thematic meaning.

In one respect this logic simply rehearses the narratologist's well-known distinction between *fabula* and *sjuzet* (Erlich, 1965, 240–1). Perhaps Herzog understands an implicit premise of narratology, that the supplanting of historical reality produced by all metaphysical longing is enabled precisely by a conflation of narrative act with story, a confusion of the story with the act of telling. Such a confusion upon which unreflexive narrative conventions subsist inevitably results in a specious form and content dichotomy. This is the dichotomous logic that facilitates the social transcendence of history through myth and the superimposition of ideological practice on the forms of social life.

Ideology is a bifurcation of lived reality into real and imaginary registers of experience. In *Heart of Glass,* Herzog's achievement as a narrative artist is to reassimilate myth to its historical exigencies, thus eliminating any form/content dichotomy by rigorously subsuming all that we see under the terms of our seeing.

The final scenes of *Heart of Glass,* though glaringly discontinuous with the narrative time of the dramatic plot, are nonetheless continuous with the narrative principle outlined above. They effectively shift the expository movement of the film into a metacritical register that supersedes any plotted catharsis. The film's coda takes the form of a mythic parable: the narrative of an island people trapped within the limitations of their physical space, longing for the courage to set out over the ocean and discover the end of the world, with all its allegorical portent of apocalypse and self-transfiguration. It is a narrative that expresses the situation of all metaphysical longing, and once again it would appear to implicate Herzog in the very wish for a visionary transcendence that the villagers have taken refuge in. But such a conclusion is once again preempted out of the same speculative habits that have been conditioned by the visual regimen preceding it. What appears in this portentous coda to be an overture to metaphysical flight is transformed into a paradoxical reflection on the sources of narrative desire that fetter such flights of fancy with the knowledge of their necessity.

In the film's coda, as in the tableau of Hias and the dwarfish villagers, the knowledge denied to the characters is almost ceremonially conferred upon the viewer. We see the islanders set out to open sea in a small boat. A final title card, without benefit of voice or character, speculates about the future of this adventure in terms that conflate putative fact with the open-ended possibilities of story-telling: "Perhaps they took it as a sign of hope that the birds followed them out to sea." Appropriately, the word *perhaps* expresses both hope and the contingency of hope, thus seeming to proclaim the much-heralded convergence of the human and the transhuman worlds. Indeed, both meanings are compacted in the superimposition of the white title card ("Perhaps they took it as a sign . . .") over the film's final image of birds following the boat out to sea. The composition collapses the literal and the imaginary in an explicitly textual figuration, rendering the conclusion of the film neither effective history nor myth but only a marker for the supersession of narrative will in all such human speculation. In narrative, the desire that takes us out of the world turns out to be only an ingenious refurbishing of the world. This remembrance is for the audience perhaps the most plausible hope Herzog could have extended at the end of such a film. For it is proffered in the understanding that every re-imagining of the world is made possible only through self-awareness of the means that are already palpable in our hands and heads. To remember that one's fate is a story one has told about oneself is to master one's fate by sustaining the narrative momentum of its telling.

It should be clear that I am not minimizing the other-worldly trajectories of Herzog's films: the exotic physical and temporal locales populated by pariahs and primitives, the circuitous plot-lines that lead beyond the horizon of cultural traditions. Rather my point is that however exotic the look of the films, they always return us to the knowledge that such other-worldly exoticism is no less a product of culture than the cultural norms it belies. Therein lies the complex understanding of cultural identity that Herzog possesses as a starting point in each film. I am not denying the sincerity of Herzog's tirelessly reiterated longing for worlds unseen. I am only insisting that such longing, at least within the rhetorical scope of the films, is consummated as a conspicuous labor of cultural production rather than an escapist illusion.

III

We have seen how the traditional cultural touchstones of sublimity, presented as intractable artifactual elements of Herzog's films, always call us hastily back from the precipice of the sublime. *The Mystery of Kaspar Hauser*, which was the original point of departure for this chapter, divulges this truism of Herzogian vision with persuasive candor in the structurally pivotal dreams of its protagonist. Kaspar's dreams awaken the viewer of Herzog's films to the knowledge that cultural innocence is only the product of cultural longings. Like the coda of *Heart of Glass*, Kaspar's dreams appear to nullify narrative time but only as they recoil upon the sources of narrative desire that they explicate in time.

Kaspar is the proverbial orphan of culture because he is incapable of rationalizing his dreams to satisfactory narrative conclusions. He does not possess the repertoire of rhetorical gestures that operate narrative closure and thus make possible a human habitation of this world. This is the mark of Kaspar's sublimity. But neither is he capable of repressing the impulse to rationalize, which is the motor of all narrative projection. Kaspar dreams three times. Just as Kaspar contains within his being the contradiction of rational and irrational nature, each dream is rendered in a mise-en-scène riven with the contradiction between visionary spectacle and the naked machinery of fictive artifice. The first dream of the far-away mountains is imaged in the half-speed sepia blinking light of antique movie projection. The dream of the Caucasus is quite clearly an old movie heavily laden with the very historical burden that we have seen the viewer obliged to take up time and time again in other films. For Herzog, character viewpoint is once again interpolated as an allegory of filmic representation and hence constitutes a return to the contemplation of the dreamer rather than the dream. As in the previous films, Herzog's mise-en-scène obtrudes knowledge of the relation between the viewer and the medium as a condition of the medium's disclosure of a world. Accordingly, the second dream is a doleful vista of a gloomy mountain ascending to the figure of death. The tableau of the dream figures attired in unmistakably modern dress, toiling upward and downward on a rocky slope, achieves by its allusion to the historical time of the viewing audience only a parodic allegory of vision rather than the visionary experience to which Kaspar wants to testify. We are reminded that the visionary is ironically the underpinning of all allegorical thought that always serves as an adequate expression only insofar as it dissimulates its true meaning.

The third and climactic dream is a narrative that reveals Kaspar's own grasp of the very narrative means that have – insofar as they have been in evidence for the viewer here – falsified the allegorical portent of the previous dreams. Evoked again in the format of the sepia-tinted beginnings of cinematic technique and vivid with the promise of vicarious adventure proffered in that technique, the third dream devolves nonetheless to a narrative development returning the narrator ineluctably to the place of narrative beginnings. Kaspar relates the plight of a lost desert caravan deluded by a mirage of mountains. A blind seer divines the true direction by tasting the sand across which they must trek. Kaspar concludes: "And they follow the old man's advice and finally reach the city in the north. And that's where the story begins. But how the story goes after they reach the city, I don't know." Like the narrative of the islanders who set out at the end of *Heart of Glass,* the desert of Kaspar's dream is a projection of narrative desire that by its mechanical default of denouement expresses not the mystic naif's sublime subversion of narrative time but only the inexhaustibility of narrative desire itself – always renewing itself out of its own calcula-tions in time. The mind of narration is a place where beginnings are eternal and ends are only instrumental pretexts for beginning again.

As we know well from Marx and from recent social theory, history is not the sum of moments. It is a lived relation of individuals to the representations that express them. Appropriately, the "visionary spectacle" of Kaspar's dreams obtrudes a distance between the audience and the character that, though it teases the parable of the Rousseauian native in its strangeness and simplicity and promises to simplify into the easy thematic of nostalgia for our lost innocence, remains inextricable in the viewing eye from the contemplative space of its own construction. Our viewing paradoxically results in our inability to find our way back to Kaspar's innocence because we are complicit in the forms of representing it, the forms of an objectifying distance that fosters not nostalgia but the responsibility of self-knowledge. The juxtaposition of the historical moment of film technology with the "visionary" introversion of Kaspar's cultural primitivism frustrates our desire to spiritualize the protagonist of this film, to abstract him from the *Weltanschauung* that seems so cruelly to denature him.

Indeed, that would be too sentimental. In Herzog's films we are, as I have tried to show, mightily constrained to ironic knowledge. It is not, however, a nihilistic irony. As Kaspar's dreams make clear, ironic knowledge constitutes an historical perspective within which the viewer can find his or her own place as a viable participant in what is seen. By history I am designating a textual discipline to which the viewer of Herzog's films is apprenticed in the self-consciousness they produce. It is by this means that the films possess a lucidity independent of the characters' metaphysical faith, their hapless longing to be in another place at another time. Indeed, the historical lucidity of the textual order in Herzog's films obtains specifically as it produces the interpreter's position external to the text he or she is reading. If this abstraction of the viewer from the text seems paradoxically to evoke the romantic sublime and the evasions of historical responsibility I have already condemned, we must observe that in Herzog's ironic sublime the interpreter is also explicitly reflected as the text's condition of existence. Thus the knowledge produced by such a text is not dissipated in the wearisome dualisms of subject and object. The viewer is not overwhelmed by the state of hallucinatory freedom that is all too often the critical advertisement for the Herzogian sublime but is rather charged with reflecting on all of the film's own textual pretexts as the first constraint of interpretation.

In all of Herzog's films perhaps the moment that declares the imperative of this textual/historical/ironical knowledge most emphatically occurs in *The Great Ecstasy of the Sculptor Steiner*. To call *Steiner* a documentary is already to have diluted its textual density, since its distinction is its clear violation of genre boundaries. It is a film in which the filmmaker himself is an anchor to the textual order insofar as he presents himself as both auteur and character. Hs is at once documentarian aesthete and self-parodying media announcer. He orchestrates the images of Steiner's balletic feats and then intrudes upon their aesthetic delicacy with flat-footed commentary that brings all the airy ease of ski-flying to earth as a laborious chore of representation.

The filmmaker's ambiguous presence stands in striking contrast to the "serious" documentary exposition of the skier's physical accomplishments, setting up an invidious comparison of the essential and the accidental, the authentic and unauthentic, the worldly ridiculous and the sobering sublime. The lyrical feats of the ski-flier Walter Steiner, whose soaring image in the film's opening seems to divest the film of all earthly bearings, inspire that longing for abstraction which is perhaps the heroic aura of all displays of athletic prowess. Indeed, as if inspired by what it sees, Herzog's camera achieves a physical mobility of its own that defies the concreteness of the perspectives within which this sport is usually represented by the sports media.

As in *Fata Morgana,* the camera in *Steiner,* alternating between poses of sincerity and irony, traverses the space between representation and the representable – between the objects in space and the narrative space that objectifies them. Following these movements, we viewers supplant the object with our own shifting perspectives on that object. Sculpture is that art form which constrains aesthetic contemplation to the materiality of human time and space. It is always produced within the mobile perspectives of the viewer. Therefore it is an unusually apt metaphor for a film that weighs heavily with an earth-bound materiality of mind, even as that mind contemplates the "miracle" of unearthly flight. It is a film that pries us from the object of our fascination, putting us at a contemplative remove that breaks the reifying spell of vicarious experience.

In the most breath-taking action sequence of Herzog's film, Steiner first rises above the camera, giving a vivid immediacy to the uncanny feat of ski-flying. But in Herzog's inimitable treatment of such action, the camera rises too, ascending into the air out of physical resources that because they remain inaccessible to the viewer are rendered virtually miraculous. The camera crosses paths with the athlete in mid air. As Steiner begins his descent, the camera supplants him in the sky, inverting our initial perspective and thus revealing at the solid factual core of the documentary record a fictive malleability. Steiner's accomplishment is not belittled in this maneuver. But the passive adoration of the documentarist's camera and the awe of the spectator/ viewer are made complicit in an awareness that belies the vicarious flight of fantasy identification excited by such images on television and in the newsreels. In the media spectacles of this sport the camera never inhabits its own perspective.

Indeed, it is precisely the obtrusive presence of the conventionally unseen mechanical trappings of newsreel production that overturns the representational priorities (e.g. the inverted perspective of camera and subject) of the visual spectacle in Herzog's film "document." The definitive moment comes when, after Steiner has suffered a seemingly catastrophic fall, the filmmaker obtrudes on camera to declare a cata- strophe of aesthetic proportions: "This could be the end of our film," Herzog soberly attests in a serio-comic confusion of subject and object that has the effect of making everything we see in this film complicit in the contrivances of conspicuous narrative necessity. Such evidence of manipulation, which makes the documentary event interchangeable with the props of melodramatic intent, compels us to attend with fresh interest to the immediacy of what is before our eyes rather than to what transcends the apparatus of our knowledge. Such, after all, are the responsibilities of self-knowledge that I spoke of earlier as a necessary corollary to the objectifying distance imposed by Herzog's self-dis- simulating mise-en-scène.

Such self-knowledge takes on particular resonance for the audience of this film because it presents a striking counterpoint to the audience *in* the film. Ski-flying is emphatically a spectator sport, denying partici- pation to the ordinary person except through the most attenuated gestures of symbolic longing. The desire for vicarious flights of fantasy identification that sustains Steiner's audience on the slopes is precisely what is denied the film audience, who, always situated and resituated within the perspectives of their amazement, only see what they see as a variable of their uniquely mobile perspective.

Steiner's relationship with the crowds on the slopes subtly parallels the relationship of the audience of the film with the audience in the film. Steiner repeatedly confesses his discomfort under the public pressure to shorten his approach to the jump and thereby to defy the limits of physical ability more spectacularly than comprehension and perhaps mortality allow. He is a prisoner of the spectatorial fantasy he creates. Clearly the best jump from the audience's point of view would be the one that culminates in the skier's death, when he would be taken up into the pure invisibility of their own longing and thus become a symbol of what they otherwise must always wait in painfully mortal time for him to accomplish. Steiner is seen in most of the film carefully contemplating the cost of such risky jumps. With great lucidity he explains to the camera that what is lost in the clouds of anxiety produced by very risky jumps is quite literally the freedom of the ski-flier to contemplate his own motions, to be effectively human in the act of superhuman courage. The ideal jump for Steiner, though it begins as a great blinding tension pressing on his skull, releases him – as he decends – into clear sight of what he is doing. This emphasis on lucidity of thought contrasts the pleasure of his art with the crowd's brutal wish for a new record – one that would be conspicuously artless in its self-subverting abstraction. At the end Steiner confesses: "I ought to be all alone in the world ... then I would not be afraid." If the source of Steiner's fear is in the minds of others who are manifestly unscrupulous in their unselfconscious desire, his true apotheosis will be to transcend the consciousness of transcendence.

Through most of the film Steiner is poised bird-like in mid air, with his head down, his body tucked under his arms, a figure of metaphoric purport, a soaring embodiment of daring will. But while such emblematic images in this film (as in most of Herzog's films) indulge the imagination of what is beyond experience, they do so only to reattach such longings to more worldly human motives, needs, and conditions. So, very much like the Herzog I have described in this chapter, Steiner trespasses beyond the ordinary not to transcend his human scale but to make of it a better measure of familiar time and place. It is therefore quite appropriate that after the title credits Herzog's film about Steiner opens not with the image of the ski-flier in full flight above the slopes, and therefore already several leaps beyond our amazement/comprehension, but rather with a shot of the hands of the wood sculptor. He holds a wooden bowl. It is carved, he says, as if an explosion had occurred. But it is an explosion detonated out of his own laborious concentration. It is an image that aptly captures the mortality of Steiner's longing. The substantiality of the sculptor's craft is the analogue not the antithesis of the ski-flier's airy bounding. For in the course of our viewing, ski-flying no less than wood sculpture comes to be understood as a reckoning with the temporal process of historical life, which is mastered only through a consciousness of time and place that is the constitutive moment of time and place.

IV

There is no doubting that Herzog's films situate the viewer uncomfortably between the human and the superhuman (the natural sublime) as though the two realms of existence demanded reconciliation. But for Herzog (unlike that romantic artist for whom nature is grandiosely and prophetically affective), the belief in the necessity of their reconciliation is coldly scrutinized as itself already an artifact of their incommensurability. Herzog seems well aware that the mystic's visionary marriage of mind and its "other" nature is already the mind's preemption of nature. Any alternative is literally unthinkable since one cannot contemplate the natural world *as* nature, and it is after all only the literally thinkable that can help us or harm us. I have never denied that the imagery of Herzog's "other" worlds thwarts a comprehension adequate to our apprehension, thus taunting us with the very overdeterminations of sublimity that would subvert our narrative will into a metaphysical abstraction. Yet we must always distinguish the overdetermination of the image in Herzog's films as simultaneously the production of a text, yielding determinate knowledge of its own albeit indeterminate articulations. Whereas in the Kantian sublime comprehension is simply outstripped by the proliferation of worlds for our apprehension, in Herzog's films comprehension sustains its dialectic with apprehension by making sensuous life both the trace and determination of the film's own textuality. In other words, apprehension is not supplanted or surpassed but included in comprehension by the constraints of a self-comprehending experience of temporality. Earlier I used the term *reparticularization* to delineate this textual operation of Herzog's film rhetoric and its temporality. In the films discussed here, even the most conceptually indeterminate (static, in narrative terms) images are always given a temporal logic by the syntax of reflexivity, the reflection of the image upon the site of its production.

Despite the burdens of self-consciousness it assumes, this aesthetic is by no means a simple redaction of Brechtian formalism unraveling the complex dialectic of ideological stances that make up the social world. After all, Herzog's films do not depict social order with even a parodic verisimilitude. If the dream of sublimity that haunts his film worlds is itself undeniably a social myth, it is the myth of the end of society and hence the end of narrative. And that is why Herzog mistrusts it. The reflexivity of Herzog's films is always emphatically a narrative practice grounded in temporal necessities. Compared with the Brechtian alienation effect, which also employs self-consciousness as a tool of cultural critique, Herzog cares less to preach a vision of utopian society (perhaps because it, too much like metaphysical idealism, vaunts the responsibilities of immediacy) than simply to practice the ways of knowing immediacy as a condition for knowing every future moment. Perhaps because Herzog, unlike the Brechtian artist, is satisfied with neither a polemical demystification of narrative and the worlds it propagates nor a simple "baring of the devices," we can observe a peculiar ethical compulsion in these films. It is perhaps most sharply focused in the prevailing mode of narrative anticlimax: think of Kaspar's incompletable dream, the elliptical coda of *Heart of Glass,* Steiner's inertia toward death without dying, and many other such demi-denouements in Herzog's films. The anticlimactic moment uniquely discharges its meaning by returning us to contemplation of the textual agency that animates it. Thus it denotes a reinvestment of narrative desire in the very materials that have already rendered their meaning as manifestly incomplete. In other words, the ethic of Herzog's films is born in a Nietzschean awareness that every narrative strategy is already the text of its "self-overcoming" if one attends to it as a text. The text's composition supersedes the meanings inscribed in it.

The much-touted speculation that Herzog's need to "live" the struggle of his films expresses his desire to transcend representation is perhaps most convincingly falsified by his own widely broadcast claims about the production values of *Aguirre, The Wrath of God.* The spectacle of the "real" Amazon documented in that film by the strenuous efforts of real people in a real jungle has become a source of boasting for the director not because it is real, but, in his own words, because it *looks like* the exorbitant Hollywood spectacle (Walsh/Ebert, 1979, 96) that he wants to belie. Appropriately, it is in the feat of representing the capabilities of representation that Herzog takes his greatest satisfaction as an artist. In light of this, perhaps we are entitled to say that the forms of representation in Herzog's films carry an historical burden most emphatically because they produce their narrative as the condition of narration itself. Any other conditions would be too abstract, rendering appearances the limit rather than the threshold of the spectator's comprehension.

Works cited

Burke, E. (1958) *A Philosophical Inquiry into the Origin of Our Ideas of the Sublime and Beautiful,* ed. J. T. Boulton, London, Oxford University Press.

Coleridge, S. T. (1907) *Biographia Literaria,* ed. J. Shawcross, London, Oxford University Press.

Erlich, V. (1965) *Russian Formalism: History and Doctrine*, The Hague, Mouton.

Kant, I. (1968) *Critique of Judgement,* trans. J. H. Bernard, New York, Hafner.

Walsh, Gene (ed.) (1979) "'Images at the Horizon': a workshop with Werner Herzog," conducted by Roger Ebert, Chicago, Facets Multimedia Center (pamphlet).

V
DOCUMENTING HERZOG:
A FILMOGRAPHY AND
SELECTED BIBLIOGRAPHY

Filmography

Heracles [Herakles]
Production: Werner Herzog, Munich, 1961/2
Screenplay: Werner Herzog
Editor: Werner Herzog
Sound: Werner Herzog
Photography: Jaime Pacheco
Music: Uwe Brandner
Assistants: Siegfried Kohlhammer, Achim von Heynitz
Cast: Mr Germany
Running time: 12 minutes
35mm, b/w
Cost: 8000 DM

Playing in the Sand [Spiel im Sand]
Production: Werner Herzog, Munich, 1964
Production Assistant: Uwe Brandner
Screenplay: Werner Herzog
Editor: Werner Herzog
Sound: Werner Herzog
Photography: Jaime Pacheco
Music: RA: Uwe Brandner
Running time: 15 minutes
35mm
Dates of filming: June, 1964
Cost: 8000 DM

The Unparalleled Defense of the Fortress Deutschkreutz [Die beispiellose Verteidigung der Festung Deutschkreutz]
Production: Werner Herzog, Munich/Arpa-Film, Munich, 1966
Screenplay: Werner Herzog
Editor: Werner Herzog
Sound: Uwe Brandner
Photography: Jaime Pacheco
Assistants: Uwe Brandner, Holger Trulzsch, Stephan Maluschek
Cast: Peter H. Brumm, Georg Eska, Karl Heinz Steffel, Wolfgang von Ungern-Sternberg

Running time: 14 minutes
35mm, b/w
Première: April 5, 1967, Oberhausen

Signs of Life [Lebenszeichen]
Production: Werner Herzog, Munich, 1967
Screenplay: Werner Herzog
Editors: Beate Mainka-Jellinghaus, Maximiliane Mainka
Sound: Herbert Prasch
Photography: Thomas Mauch with Dietrich Lohmann
Assistants: Florian Fricke, Thomas Hartwig, Bettina Von Waldthausen,
    Ina Fritsche, Tasos Karabelas, Mike Piller, Friederike Pezold, Martje
    Grohmann
Music: Stavros Xarchakos
Cast: Peter Brogle, Wolfgang Reichmann, Athina Zacharopoulos,
    Wolfgang von Ungern-Sternberg, Wolfgang Stumpf, Florian Fricke,
    Werner Herzog
Première: June 25, 1968, Berlin
Available in 16mm
Dates of filming: June–July, September 1967
Awards: Carl Mayer-Drehbuchpreis 1963 for Werner Herzog, IFF Berlin
    1968: Silberner Bar (Regie), Deutscher Filmpreis 1968: Filmband in
    Silber

Last Words [Letzte Worte]
Production: Werner Herzog, Munich, 1967/8
Screenplay: Werner Herzog
Editor: Beate Mainka-Jellinghaus
Sound: Herbert Prasch
Photography: Thomas Mauch with Dietrich Lohmann
Assistant: Nicos Triandafylidis
Cast: Inhabitants of Crete and Spinalonga
Running time: 13 minutes
Première: April 4, 1968, Oberhausen
Available in 16mm
Dates of filming: summer 1967
Awards: Kurtzfilmtage Oberhausen 1968
Cost: 1200 DM

Precautions Against Fanatics [Massnahmen Gegen Fanatiker]
Production: Werner Herzog, Munich, 1968
Screenplay: Werner Herzog

Editor: Beate Mainka-Jellinghaus
Sound: Werner Herzog
Photography: Dietrich Lohmann, Jörg Schmidt-Reitwein
Cast: Petar Radenkovic, Mario Adorf, Hans Tiedemann, Herbert Hisel,
   Peter Schamoni
Running time: 11 minutes
Première: March 28, 1969, Oberhausen
Available in 16mm
Dates of filming: September–October 1968
Cost: 28,000 DM

The Flying Doctors of East Africa [Die fliegenden Ärzte von Ostafrika]

Production: Werner Herzog, Munich, 1968/9
Screenplay: Werner Herzog
Editor: Beate Mainka-Jellinghaus
Sound: Werner Herzog
Photography: Thomas Mauch
Assistants: Leonore Semler, Hans von Mallinckrodt (Flying Doctors
   Service)
Cast: Dr Rottcher, Dr Michael Wood, Dr Ann Spoery, Dr Keisler, Betty
   Miller, James Kabale
Running time: 45 minutes
35mm
Dates of filming: October–November 1968

Fata Morgana

Production: Werner Herzog, Munich, 1968/70
Screenplay: Werner Herzog
Editor: Beate Mainka-Jellinghaus
Sound: Werner Herzog
Photography: Jörg Schmidt-Reitwein
Music: Georg Friedrich Handel, Wolfgang Amadeus Mozart, Blind Faith,
   François Couperin, Leonard Cohen
Cast: Wolfgang von Ungern-Sternberg, James William Gledhill, Eugen
   des Montagnes
Running time: 79 minutes
Première: May 17, 1971, Cannes
German première: June 4, 1971, Hof
Available in 16mm
Dates of filming: November 1968, May–September 1969, December
   1969

Even Dwarfs Started Small [Auch Zwerge haben klein angefangen]
Production: Werner Herzog, Munich, 1969/70
Screenplay: Werner Herzog
Editor: Beate Mainka-Jellinghaus
Sound: Herbert Prasch
Photography: Thomas Mauch with Jörg Schmidt-Reitwein
Assistants: Ina Fritsche, James William Gledhill, Martje Grohmann, Wolfgang von Ungern-Sternberg
Music: Florian Fricke and Spanish folk-music
Cast: Helmut Doring, Paul Glauer, Gisela Hertwig, Hertel Minkner, Gertraud Piccini, Marianne Saar, Brigitte Saar, Gerd Gickel, Erna Geschwendtner, Gerhard Marz, Alfredo Piccini, Erna Smollartz, Lajos Zsarnoczay
Running time: 96 minutes
Première: May 8, 1970, Cannes
German première: May 30, 1970, Hof
Available in 16mm
Dates of filming: November–December 1969

Impeded Future [Behinderte Zukunft]
Production: Werner Herzog, Munich, 1970
Screenplay: Werner Herzog (after an idea by Hans Peter Maier)
Editor: Beate Mainka-Jellinghaus
Sound: Werner Herzog
Photography: Jörg Schmidt-Reitwein
Narrator: Rolf Illig
Running time: 62 minutes
Available in 16mm
Dates of filming: summer 1970
Cost: 40,000 DM

Land of Silence and Darkness [Land des Schweigens und der Dunkelheit]
Production: Werner Herzog, Munich, 1970/1
Screenplay: Werner Herzog
Editor: Beate Mainka-Jellinghaus
Sound: Werner Herzog
Photography: Jörg Schmidt-Reitwein
Music: Johann Sebastian Bach, Antonio Vivaldi
Cast: Fini Straubinger, Heinrich Fleischmann, Vladimir Kokol, M. Baaske, Resi Mittermeier

Running time: 85 minutes
Première: October 8, 1971, Mannheim
Available in 16mm
Dates of filming: October 1970–January 1971
Cost: 40,000 DM

Aguirre, the Wrath of God [Aguirre, der Zorn Gottes]

Production: Werner Herzog, Munich/Hessischer Rundfunk, Frankfurt, 1972
Screenplay: Werner Herzog
Editor: Beate Mainka-Jellinghaus
Sound: Werner Herzog
Photography: Thomas Mauch with Francisco Joan and Orlando Macchiavello
Assistants: Martje Grohmann, Dr Georg Hagmuller, Ina Fritsche, Rene Lechleitner
Music: Popol Vuh
Cast: Klaus Kinski, Helena Rojo, Del Negro, Ruy Guerra, Peter Berling, Cecilia Rivera, Daniel Ades, Edward Roland, Armando Polanah, Daniel Farfán, Alejandro Chavez, Antonio Marquez, Julio Martinez, Alejandro Repullés, Indianer de Kooperative Lauramarca
Running time: 93 minutes
Première: December 29, 1972, Cologne
Available in 16mm
Dates of filming: January–February 1972

The Great Ecstasy of the Sculptor Steiner [Die Grosse Ekstase Des Bildschnitzers Steiner]

Production: Werner Herzog, Munich, 1974
Screenplay: Werner Herzog
Editor: Beate Mainka-Jellinghaus
Sound: Benedikt Kuby
Photography: Jörg Schmidt-Reitwein with Francisco Joan, Frederik Hettich, Alfred Chrosziel, Gideon Meron
Music: Florian Fricke, Popol Vuh
Cast: Walter Steiner
Running time: 45 minutes
Première: November 14, 1974, Munich
Available in 16mm
Dates of filming: September, December 1973; January, March 1974
Cost: 50,000 DM

The Mystery of Kaspar Hauser; literal translation is **Every Man For Himself and God Against All [Jeder für sich und Gott gegen alle]**
Production: Werner Herzog, Munich, 1974
Screenplay: Werner Herzog
Editor: Beate Mainka-Jellinghaus
Sound: Haymo Henry Heyder
Photography: Jörg Schmidt-Reitwein
Music: Johann Pachelbel, Orlando di Lasso, Tommaso Albinoni, Wolfgang Amadeus Mozart
Cast: Bruno S., Walter Ladengast, Brigitte Mira, Hans Musäus, Willy Semmelrogge, Michael Kroecher, Henry van Lyck, Enno Patalas, Volker Elis Pilgrim, Volker Prechtel, Gloria Doer, Helmut Döring, Kidlak Tahimik, Andi Gottwald, Herbert Achternbusch, Wolfgang Bauer, Walter Steiner, Florian Fricke, Clemens Scheitz, Johannes Buzalski, Willy Meyer-Furst, Alfred Edel, Franz Brumbach, Herbert Fritsch, Wilhelm Bayer, Peter Gebhart, Otto Heinzle, Reinhard Hauff
Running time: 109 minutes
Première: November 1, 1974, Dinkelsbuhl
Available in 16mm
Dates of filming: June–August 1974
Awards: Deutscher Filmpreis 1975: Filmband in Silber, Filmband in Gold, Filmband in Gold for Beate Mainka-Jellinghaus, Editor, IFF Cannes 1975 Sonderpreis der Jury
Cost: 850,000 DM

How Much Wood Would A Woodchuck Chuck
Production: Werner Herzog, Munich, 1976
Screenplay: Werner Herzog
Editor: Beate Mainka-Jellinghaus
Sound: Werner Herzog
Photography: Thomas Mauch with Francisco Joan and Edward Lachmann
Music: Shorty Eager and the Eager Beavers
Cast: Ralph Wade, Alan Ball, Steve Liptay, Abe Diffenbach
Running time: 46 minutes
Première: September, 1976
Available in 16mm
Dates of filming: September 1975, June 1976

No One Will Play with Me [Mit mir will keiner spielen]
Production: Werner Herzog, Munich, 1976

Screenplay: Werner Herzog
Editor: Beate Mainka-Jellinghaus
Sound: Haymo Henry Heyder
Photography: Jörg Schmidt-Reitwein
Running time: 14 minutes
Available in 16mm
Dates of filming: January–February 1976

Heart of Glass [Herz Aus Glas]

Production: Werner Herzog, Munich, 1976
Screenplay: Herbert Achternbusch and Werner Herzog
Editor: Beate Mainka-Jellinghaus
Sound: Haymo Henry Heyder
Photography: Jörg Schmidt-Reitwein with Michael Gast
Assistants: Claude Chiarini, Ina Fritsche, Alan Greenberg, Patrick Leray
Music: Florian Fricke, Thomas Brinkley, Popol Vuh and the Studio of
  Early Music
Cast: Josef Bierbichler, Stefan Güttler, Clemens Scheitz, Volker
  Prechtel, Sepp Muller, Sonja Skiba, Brunhilde Klockner, Wolf
  Albrecht, Thomas Brinkley, Sterling Jones, Richard Levitt, Andrea
  von Ramm, Janos Fischer, Wilhelm Friedrich, Edith Gratz, Alois
  Hruschka, Egmond Hugel, Wolfram Kunkel, Werner Lederle, Agnes
  Nuissl, Helmut Kossick, Amad Ibn Ghassem Nadij, Bernhard Schabel,
  Friedrich Steinhauer, Joschi Arpa, Claude Chiarini, Martje Grohmann,
  Werner Herzog, Alan Greenberg, Helmut Krüger, Karl Kaufmann,
  Walter Schwarzmeier, Arno Vahrenwald, Detlev Weiler, Siegfried
  Wolf, Karl Yblagger
Running time: 94 minutes
Première: November 12, 1976, Paris
German Première: December 17, 1976
Available in 16mm
Dates of filming: August 1975, March 15–April 22 1976, April–May 1976
Awards: Deutscher Filmpreis 1977: Filmband in Gold (Kamera) for
  Schmidt-Reitwein
Cost: 700,000 DM

La Soufrière

Production: Werner Herzog, Munich, 1976
Screenplay: Werner Herzog
Editor: Beate Mainka-Jellinghaus
Sound: Werner Herzog
Photography: Jörg Schmidt-Reitwein, Edward Lachmann

Music: Sergei Rachmaninoff, Felix Mendelssohn-Bartholdy, Johannes Brahms, Richard Wagner
Running time: 31 minutes
Première: March 1977, Bonn
Available in 16mm
Dates of filming: August, 1976
Cost: 45,000 DM

Stroszek
Production: Werner Herzog, Munich/ZDF television, 1976
Screenplay: Werner Herzog
Editor: Beate Mainka-Jellinghaus
Sound: Haymo Henry Heyder and Peter van Anft
Photography: Thomas Mauch and Edward Lachmann with Wolfgang Knigge
Assistants: Peter Holz and Stephano Guidi
Music: Tom Paxton, Chet Atkins, Sonny Terry
Cast: Bruno S., Eva Mattes, Clemens Scheitz, Wihelm von Homburg, Burkhard Driest, Pitt Bedewitz, Clayton Szlapinski, Ely Rodriguez, Alfred Edel, Scott McKain, Ralph Wade, Vaclav Vojta, Michael Gahr, Yücsel Topcugürler, Bob Evans
Running time: 108 minutes
Première: May 20, 1977, Munich
Available in 16mm
Dates of filming: November 16–December 31 1976, February 17–18 1977
Awards: Preis der deutschen Filmkritik 1978
Cost: 900,000 DM

Nosferatu, the Vampire [Nosferatu – Phantom der Nacht]
Production: Werner Herzog, Munich/ZDF television, 1978
Screenplay: Werner Herzog, based on the film *Nosferatu, a Symphony of Terror* by F. W. Murnau and the novel *Dracula* by Bram Stoker
Editor: Beate Mainka-Jellinghaus
Sound: Harald Maury
Photography: Jörg Schmidt-Reitwein with Michael Gast
Music: Popol Vuh, Florian Fricke, Richard Wagner, Charles Gounod, Vok Ansambl Gordela
Cast: Klaus Kinski, Isabelle Adjani, Bruno Ganz, Roland Topor, Jacques Dufilho, Walter Ladengast, Dan van Husen, Carsten Bodinus, Martje Grohmann, Ryk de Gooyer, Clemens Scheitz, Bo van Hensbergen, John Leddy, Margriet van Hartingsveld, Tim Beekman, Beverly

Walker, Rudolf Wolf, Johan te Slaa, Claude Chiarini, Stefan Husar, Roger Berry Losch, Werner Herzog, Michael Edols, Gisela Storch, Anja Schmidt-Zähringer, Martin Gerbl, Walter Saxer, Ja Groth, Dominique Colladant

Running time: 107 minutes

Première: January 10, 1979, Paris

German première: February 23, 1979, Berlin

Available in 16mm

Dates of filming: May 1–July 6 1978

Awards: IFF Berlin 1979: Silberner Bär (Ausstattung) for Henning von Gierke for set design, Deutscher Filmpreis 1979: Filmband in Gold for Klaus Kinski, Cartagena 1980 for Klaus Kinski

Cost: 2,500,000 DM

Woyzeck

Production: Werner Herzog, Munich/ZDF television, 1978

Screenplay: Werner Herzog, based on the drama fragment by Georg Büchner

Editor: Beate Mainka-Jellinghaus

Sound: Harald Maury

Photography: Jörg Schmidt-Reitwein with Michael Gast

Music: Fiedelquartett Telč, Benedetto Marcello, Antonio Vivaldi

Cast: Klaus Kinski, Eva Mattes, Wolfgang Reichmann, Willy Semmelrogge, Josef Bierbichler, Paul Burian, Volker Prectel, Dieter Augustin, Irm Hermann, Wolfgang Bächler, Rosemarie Heinikel, Herbert Fux, Thomas Mettke, Maria Mettke

Running time: 81 minutes

Première: May 22, 1979, Cannes

German première: May 25, Berlin, Munich, Frankfurt

Available in 16mm

Dates of filming: July 13–August 3 1978

Awards: IFF Cannes 1979 for Eva Mattes

Cost: 900,000 DM

God's Angry Man [Glaube und Währung]

Production: Werner Herzog, Munich, 1980

Screenplay: Werner Herzog

Editor: Beate Mainka-Jellinghaus

Sound: Walter Saxer

Photography: Thomas Mauch

Cast: Gene Scott

Running time: 46 minutes

Available in 16mm

Huie's Sermon [Huie's Predigt]
Production: Werner Herzog, Munich, 1980
Screenplay: Werner Herzog
Editor: Beate Mainka-Jellinghaus
Sound: Walter Saxer
Photography: Thomas Mauch
Cast: Bishop Huie L. Rogers
Running time: 42 minutes
Available in 16mm

Fitzcarraldo
Production: Werner Herzog Filmproduktion, Lucki Stipitic, Project Film
production, Filmverlag Der Autoren, Munich, ZDF television, and
Wildlife Films, Peru, S.A.
Screenplay: Werner Herzog
Editor: Beate Mainka-Jellinghaus
Sound: Juarez Dagoberto, Zeze d'Alice
Photography: Thomas Mauch, Rainer Klausmann
Music: Popol Vuh, Giuseppe Verdi, Vincenzo Bellini, Richard Strauss,
Ruggiero Leoncavallo, Giacomo Meyerbeer, Jules Massenet
Cast: Klaus Kinski, Claudia Cardinale, Jose Lewgoy, Miguel Angel
Fuentes, Paul Hittscher, Huerequeque Enrique Bohoruez, Grande
Othelo, Peter Berling, David Perez Espinoza, Milton Nascimento, Rui
Polanah, Salvador Godinez, Dieter Milz, Bill Rose, Leoncio Bueno
Opera in Manaus: Werner Schroeter
Running time: 158 minutes
Première: March 5, 1982, Munich
35mm
Dates of filming: January–February 1981, April–July 1981, October–
November 1981
Awards: Deutscher Filmpreis 1982: Filmband in Silber (Programm-
fullender Spielfilm); IFF Cannes 1982; for production, IFF San
Sebastian 1982: Preis des Internationalen katholischen Filmburos
(OCIC)

Where the Green Ants Dream [Wo du grünen Ameisen traümen]
Production: Werner Herzog, Munich/ZDF television, 1983/4
Screenplay: Werner Herzog
Editor: Beate Mainka-Jellinghaus
Sound: Claus Langer
Photography: Jörg Schmidt-Reitwein, Michael Edols
Music: Gabriel Fauré, Ernst Bloch, Klause-Jochen Wiese, Richard

Wagner, Aboriginal music by Wandjuk Marika

Cast: Bruce Spence, Wandjuk Marika, Roy Marika, Ray Barrett, Norman Keye, Colleen Clifford, Ralph Cotterill, Nicolas Lathouris, Basil Clarke, Ray Marshall, Dhungula I. Marika, Gary Williams, Tony Llewellyn-Jones, Marraru Wunungmurra, Robert Brissenden, Susan Greaves, Michael Glynn, Michael Edols, Noel Lyon, Max Fairchild, Bob Ellis, Trevor Oxford, Hugh Keays-Byrne, Andrew Mack, Maria Stratford, Michael Mandalis, Anastasios Chatzidimpas, Paul Cox, Philip Radke, Rickey & Ronnie, James Ricketson, Christopher Cain, Paul Donazzan, Tim Cartwright, Michael Glynn

Running time: 103 minutes

Première: May 14, 1984, Cannes

German première: June 26, 1984, Munich

35mm

Awards: Deutscher Filmpreis 1984: Filmband in Gold (Abendfüllender Spielfilm); Filmband in Gold for Photography for Jörg Schmidt-Reitwein

Cost: 2,800,000 DM

Ballad of the Little Soldier [Ballade vom kleinen Soldaten]

Production: Werner Herzog, Munich, 1984

Screenplay: Werner Herzog

Editor: Maximiliane Mainka

Sound: Christine Ebenberger

Photography: Jorge Vignati, Michael Edols

Narrator: Werner Herzog

Running time: 46 minutes

Première: October, 1984, Hof

Available in 16mm

Dates of filming: February 1984

Cost: 220,000 DM

The Dark Glow of the Mountains [Gasherbrum – Der leuchtende Berg]

Production: Werner Herzog, Munich, 1984

Screenplay: Werner Herzog

Editor: Maximiliane Mainka

Sound: Christine Ebenberger

Photography: Rainer Klausmann, Jorge Vignati

Music: Popol Vuh, Florian Fricke, Renate Knaup, Daniel Fichelscher

Cast: Reinhold Messner, Hans Kammerlander

Running time: 45 minutes

Première: February 18, 1985, Berlin
Available in 16mm
Dates of filming: summer, 1984
Cost: 200,000 DM

Films featuring Herzog

Geschichten vom Kubelkind
Production: Edgar Reitz, Ula Stockl, 1968/70
Cast: Kristine de Loup, Werner Herzog

Anderthalb Tage FuBweg
Production: György Polnauer, 1973/4.
Cast: Werner Herzog

Was ich bin, sind meine Filme
Production: Christian Weisenborn, Erwin Keusch, 1976/8
Cast: Werner Herzog, Bruno S., Thomas Mauch, Eva Mattes, Burkhard
    Driest, Wilhelm von Homburg

Werner Herzog Eats His Shoe
Production: Les Blank, 1979/80
Cast: Werner Herzog

Burden of Dreams [Die Last der Traüme]
Production: Les Blank, 1981/2
Cast: Werner Herzog, Klaus Kinski, Claudia Cardinale, Jason Robards
    Jr, Mick Jagger, Alfredo de Rio Tambo, Angela Reina, Carmen Correa,
    Elia de Rio Ena, David Perez Espinosa, Miguel Angel Fuentes, Paul
    Hittscher

Chambre 666. N' importe quand ...
Production: Wim Wenders, 1982

Man of Flowers
Production: Paul Cox, 1983
Cast: Norman Kaye, Alyson Best, Chris Haywood, Werner Herzog

Tokyo-Ga
Production: Wim Wenders, 1983/5
Cast: Chishu Ryu, Yuharu Atsuta, Werner Herzog

Land of Bitterness and Pride
Production: Nina Gladitz, 1984

Selected bibliography

Andrews, N. (1978) "Dracula in Delft," *American Film*, 4 (1), 32–8.

Bachmann, G. (1977) "The Man on the Volcano: a Portrait of Werner Herzog," *Film Quarterly*, 31 (1), 2–10.

Barthleme, D. (1979) "The Earth as an Overturned Bowl," *New Yorker* (September 10), 120–2.

Benelli, D. (1977) "Mysteries of the Organism: Character Consciousness and Film Form in *Kaspar Hauser* and *Spirit of the Beehive*," *Movietone News*, 54 (June), 28–33.

—— (1977) "The Cosmos and its Discontents," *Movietone News*, 56 (November), 8–16.

Benson, S. and M. Karman (1976) "Herzog," *Mother Jones* (November), 40–5.

Blank, L. and J. Bogan (eds) (1984) *Burden of Dreams: Screenplay, Journals, Photographs*, Berkeley CA, North Atlantic.

Cairns, F. (1981) *"Fitzcarraldo,"* *Sight and Sound* (Summer), 180–1.

Canby, V. (1970) *"Even Dwarfs Started Small,"* *New York Times* (September 17).

—— (1971) *"Fata Morgana,"* *New York Times* (October 8).

—— (1977) *"Aguirre, the Wrath of God:* Haunting Film by Herzog," *New York Times* (April 4).

—— (1977) "Herzog's Pilgrims Hit the US," *New York Times* (July 13).

—— (1983) "Werner Herzog's Documentaries," *New York Times* (July 20).

Carrère, E. (1982) *Werner Herzog*, 'Cinégraphiques Series,' Paris, Edilig.

Carroll, N. (1985) "Herzog, Presence, and Paradox," *Persistence of Vision*, 2 (Fall), 30–40.

Cleere, E. (1980) "Three Films by Werner Herzog: Seen in the Light of the Grotesque," *Wide Angle*, 3 (4), 12–19.

Coleman, J. (1984) "Films: Hit or Miss," *New Statesman*, 108 (October 19), 36–7.

Combs, R. (1980) "Werner Herzog," in Richard Roud (ed.) *Cinema: A Critical Dictionary*, 2 vols, New York, Viking, 486–7.

Corrigan, T. (1983) *New German Film: The Displaced Image*, Austin, University of Texas Press.

Cott, J. (1976) "Signs of Life," *Rolling Stone* (November 18), 48–56.

Coursen, D. (1979) "Two Films by Werner Herzog," *Cinemonkey*, 16 (Winter), 22–4.

Csicsery, G. (1986) *"Ballad of the Little Soldier:* Werner Herzog in a Political Hall of Mirrors," *Film Quarterly*, 39 (2) (Winter), 7–15.

Davidson, D. (1980) "Borne Out of Darkness: The Documentaries of Werner Herzog," *Film Criticism*, 5 (Fall), 10–25.

Dawson, J. (1977) "Herzog's Magic Mountain," *Sight and Sound*, 47 (Winter), 57–8.

Denby, D. (1977) "The Germans Are Coming! The Germans Are Coming!," *Horizon*, 20 (September), 88–93.

Dorr, J. (1972) *"Even Dwarfs Started Small,"* *Take One*, 3 (6), 35–6.

Dost, M., F. Hopf and A. Kluge (1973) *Filmwirtschaft in der BRD und in Europa: Gotterdämmerung in Raten*, Munich, Hanser.

Eder, R. (1977) "A New Visionary in German Films: Werner Herzog," *New York Times* (July 10), 24–6 ff.

Eisler, K. (1974) *"Aguirre: the Wrath of God,"* *Movietone News*, 29 (January-February), 43–4.

—— (1974) "Offing the Pig: *Even Dwarfs Started Small,"* *Movietone News*, 36 (October), 8–11.

Eisner, L. (1974) "Herzog in Dinkelsbuehl," *Sight and Sound*, 43 (Autumn), 212–13.

Elsaesser, T. (1974) "The Cinema of Irony," *Monogram*, 5, 1–2.

Fell, J. (1979) *"Heart of Glass,"* *Film Quarterly*, 32 (Spring), 54–5.

Finger, E. (1979) "Kaspar Hauser Doubly Portrayed: Peter Handke's *Kaspar* and Werner Herzog's *Every Man for Himself and God Against All,"* *Literature/Film Quarterly*, 7 (3), 235–43.

Fisher, R. and J. Hembus (1981) *Der neue deutsche Film 1960–1980*, Munich, Goldmann.

Forbes, J. (1977) *"Heart of Glass,"* *Sight and Sound*, 46 (Autumn), 255–6.

Franklin, J. (1983) *New German Cinema: From Oberhausen to Hamburg*, Boston, Twayne.

Gambaccini, P. (1980) "The New German Film Makers," *Horizon*, 23 (June), 22–3.

Gilliatt, P. (1977) "Gold," *New Yorker* (April 11), 127–8.

—— (1977) "Hurrah," *New Yorker* (July 25), 74–7.

—— (1978) "Check," *New Yorker* (May 22), 115–16.

Gitlin, T. (1984) *"Fitzcarraldo,"* *Film Quarterly*, 37, 2 (Winter), 50–4.

Goodwin, M. (1982) "Herzog. The God of Wrath," *American Film*, (June), N.P.

Greenberg, A., H. Achternbusch and W. Herzog (1976) *Heart of Glass,*

Munich, Skellig.

Greenberg, A. (1977) "Notes on Some European Directors," *American Film* (October), 49–53.

Grosoli, F. (1981) *Werner Herzog,* Florence, La Nuova Italia.

Herzog, W. (1976) "Why Is There 'Being' at all Rather than Nothing?," trans. Stephen Lamb, *Framework,* 3 (Spring), 24–7.

—— (1980) *Of Walking in Ice,* trans. by Alan Greenberg and Martje Grohmann, New York, Tanam.

—— (1980) *Screenplays,* trans. by Alan Greenberg and Martje Herzog, New York, Tanam.

In German:

—— (1964) "Neun Tage eines Jahres," *Filmstudio,* 44 (September).

—— (1964) "Rebellen in Amerika," *Filmstudio* (Frankfurt/Main), 43 (May).

—— (1968) "Mit den Wolfen heulen," *Filmkritik,* 7 (July).

—— (1974) *Vom Gehen im Eis,* Munich, Hanser.

—— (1974) "Warum ist überhaupt Seiendes und nicht vielmehr Nichts?" *Kino* (West Berlin), 12 (March-April).

—— (1977) Drehbücher I: *Lebenszeichen: Auch Zwerge haben klein angefangen: Fata Morgana,* Munich, Skellig.

—— (1977) Drehbücher II: *Aguirre, der Zorn Gottes: Jeder für sich und Gott gegen alle; Land des Schweigens und der Dunkelheit,* Munich, Skellig.

—— (1977) "Die Bestie und der Brave Erlebnisse" mit dem Fußballtrainer Rudi Gutendorf, *Der Abend* (West Berlin), v. 4.2.

—— (1978) "Faszination über ein Sterben. Australische Ureinwohner im Film *Floating* und *Lalai Dreamtime,*" *Suddeutsche Zeitung,* v. 1.2.4.

—— (1978) "Vom Ende des Analphabetismus. Paolo und Vittorio Tavianis grosser Film *Padre Padrone,*" *Die Zeit,* v. 24. 11.

—— (1979) Drehbücher III: *Stroszek, Nosferatu:* Zwei Filmerzahlunger, Munich, Hanser.

—— (1982) *Fitzcarraldo: Erzählung,* Munich, Hanser.

—— (1982) *Fitzcarraldo Filmbuch,* Munich, Schirmir/Mosel.

—— (1984) *Wo die grunen Ameisin traümen: Filmerzählung,* Munich, Hanser.

Hoberman, J. (1978) "Over the Volcano," *Village Voice* (May 22), 48.

—— (1983) "The divine connection," *Village Voice* (July 26), 51.

—— (1985) "Obscure objects of desire," *Village Voice* (February 19), 61.

Horak J.-C. (1979) "Werner Herzog's *Ecran absurde,*" *Literature/Film*

Quarterly, 7 (3), 223–34.

Jansen, P. and W. Schütte (eds) (1976) *Herzog/Kluge/Straub*, Munich, Hanser.

—— (1979) *Werner Herzog*, Munich, Hanser.

Kael, P. (1975) "Metaphysical Tarzan," *New Yorker* (October 20), 142–9.

Kauffmann, S. (1975) "Secret Places, Secret Parts," *New Republic* (November 1), 22–3.

Kawin, B. (1980) "Nosferatu," *Film Quarterly* (Spring), 45–7.

Kent, L. (1977) "Werner Herzog: 'Film Is Not the Art of Scholars. But of Illiterates'," *New York Times* (September 11).

Kolker, P. (1983) *The Altering Eye: Contemporary International Cinema*, New York, Oxford University Press.

Lloyd, P. (1974) "Objectivity as irony: Werner Herzog's *Fata Morgana*," *Monogram*, 5, 8–9.

McCormick, R. and P. Aufderheide (1978) "Werner Herzog's *Heart of Glass* – Pro and Contra," *Cineaste*, 8 (4), 32–4.

Melzer, H. E. *et al.* (1981) *Die Aguaruna und der Zorn des Werner Herzog*, Munich, Lateinamerika-Komitee.

Mitgutsch, W. (1981) "Faces of Dehumanization: Werner Herzog's Reading of Buchner's *Woyzeck*," *Literature/Film Quarterly*, 11 (3), 152–60.

Morris, G. (1977) *"Stroszek," Take One* (November), 8–9.

—— (1978) "Werner Herzog," in Peter Cowie (ed.) *IFG 1979*, London, Tantivy, 28–33.

Nothangel, K. (1985) "Werner Herzog," in Hans-Michael Bock (ed.) *Cinegraph*, Munich: edition, text & kritik, 183ff.

O'Toole, L. (1979) "The Great Ecstasy of the Filmmaker Herzog," *Film Comment* (November-December), 34–9.

—— (1979) "I Feel That I'm Close to the Center of Things," *Film Comment*, 15 (6) (November-December), 40–50.

Overbey, D. (1975) *"Every Man for Himself," Sight and Sound*, 44 (2) (Spring), 73–5.

Payne, R. (1985) "New German Cinema/Old Hollywood Genres," *USC Spectator*, 5 (1) (Fall), 8–11.

Perlmutter, R. (1979) "The Cinema of the Grotesque," *Georgia Review*, 33 (1), 169–93.

Peucker, B. (1984) "Werner Herzog: In Quest of the Sublime," in Klaus Phillips (ed.) *New German Filmmakers*, New York, Ungar, 168–94.

—— (1986) "Invalidating Arnim: Herzog's *Signs of Life* (1967)," in Eric Rentschler (ed.) *German Film and Literature: Adaptations and Trans-*

formations, New York/London, Methuen.

Pflaum, H. and H. Prinzler (1983) *Cinema in the Federal Republic of Germany. The New German Film: Origins and Present Situation. A Handbook*, trans. by Timothy Nevill, Bonn, Inter-Nationes.

Rentschler, E. (1980) "West German Film in the 1970's," special issue of *Quarterly Review of Film Studies*, 5 (2) (Spring).

—— (1981/2) "American Friends and the New German Cinema: Patterns of Reception," *New German Critique*, 24–5 (Fall/Winter), 7–35.

—— (1984) *West German Film in the Course of Time: Reflection on the Twenty Years since Oberhausen*, Bedford Hills NY, Redgrave.

—— (1985) "How American Is It: The US as Image and Imaginary in German Film," *Persistence of Vision*, 2, 5–18.

—— (ed.) (1986) *German Literature and Film: Adaptations and Transformations*, New York/London, Methuen.

Rogers, T. (1979) *"Nosferatu the Vampyre," Films in Review*, 30 (December), 27.

Rosenbaum, J. (1977) "Steiner," *Monthly Film Bulletin* (January), 7.

Sarris, A. (1977) "Werner Herzog Makes a Real Movie," *Village Voice* (August 1), 33 and 37.

Siegel, J. (1976) *"The Mystery of Kaspar Hauser," Film Heritage*, 11 (2) (Winter), 45–6.

Silverman, K. (1981/2) "Kaspar Hauser's 'Terrible Fall' into Narrative," *New German Critique*, nos 24–5 (Fall/Winter), 73–93.

Simon, A. (1975) "Werner Herzog's *Aguirre, the Wrath of God*," *Monogram*, 6, 26–7.

Simon, J. (1975) "Cinematic Illiterates," *New York* (October 20), 86–7.

Strick, P. (1979) *"Nosferatu – The Vampyre," Sight and Sound* (Spring), 127–8.

Thomson, D. (1980) "The Many Faces of Klaus Kinski," *American Film* (May), 22–7.

—— (1981) "Werner Herzog," in *A Biographical Dictionary of Film* (2nd rev. edition), New York, Morrow.

Todd, J. (1981) "The Classic Vampire," in M. Klein and G. Parker (eds). *The English Novel and the Movies*, New York, Ungar, 197–210.

Trojan, J. (1979) *"How Much Wood Would A Woodchuck Chuck," "La Soufrière," Take One* (January), 11–13.

Van Wert, W. (1980) "Hallowing the Ordinary, Embezzling the Everyday: Werner Herzog's Documentary Practice," *Quarterly Review of Film Studies*, 5(2) (Spring), 183–90.

Viseur, R. de le and W. Schmidmaier (1977) *"Playboy* interview: Werner

Herzog," *Playboy* (German edition) (January), 29–37.

Vogel, A. (1971) "In Paradise Man Is Born Dead," *Village Voice* (November), 88

—— (1977) "Herzog in Berlin," *Film Comment,* 13 (5) (October), 37–8.

—— (1981) "On Seeing a Mirage," *Film Comment* (January/February), 76–8.

Walker, B. (1978) "Werner Herzog's *Nosferatu,*" *Sight and Sound* (Autumn), 202–5.

Waller, G. (1980) "Satire and the Grotesque in Herzog's Even Dwarfs Started Small," *Proceedings of the Fifth Annual Purdue University Conference on Film,* West Lafayette, Purdue University, 3–10.

—— (1980) "The Great Ecstasy of the Woodsculptor Steiner: Herzog and the Stylized Documentary," *Film Criticism* (Fall), 26–35.

—— (1981) "*Aguirre, the Wrath of God*: History, Theatre, and the Cinema," *South Atlantic Review,* 46 (2) (May), 55–69.

Walsh, G. (ed.) (1979) "'Images at the Horizon': a workshop with Werner Herzog," conducted by Roger Ebert, Chicago, Facets Multimedia Center (pamphlet).

Young, V. (1977) "Much Madness: Werner Herzog and Contemporary German Cinema," *Hudson Review,* 30 (3), 409–14.

—— (1983) "Film Chronicle: Dying Is Easy," *Hudson Review,* 24–5 (Fall/Winter), 7–35.

Index